D1615125

The West Coast Pacifics

The West Coast Pacifics

J. F. Clay & J. Cliffe

LONDON

IAN ALLAN LTD

First published 1976

ISBN 0 7110 0691 1

© Ian Allan Ltd 1976

Published by Ian Allan Ltd, Shepperton, Surrey,
and printed in the United Kingdom by
J. G. Eccles, Inverness

Contents

Preface

The West Coast route to Scotland called for hard locomotive work. Many designs were built to overcome the difficulties and the culmination of British steam power is personified in the various Pacific locomotives which worked over this line. The 'Duchess' class, first built by the LMS and operated by BR up to 1964 were, in the opinion of many, the most impressive-looking express locomotives ever to have run in Britain. The magnificent appearance of these locomotives was matched by performance on the road which, at its best, was unsurpassed by any British express locomotives.

It has been the aim of the writers of this book to tell the story of the West Coast Pacifics against the general background of Pacific locomotives in this country and abroad. There has been no attempt to put across a claim for supremacy in every aspect of design, but a picture emerges of a class of locomotives with much to commend it. In the case of the final 'Duchess' design there was more good than bad.

In all books of this kind it has to be accepted that there is a certain degree of uncertainty even in the published official records. We have presented a story which we think is largely authentic, but in some aspects of dimensional history there are points of doubt where a decision has had to be made between conflicting sources of information. We hope that we have chosen correctly when faced with alternatives.

The logs of performance are subject to the usual hazards of what is not a completely exact science. We have tried to find new aspects of performance and some logs are here published for the first time. In many cases we have managed to contact the original recorders, who have re-checked their original notebooks, with the result that some speeds and train weights are slightly different from figures published earlier. We do not claim complete accuracy even after this, but we submit that the errors remaining are small and of minor significance. No log published in this book is in conflict with the standards of power and speed proved by official tests.

Our thanks are due to a number of serving and retired railwaymen and to some talented and well-informed laymen. Among these we are most grateful to former LMS officers Messrs D. S. M. Barrie, R. C. Bond and E. S. Cox. Mr Cox was intimately concerned with the design of various Pacific projects of the 1920s which did not reach fulfilment and his informative letters and his permission for us to quote from his various Ian Allan books are much appreciated. We owe an equal debt of gratitude to serving railwaymen P. J. Coster and G. A. Yeomans for information and assistance. P. H. V. Banyard, a retired Locomotive Inspector of vast experience, is thanked for his valued critical comments on the various Pacific designs of all Regions. H. A. Gamble, the founder of the Leicester Railway Society, has read the script and made helpful suggestions and we are also most grateful to Norman Harvey, D. H. Landau, Gp Capt J. N. C. Law and K. R. Phillips for their help in the assessment of locomotive performance. J. D. Cliffe has assisted with information on obscure points of dimensional history. We thank the Editor of the *Railway Magazine* for his permission to quote from past issues.

Beyond those who have assisted directly with the book there is a vast army of known and unknown railwaymen and others who have, through the years, contributed to background knowledge which has helped us to see the story of the West Coast Pacifics with some degree of perspective.

Our thanks go out once more to the photographers whose art has brought the story to life and especially to T. G. Hepburn, not only for his fine prints but for the pleasure of his company on photographic expeditions in the years now long gone by.

Leicester, May 1975   *J. F. Clay*
London, May 1975   *J. Cliffe*

CHAPTER ONE

The History of the
Pacific Type

The 4-6-2 or Pacific type of locomotive dominated express practice for many years in many lands and it still ran a large mileage after it had been outclassed, especially in America, by the larger 4-6-4, 4-8-2 and 4-8-4 types. In Britain the Pacific held its place as the premier express type right up to the end of steam, as only one 4-6-4 was actually built while the 4-8-2 and 4-8-4 types, although considered, never left the drawing boards. The last high-speed steam locomotives to be built anywhere were German Pacifics, the two experimental Class 10s built by F. Krupp in 1957.

The first 4-6-2 type of locomotive to be built was an American experimental engine designed by G. S. Strong in 1886. The firebox had two horizontal corrugated flues similar to those used in marine practice. This was too wide to be located between the trailing pair of driving wheels and as it projected behind them, it needed a pair of carrying wheels to support it: and so the 4-6-2 wheel arrangement was born of necessity. The locomotive and its patent firebox failed and had little immediate impact. The first Pacific locomotives built as a class was the Class Q for the New Zealand Government Railways, erected by Baldwin in 1901, which anticipated by a small margin a class built for the Missouri Pacific Railroad.

There are conflicting opinions as to the origin of the name "Pacific" for the 4-6-2 type. It has been suggested that because New Zealand, the destination of the first class of the type, is in the Pacific Ocean the name followed naturally. Others believe that it came from the railroad in the US which first ordered a class of 4-6-2s, the Missouri Pacific. But the third suggestion is perhaps the most convincing, this is that the first 4-4-2 express locomotives were built for the Atlantic Coast Line and gained the name "Atlantics" and when the larger 4-6-2 type followed it was natural for them to take the name of the larger ocean and become "Pacifics". There is no evidence that the name was ever associated with the original experimental 4-6-2 of 1886 which pre-dated the first Atlantics.

The Pacifics built for New Zealand and the Missouri Pacific owed their origin to the natural process of evolution from the 2-4-2 Columbia type, the 4-4-2 Atlantic and the 2-6-2 Prairie type. These types had all been tried in the US and they permitted the use of the wide firebox.

The 2-4-2 was soon outclassed as being too small and its riding at high speeds was suspect. The 4-4-2 had a longer vogue and it achieved some success on the easily graded routes, but its lack of adhesion was a handicap. The 2-6-2 started with a blaze of glory, especially on the Lake Shore and Michigan Southern, but fears for its stability and a number of derailments gave it a short life on the fastest trains. The 4-6-2 appeared to present a combination of all the best qualities and a total of 6800 was reached in the US, almost as many as all the other wide-firebox express types put together. It was outclassed for the fastest and heaviest duties from the late 1920s onwards by the 4-6-4 on the level routes and by the 4-8-2 and 4-8-4 on the heavier grades. The 4-8-4 was still being developed when the diesels took over. A similar position existed in Europe, where the Pacific reached its highest refinement of design in the compound Pacifics designed by A. Chapelon for the Paris Orleans Railway and later used on other French railways. In Britain, where for many years there was an abundance of good quality coal, the Pacific had a slow start against some very efficient 4-6-0s.

The wide firebox 4-6-2 could be called "the true Pacific", but there was a minority of 4-6-2 engines which retained the narrow firebox. These engines had evolved from the 4-6-0 rather than from the Atlantic or the 2-6-2. Viewed in side elevation, they appear trying to be 4-6-0s but just failing and having to accept a rear pair of carrying wheels with some reluctance. The most notable of such engines were the various classes of 4-6-2 compounds used on the French Nord before the Chapelon 231Es were built. The final design was the Collin Super Pacific, which could have been 4-6-0s had greater axle loading been permitted. Had Collin had the axle loading permitted to Collett when he designed the GWR 4-6-0 'Kings' he could have spaced his axles in a similar way to the British engine and have produced a 4-6-0. Some 4-6-2s built by British firms for railways in South America resemble over-grown 4-6-0s and a British railway might have had such an engine had the Great Central 4-6-2 mentioned on page 326 of George Dow's *Great Central Railway* Vol 3 (Ian Allan 1965) materialised. The West Coast Pacifics were all of the "true" wide-firebox type.

The first Pacific in Europe was built in 1907 for the Paris Orleans Railway in France and pre-dated a Pacific built in South Germany by a narrow margin. In 1908 the first British Pacific was built for the Great Western Railway by George Jackson Churchward. This engine was largely experimental and various theories have been advanced for the construction, by Britain's most able designer, of an engine for which there was no immediate need. The GWR Pacific was named *The Great Bear* and it was limited to the London-Bristol route because of weight and clearance restrictions. It never outclassed the Churchward 4-6-0s in performance. Here, perhaps, lay the origins of the resistance to Pacifics which was strong in Britain for many years. *The Great*

Bear was loved by the general public and by the GWR publicity people and it enjoyed its role as "Britain's Largest Express Locomotive" unchallenged for 14 years, so that it almost seemed to be an act of irreverence when the Great Northern built a Pacific in 1922. The Great Northern and North Eastern Pacifics were different from *The Great Bear* in that they were intended for production in quantity; they were built to fill a need and relieve overloaded Atlantic-type engines.

The Pacific type had its good qualities and, like everything else in the universe, had defects which ultimately led to its replacement. The large boiler with its wide firebox promised an ample supply of steam and a large thermal storage capacity which could be built up during easy running and drawn on when a hard effort was required. The wheel arrangement allowed for an excellent vehicle, as engines with an idle carrying axle under the cab normally rode better than those with driving wheels at the rear. While that is a valid statement of fact in general terms, it must be emphasised that there could be exceptions. There were Pacifics which were bad-steaming engines and there were 4-6-0s which steamed magnificently; there were bad-riding Pacifics and good riding 4-6-0s; but a Pacific, designed with the best science of its day, would outclass the best 4-6-0 at high sustained horsepower at speed and would give a more comfortable ride to its crew while doing so. The wide firebox promised to be less exacting in its choice of fuel, but here again there were exceptions; some coal was so bad that even the wide-firebox designs could do little with it. This was destined to affect the West Coast Pacifics as well as others.

The steaming capacity and good riding of the Pacific type made this an ideal engine for very high speeds. In Britain the only authentic speeds of over 110mph were attained by Pacifics. In the whole world the only engines which have topped this maximum have either had a two-wheeled or a four-wheeled trailing truck. In the realm of power in relation to size, however, the world records are held by the 4-8-0 compounds designed by A. Chapelon which surpassed, in this criterion of performance, the same designer's Pacifics. In Britain, in regular everyday service it was the practice to work 4-4-0 and 4-6-0 locomotives harder, in relation to their size, than Pacifics. On the West Coast no class of Pacific was ever worked as hard continuously every day over a period of years as were the LNWR 4-4-0s of the 'George the Fifth' class from their inception in 1910 until wartime restrictions caused an easing-off in 1916. In LMS and LMR days, although the Pacifics regularly produced more actual power than the 'Royal Scot' 4-6-0s, it is doubtful if they were ever worked as hard, relatively to their size, in everyday service.

There were two reasons for this. The Pacific's usually had about 65% of their total weight available for adhesion; this was better than the 50% of the 4-4-2 Atlantic, or their more recent rivals the 4-6-4s, but it was inferior to the 75% or so of the average 4-6-0. This meant

11

in practice that the 4-6-0 and the 4-8-0 could be expected to utilise the full output of the boiler without fear of slipping, while a Pacific could give trouble at starting or on very heavy grades at low speeds. The Pacific was better as a runner than as a puller. It was easier for one fireman to feed the narrow box of a 4-6-0 than the much larger firebox of a Pacific. In the US some help was given to engines with two-or four-wheeled trailing trucks by the use of the booster engine on one of the carrying axles. This could be cut in at starting or when speed was low near the crest of a steep bank, or when the approach to a climb was balked by a slack. Large-boilered American engines, such as the 4-6-4 Hudsons of the New York Central, could haul at speed any load which their boosters allowed them to start and such engines were worked relatively as hard for their size as European 4-6-0s. They were, of course, mechanically fired. Some experimental work was done by Gresley with boosters on Atlantic-type engines, but it was never extended to Pacifics. There were times when an efficient booster would have been a great help to British Pacifics.

It has been suggested that a prime cause of the slipping by Pacifics at starting was due to the backwards pull on the rear drawbar causing a downward pull on the idle trailing axle and a corresponding lightening of the load on the coupled axles further forward. This theory has been disputed, but whatever argument there may be about the cause, the effect is beyond doubt. It could be observed from the platform end by anyone who spent any time watching the departure of trains. A 4-6-0 almost always got away with less slipping than a Pacific. It was said that any downward pull on the rear end of a 4-6-0 merely put more effective weight on the rear pair of coupled wheels. It could not have merely been a matter of the adhesion factor, because the GWR 'Kings' had no more weight in relation to tractive effort than a number of Pacific classes which were obviously less sure-footed. An alternative suggestion has been that the whole secret lay in regulator design, but alternative designs of regulator have been tried on Pacifics without complete success. The largest type of Pacific built for the West Coast route, the 'Duchess' class, had a particularly bad reputation for slipping, but it is doubtful if they were really any worse than contemporary Pacifics on other British lines.

Once having got away, a Pacific, by reason of its large boiler, could usually catch up a 4-6-0 within a few miles, even though the smaller engine had made a quicker initial start. The smaller engine would need to be notched up earlier to avoid too great a drain of steam as speed rose. A more serious operational problem was slipping on the banks in wet weather. The atmospheric conditions over the Cumbrian fells or the Scottish Uplands could be daunting. There are well-documented examples of free-steaming Pacifics with willing crews having to be eased to a level of output well below their maximum in misty weather on Shap or Beattock. Under these circumstances the banker had sometimes to be called when the load was relatively moderate in comparison with those handled with success under favourable conditions. The Pacific type was an admirable choice in view of the long continuous runs from Euston to Glasgow, or for high sustained speed from Carnforth to Euston, but an eight-coupled design would have been closer to the ideal over the banks.

The very length of a Pacific was a design problem. In many cases their introduction meant capital expenditure on longer turntables and such considerations delayed the building of Pacifics while there was a case for a good 4-6-0. The length of the boiler barrel was also a problem and some of the early designs, both those actually built and those which were only contemplated, offended the basic principles of good practice in this respect. Tube lengths of 22ft or over were less effective than those several feet shorter, as the section of tube furthest from the firebox was of little value as heating surface. The same thing applied to large superheating surfaces, where in some cases it emerged that the elements could have been shortened, reducing the heating surface on paper but increasing the temperature of the steam. At a very late hour in the history of steam, research undertaken in France under the leadership of A. Chapelon suggested that if the problems of draughting had been understood earlier and the correct proportions of tube diameter to tube length had been applied to some earlier designs, then much better steaming could have been obtained. Some designers sought to reduce tube length to a reasonable figure by using a combustion chamber on the firebox or by recessing the smokebox backwards into the boiler. The problems of bad steaming did not automatically vanish when the 4-6-2 wheel arrangement was adopted.

There has been much debate over the years about the relative efficiencies of the wide and narrow fireboxes. It has been pointed out that the world record for power for size and for coal per drawbar hp hour was held by the Chapelon 4-8-0s rebuilt from Pacifics of the Paris Orleans Railway. As far as can be deduced from the published test results it would appear that the power/weight claim for the Chapelon 4-8-0s can be sustained, but they were equalled in power per unit of fuel burnt by other French compounds, such as the 141P 2-8-2 engines which had the wide round-top firebox and piston valves. It may be claimed that there was no special advantage to be gained by the wide firebox in actual fuel economy, nor need there have been any disadvantage. A more important question, but one more difficult to assess, was that of boiler maintenance cost. It has been claimed that the wide-firebox engines, producing a given volume of steam at a moderate firing rate in terms of lb of coal per sq ft of grate area, were lower in boiler maintenance costs than a 4-6-0 whose smaller boiler had to be fired at a higher combustion rate to obtain the same amount of steam. On this question no definitive ruling can be given, as comparative figures for boiler maintenance costs are not available.

All that can be said is that the rate of firing per square foot of grate area on the most strenuous test ever given to a West Coast Pacific on the main line was relatively moderate despite the high power output.

The wide firebox of the Pacific type, as compared with the narrow box of most 4-6-0s, promised a more ample supply of steam. The rear carrying wheels, in theory at least, allowed space for the use of an ashpan with a good air supply. In practice this was not always realised in Britain and our Pacifics in general suffered from poor ashpan design with inadequate air supply at the rear and sides of the grate. Often there was only a front damper and nothing like the side air inlets and overhanging side ashpans, as used, for example, in France and Germany, were ever seen in this country. It is true, of course, that the British loading gauge was more restrictive in this respect. The tendency to weight transfer at starting was counteracted abroad by the adoption of compensated springing with equalising beams and this again was a feature not found on British Pacifics. A possible argument against the necessity of this type of suspension was the supposedly better British track.

The Pacific type of locomotive was not the complete answer to all operating problems, but over a large percentage of the British main lines it was perhaps the best compromise solution. There was a strong case for Pacifics on the West Coast Route; they did much useful work that would have been beyond the capacity of the best 4-6-0s — and here it must be remembered that the Converted 'Royal Scots' were among the best 4-6-0s in Europe. The West Coast authorities, however, did not accept the Pacific as the universal type of express engine and they did not flood the railway with 4-6-2s. They sought, rather to keep a balance between Pacifics and 4-6-0s, with just enough of the larger engines to cover the cream of the traffic. They saved capital by not buying so many of the more expensive Pacifics, but there was the disadvantage of needing firemen to master the different techniques of firing both wide and narrow fireboxes. The question of whether the West Coast built the correct number of Pacifics has long been debated and during the war critics pointed to the East Coast's large fleet of Pacifics and 2-6-2s as an example of a railway with a wise motive power policy; but in peacetime the absurdity of a Pacific shunting a country goods yard was not a common feature of West Coast operating.

CHAPTER TWO

The Locomotive Problems of the West Coast Route

A traveller over the West Coast Route today, who romps over the summits of the former LNWR and Caledonian main lines at 90mph behind an electric locomotive smaller than the coaches it hauls, may be pardoned if he wonders why train operation was ever considered to be difficult. The fundamental question affecting the speed which is possible on steeply rising gradients is not, however, whether the locomotive is steam, diesel, gas turbine or electric, it is the ratio of power to weight which is all important. The electric locomotive has a big advantage here because it transmits power which is produced in an external source, while the other types of locomotive produce power from within themselves. The desirability of separating heavy power-producing machinery from the moving vehicles was recognised even by the early pioneers, some of whom advocated cable haulage or the atmospheric system for steep gradients. In the very beginning the first trains from Euston were hauled to the top of Camden Bank by a stationary engine and cable.

The fact that cable haulage was employed on Camden Bank was evidence that Euston station was opened at an early date, for the bank is not long and only part of it is as steep as 1 in 70. Had the line been built a mere five, or at most ten, years later the need for rope haulage would never have entered anyone's head. Not many years after the opening of Euston station, gradients as steep as Camden Bank but extending for ten times the distance were accepted for locomotive haulage on other parts of the West Coast Route. This frequently meant rear-end banking assistance on the heavier trains and it was not long before this replaced rope haulage on Camden Bank.

Once a train on the London and Birmingham Railway had reached the top of Camden Bank it faced little more than slight gradients. Robert Stephenson had engineered the line in accordance with the ideas of the 1830s, when the ability of locomotives to climb severe gradients was a matter of some doubt. Had the line been built later the gradients might have been slightly more difficult and the earth-works such as Tring Cutting less impressive. It is, perhaps, significant that the four main lines entering London from the north were in ascending order of difficulty of grading. The LNWR was easiest, followed by the GNR, the Midland and the Great Central, which was the most difficult. In part this was the result of the GCR being last in the field after the easier routes had been taken by others, but in part it was due to the GCR being built in an age when locomotives were more capable.

The same general pattern of easy gradients was continued along the Trent Valley line. The first slight deviation from the general pattern of a ruling grade of 1 in 300 or easier was Madeley Bank as the line descended towards Crewe, where there is a stretch of 1 in 177. Madeley Bank was the scene of the highest speed ever attained by steam on the West Coast Route and in the other direction it could be some handicap to a heavily-loaded southbound train, especially if the engine was starting cold from Crewe.

North of Crewe, through industrial Lancashire, the same general characteristic grading continues, broken only by a short 1 in 104 for 1¾ miles of Boar's Head Bank, which could be troublesome because the Wigan slack could balk the ascent, in contrast to the mile of 1 in 135 to the bridge over the Manchester Ship Canal near Acton Grange, which could be rushed and was hardly noticed. North of Boar's Head was a corresponding fall from Coppull to Balshaw Lane. Southbound trains stopping at Lancaster had a troublesome mile of 1 in 98 between the station and Lancaster No 1 Box, but the real change in character does not come until after Carnforth. For 236½ miles the line had no exceptional gradients, but also there were no chances of coasting downhill at a reasonably high speed while water level or boiler pressure recuperated. Throughout its history as a steam-operated line the West Coast Route, even south of Carnforth, has demanded a high standard of enginemanship because of the high sustained speeds required from engines hauling heavy loads.

Approaching Carnforth the sight of the mountains ahead indicates the radical change in the nature of the line, which was recognised throughout history by lower maximum loads being permitted for the various locomotive classes. In 31½ miles from Carnforth to Shap Summit the line rises 890ft. The name "Shap Summit" has romantic associations and in the minds of the general public it has become the criterion of the sternest battle ever fought between engine and gravity when, in actual fact, it is not the most difficult obstacle to the London-Glasgow expresses. The difficulty of the ascent in the days of steam was eased by a few "breathers", which allowed the engine to gain a little more impetus with which to charge the next up grade. Nevertheless the ascent was not to be despised when every ounce of steam had to be gained by a man with a shovel who had little respite during an ascent which rarely took less than 35min and often extended to 45-50min with heavy trains. Carnforth to Shap Summit called for the best from engines and men. The really heavy grade is the 4¼ miles of 1 in 75 from Tebay to the Summit and rear-end assistance was sometimes given over this section to trains making the rest of the ascent unassisted. This was regular practice on loose-coupled freight trains, partly as an insurance against a breakaway. A badly steaming engine could perhaps be more of a liability on the 13mile climb from Milnthorpe to Grayrigg which, although not so steep, required a longer sustained effort. Some heavy trains took a pilot engine from Oxenholme over the whole of the climb. Apart from the fight against gravity the mountain mists could wet the rails, causing engines to slip, and this worry has not completely vanished even with today's electrics.

The LNWR, with some justification claimed to be "England's Premier Line" and with equal reason the Caledonian could claim a similar position among Scottish railways. There were few points of similarity between the northern and southern partners in their locomotive policies, but they both required high standards of performance. The line north from Carlisle for the first 40 miles has a ruling grade of 1 in 200 and in this respect resembles the GNR section of the East Coast rather than the LNWR. There are ascents between Carlisle and Beattock equal to the famous climb from Peterborough to Stoke on the East Coast, but when seen on the profile they appear almost level compared with the towering ascent of Beattock Bank. This is more difficult than Shap, although only one short stretch of 1 in 69 is actually steeper. The difficulty of Beattock lay in its sustained climb for 10 miles. In LMS days engines were allowed slightly higher unassisted loads over Shap than over the Scottish Bank. In one way, however, the concentration of the grade into these 10 miles was an operational advantage; a locomotive could haul a heavy train out of Carlisle and be assisted in the rear for these 10 miles only, managing comfortably enough elsewhere. Had the climbs been spread as with Shap and Grayrigg banks more trains might have needed double-heading throughout. The descent from Beattock to Glasgow is more broken and less steep, and both in Caledonian and in LMS days much heavier loads were worked by one engine in the southbound direction.

The West Coast Route had more severe gradients than the East Coast, but easier gradients and shorter mileage than the Midland/ North British route to Edinburgh, and it was shorter and less handicapped by service slacks than the Midland/G&SWR line to Glasgow. The West Coast offered the quickest route to Glasgow and it could compete for the Edinburgh and Aberdeen traffic. The East Coast could not seriously challenge for the Glasgow traffic. The net result was that, despite its more severe grades, the West Coast was in a good competitive position to take a generous share of the Scottish traffic. The fact that there was so much traffic called for powerful engines. During parts of its history the West Coast did not have the engines it really needed, but at other times it was well supplied.

For much of its history the LNWR was a small-engine line. This began with the four-wheeled engines of the London & Birmingham Railway. There are recorded occasions of four of the Bury four-

17

wheelers being employed on one train. During the McConnell regime engines were built at Wolverton comparable with anything else on the narrow gauge, but when Wolverton was made subservient to Crewe the small engine policy again dominated. Sir Richard Moon had ideas for rigid economy and he considered that 40mph was fast enough for an express. At these speeds the relatively small Ramsbottom 2-2-2 and 2-4-0 locomotives were capable of hauling fairly heavy loads. These low standards could hardly have been expected to survive in a competitive world and by the time Webb was in charge faster trains were needed. The Caledonian had strangely enough handled its Scottish traffic over Beattock quite well with 2-2-2, 8ft, singles although rear-end assistance was needed on the bank itself.

Despite their longer and more difficult route to Edinburgh the West Coast Companies were unwilling to take a second place in the contest for this traffic and in 1888 The Races to Edinburgh took place. By this time four-coupled engines were available, but the race trains were usually worked by 2-2-2 singles from Euston to Crewe and by the Caledonian 4-2-2 single No 123 over Beattock and Cobbinshaw summits. Only on the Crewe-Carlisle section did the four-coupled engine dominate. The net result of the Race to Edinburgh was to reduce the record time of a light train from London to 7½hr and the daily schedule to 8½hr. There matters rested until 1895, when the Races to Aberdeen took place. During this stirring contest standards were established that were destined to govern train operation until the 1930s, when Pacific-type locomotives were working on both East and West Coast routes. The West Coast, despite greater distance and more difficult gradients, established the fastest time to Aberdeen in 1895, but they did this with a load 40% lighter than the East Coast train, which itself was hardly a commercial load.

From the locomotive standpoint, however, the Race to Aberdeen had been a stimulating occasion. The West Coast had, in 1895, abandoned single-driving locomotives and their race train weighing a mere 72 tons was hauled from Euston to Crewe by the Webb compound locomotive *Adriatic* with two pairs of uncoupled driving wheels. Although this engine ran well, it was outclassed by the smaller 2-4-0 engine *Hardwicke*, which ran from Crewe to Carlisle in 126min for 141½ miles with a sensational average of 62½mph from Carnforth to Shap Summit. This uphill speed over a 915ft summit captured public imagination, but one contemporary writer, the late Rev. W. J. Scott, was aware of the true point at issue when he wrote that, given a large enough engine and a light enough load, gradients could be climbed as fast as was desired.

The locomotives of the Caledonian were destined to influence British practice more than those of the LNWR during the final years of the 19th and the opening years of the 20th Century, because Webb got involved in an unrewarding venture into locomotive compounding which proved to be a blind alley, while the St Rollox authorities followed a broad simple road to success. The West Coast Race train was taken north from Carlisle by a simple 4-4-0 No 90, which ran through non-stop to Perth 150.8 miles in 149½min. Although this was not as fast as the LNWR run over Shap, it was a notable feat in that the whole run was made on one tender of water, as the Caledonian had no water troughs. Driver Crooks had performed a great feat of enginemanship, which was not fully appreciated by all contemporary writers. A similar engine built by John Lambie covered the final 89.7 miles in 80½min.

The Drummond and Lambie 4-4-0 engines represented much the type of locomotive needed in those days, simple and reliable and fast with moderate loads. Train loads were, however, growing rapidly and greater demands on motive power were constantly being made. In 1896 a big step forward was made when J. F. McIntosh placed a larger boiler on the same basic type of 4-4-0 and produced the first 'Dunalastair' class which was destined to influence British locomotive practice considerably during the years round the turn of the century. During the summer of 1896 the 'Dunalastairs' were performing work on the down 'Tourist Express' every night which approached the speeds of the race trains of the previous years with twice the load. During the subsequent years McIntosh built a series of enlarged 4-4-0s following the basic 'Dunalastair' theme.

Meanwhile the LNWR was groaning under the difficulties caused by Webb's ill-starred experiments with compounding. Admittedly, a number of good runs were recorded by the Webb compounds, especially the three-cylinder 'Teutonic' class, but the later and larger engines did not fully justify expectations and the General Manager, in October 1901, imposed the notorious ":17" rule, which in effect meant that most of the best trains had to be double-headed. Train operation, especially over the northern section, became very difficult and operating officers must have envied the Caledonian's stock of reliable 4-4-0s. In May 1903 Webb retired and was replaced by George Whale from the Running Department.

Whale was faced with the task of restoring adequate motive power to the LNWR. This he did by abandoning compounding and building the 'Precursor' class 4-4-0s, a design of monumental simplicity capable of standing considerable overload. These engines solved the motive power problem south of Crewe by their ability to handle 400ton loads without assistance, but north of Carnforth they frequently needed rear end assistance from Tebay to the Summit. Whale built a 4-6-0 version of the same general theme, the 'Experiment' class, for work over the northern section. By this time the Caledonian had also built a few large 4-6-0s, first Nos 49 and 50 and the 903 'Cardean' class. These were among the largest express engines of their day and they could work loads of 400 tons out to the foot of Beattock Bank in the scheduled 45min for the 39.7 miles; after this the bank could be climbed in good style with rear-end assistance.

To outward appearances the situation was well in hand, but the limitations of the saturated express engine with the classical valve design was becoming evident to the practical operating men. The 'Cardeans' could burn coal faster than one man could normally be expected to fire them and the results obtained on a special test run could not be repeated in regular everyday service. In 1907 Charles Rous-Marten, the leading writer on the locomotive engine, made the first published reference to Pacific locomotives on the West Coast Route when he foretold, in 1907, the use of 4-6-2s with two cylinders 20in by 28in, a boiler of 5ft 6in in diameter with a heating surface of 2500-3000sq ft and 225lb/sq in boiler pressure. His estimate of 77 to 80 tons weight for such an engine is distinctly on the low side, especially if an adequate firebox was to be included, but he had the vision to see the need for 500 ton loads unassisted over Shap in the not too distant future. It would appear that this prediction was solely Rous-Marten's own idea there is no evidence that anything of the sort was contemplated either by Crewe or St Rollox at this time; he was influenced by rumours of a Pacific materialising at Swindon, but by the time *The Great Bear* was built, in the following year, Rous-Marten was dead. It is quite likely that his Pacific, if built, would have taken its 500ton train over Shap under test conditions, but its success in everyday running is a much more doubtful proposition. Firemen, who were already fully extended on the 'Cardeans' or the 'Experiments', could hardly have kept pace with the demands of a Pacific burning coal at the rate of 5lb/dbhp hr and developing 1500ihp for 45min on the climbs to Shap north or south. The problems of slipping in misty weather with Pacifics was hardly realised in those days, although Rous-Marten did forecast 60 tons adhesion weight on the driving axles. Before a Pacific could have been a practical proposition on the West Coast Route the basic thermal efficiency of the steam locomotive needed to be improved.

There were ways in which this could have been done and the West Coast authorities looked to the experience of other railways in seeking a solution. During the closing years of his life the late C. Rous-Marten respected the locomotive performance on the Caledonian Railway as much as any British railway, but his greatest admiration was given to the work of the De Glehn type four-cylinder compounds in France, especially the Atlantics of the Nord. Churchward on the GWR had tried three of these engines but had found that, although they ran well under test conditions, they showed no practical advantage over his own Atlantics and 4-6-0s. The Caledonian was impressed by the De Glehn compounds and a design for a four-cylinder compound Atlantic was prepared in 1905. This would have been a very handsome engine, but its adhesion weight of 36½ tons would have made it less effective than the simple 4-6-0s on the banks. There were rumours that Crewe contemplated a three-cylinder compound on the Smith system at about the same period, but there is little doubt that their experience with the Webb compounds had left the LNWR with enthusiasm for the simple engine. In LMS days Smith compounds of Midland design were destined to run on LNWR and Caledonian lines.

Greater efficiency could have been obtained by adopting the rationally-designed Churchward type engines as used on the GWR. In 1910 a GWR four-cylinder 4-6-0 No 4005 *Polar Star* ran trials on the LNWR main line. It performed its work with quiet mastery — in fact, its running was so silent in comparison with the noisy exhaust of the LNWR engines that it was accused of being a menace to platelayers. Although the LNWR authorities were impressed by this engine it is doubtful if they had realised the true secret of its success, which lay in the long-lap, long-travel valves. They shrank from using the high boiler pressure of 225lb/sq in, not realising that this was not essential and that cylinder, valve and front end improvements based on Swindon practice could have been used in one of their own 175lb pressure engines. Ultimately the LNWR built their own four-cylinder 4-6-0 but of a design very different from the GWR 'Star'.

Salvation came to the LNWR from German locomotive practice with the introduction of superheating. The economy of this had been demonstrated on LNWR metals by the LB&SCR 4-4-2 tank engine No 23. In 1909, No 23 showed its moderate coal consumption and still more moderate water consumption on the LNWR 'Sunny South Special', which it worked through from Brighton to Rugby. Superheating did not have to be an alternative to compounding nor to the Churchward-type engine — in fact, superheated versions of the GWR 4-6-0s and the French De Glehn compounds progressed to great heights of efficiency and performance; but superheating also offered a cheap quick way of improving the existing locomotive stock at a minimum of capital cost. This was the policy which C. J. Bowen-Cooke, who had succeeded Whale at Crewe, adopted.

In 1910 Bowen-Cooke built No 2663 *George the Fifth*, a superheated 4-4-0 of the same general size and mechanical design as the 'Pre cursors', but having a much superior design of piston valves instead of the flat valves of the Whale engine. It is claimed that Dr Schmidt supervised valve design of the engine into which his superheater was to be introduced. The net result was an engine which could produce considerable power for its size and which could run with reasonable economy, at least when in good condition. The 'George the Fifth' class 4-4-0 were, on the basis of performance in relation to engine weight, among the best locomotives ever to have run anywhere in Britain. During the years 1910-1916, when wartime restrictions limited their opportunities, there were no British locomotives which performed superior work in everyday service and it was only at holiday weekends, when 500ton loads were carried on the GWR West of England main

21

line, that the sustained power outputs of the 'Georges' were exceeded anywhere in Britain. The 'Georges' showed their ability to work loads of 400-450 tons south of Crewe on 55-57mph schedules and north of Preston they could keep time on a schedule of 104min for the 90.1 miles from Preston over Shap to Carlisle with loads of from 350 to 400 tons. The superheated 4-4-0s outclassed the saturated 4-6-0 'Experiments', not only south of Crewe but also over the banks.

The 'Georges' were soon followed by the 4-6-0 'Prince of Wales' class, which was a superheated version of the 'Experiments'. Although the 'Princes' never seemed quite to match the brilliance of the 'Georges' they were a more useful general-purpose engine with a wider route availability and finally a total of 246 were built. Despite the success with which the 'Georges' and 'Princes' were worked so close to their maximum possible output for several years, Mr Bowen-Cooke had realised that a more powerful 4-6-0 was desirable to meet increasing loads with a greater margin of potential power over everyday requirements. A four-cylinder 4-6-0 design was chosen, but the divided drive of the GWR 'Star', in its turn derived from the De Glehn compounds, was rejected in favour of all four cylinders driving the leading axle. This arrangement was superior in balancing and accessibility, but the axle had to be strong.

The LNWR 'Claughton' class 4-6-0s proved to be at least the equals of the GWR 'Stars' in maximum hp output under test conditions, but the Swindon engines would take points for economy and for consistency in service. With the 'Claughton' class the LNWR, which carried the heaviest express passenger traffic in Britain, at last had one of Britain's most powerful locomotives with which to do so. It would appear, however, from the design of the 'Princes' and 'Claughtons' that Crewe did not realise what a good engine they had in the 'George the Fifth' class because the valve and front-end design of the 4-6-0s were inferior. Neither the 'Prince' nor the 'Claughton' surpassed the average work of the 'Georges' in ordinary everyday service, although the 'Claughtons' could do so when extended.

Superheating was also introduced on the Caledonian 4-4-0s and 4-6-0s during the same period, but the impact was less dramatic than on the LNWR. The superheated Caledonian engines burnt less coal than the saturated engine, but they were not called upon to work any harder. Despite the good work done by the Caledonian engines, J. F. McIntosh realised that increasing traffic would demand more powerful locomotives. Following the trial running of *Polar Star* on the LNWR he considered the possibility of a four-cylinder 4-6-0 which would have matched the 'Claughtons', but finally he was won over to the idea of a four-cylinder Pacific and a drawing dated 8th October 1913 has survived.

This is the first Pacific designed for the West Coast Route by an actual railway drawing office. The engine would have been slightly bigger than the project by the technical journalist, C. Rous-Marten, with a 5ft 8in boiler, a 37sq ft grate and a total heating surface of 3114sq ft. The boiler barrel would have been 22ft between tube-plates and the record of other Pacifics suggests that this might have been excessive. The intention was to build four Pacifics to deal with the cream of the West Coast traffic. The design might well have given trouble with slipping on Beattock Bank and would almost certainly have needed rear-end assistance with the 500ton loads it could, presumably, have hauled from Carlisle to Beattock. Neither Dugald Drummond nor J. F. McIntosh, who both in their day built such good 4-4-0s for the Caledonian, showed the same ability in building large locomotives. After the war W. Pickersgill built four large three-cylinder 4-6-0s of the 956 class, but they were disappointing in performance and had little impact on the West Coast services.

Such, then, was the outline pre-1923 history of the West Coast route and its locomotives. It is the story of a fight against increasing loads in which there was never a final victory, but as a containing action it had its brilliant moments, such as the 'Dunalastairs' around the turn of the century or the 'Georges' during the years 1910-1916. The Pacific type had little impact, being represented by two ghost locomotives, one the dream of a writer and the other a scheme of a professional engineer which reached only an early stage of designing. Neither of these ghosts really had great hopes of success and it was not until another 20 years had passed and the LMS group was 10 years old that the first Pacific was translated from paper to steel. These 10 years were destined to be years of internal conflict.

CHAPTER THREE

The Ancestry of the
West Coast Pacifics

The chain of events which led to the building of the first West Coast Pacific in 1933 originated over 30 years earlier. It was around the turn of the century that standard values, destined ultimately to influence the LMS, were first established. It was not, however, on any of the lines amalgamated in 1923 to form the LMS that these events took place, for the ancestry of the first LMS Pacific has first to be sought on the Great Western Railway. In 1900 William Dean was still in charge at Swindon, but owing to ill health he was deputing an increasing amount of work to his second-in-command, George Jackson Churchward, a man destined in later years to become generally accepted as the greatest locomotive engineer that Britain produced in the 20th Century. Among the more promising younger men on the GWR was W. A. Stanier, who in 1900 left the drawing office to take up the appointment of Inspector of Materials.

The young Stanier had been in the drawing office as Churchward's first experiments in boiler design were made. Although the first engines to carry his boilers were ascribed to William Dean, the domeless boilers were in great contrast to that designer's earlier traditional locomotives. In 1902 Stanier was again promoted to Technical Inspector to the Divisional Locomotive Carriage and Wagon Superintendent, Swindon. The variety of experience gained from these three appointments formed an invaluable background for one who was later destined to be in charge of a railway larger than anyone imagined in the early 1900s. This experience was widened still further when Churchward was in charge and he sent Stanier to London as assistant to John Armstrong, Divisional Locomotive, Carriage and Wagon Superintendent at Westbourne Park. This appointment was also relatively short-lived, as in April 1906 he was recalled to Swindon as Assistant to the Locomotive Works Manager, a job which lasted still less time as in October 1906 Stanier was made Divisional Locomotive Superintendent at Swindon.

All this varied experience was acquired at a most momentous period of Great Western history, as Churchward was building the most efficient locomotives which Britain had seen up to that time and many years were destined to pass before they were matched by any built elsewhere in this country. A keen young engineer must have found the first decade of the 20th Century a most stimulating period. Churchward took a long hard look at the best locomotives in the United States and in Europe and grafted their best features into his own. At this period the reputation of the De Glehn four-cylinder compounds of the French Nord was very high and Churchward bought one of these for trial running on the GWR. This engine was No 102 *La France* and it was followed by two larger French compound Atlantics similar to those used on the Paris-Orleans Railway. These engines ran well on the GWR, especially when new and in the hands of regular crews, but they showed no significant improvement on the simple Atlantics of Churchward's own design. Some features of the French engines were, however, considered to be worthy of adoption.

The French compounds had divided drive with the outside high-pressure cylinders driving the second pair of wheels and the inside low-pressure pair driving the leading axle. This cylinder arrangement was adopted by Churchward for his own four-cylinder simple Atlantic, No 40 *North Star*, which was later rebuilt as a 4-6-0 and formed the prototype of a long line of four-cylinder 4-6-0s. Churchward insisted on having the connecting rods of equal length and this meant setting the outside cylinders back level with the rear pair of bogie wheels. This was a point of weakness in that the cylinders were located at a point where the frames were less deep, being cut away to allow free side play for the bogie. Churchward also believed in having the centre line of the cylinders parallel with the rail. In this he was helped by the slightly more generous GWR clearances, but the relatively small cylinders which had to be used when the De Glehn layout was adopted made high boiler pressures essential. In the early 1900s these were purely GWR problems, but 30 years later they were to become issues which had to be resolved by a former GWR engineer faced with the problem of building a Pacific for the LMS.

Comparative running of Atlantic and 4-6-0 express engines on the GWR resulted in a victory for the six-coupled engines and the GWR was destined to become the railway on which the 4-6-0 was developed to the maximum size possible in this country. It would probably be true to say that the success of the GWR 4-6-0 was a most potent influence on British locomotive practice, having the effect of delaying Pacific construction for several years. It is ironical that the railway whose 4-6-0s persuaded others not to build Pacifics was itself the first railway in Britain to build one. This engine emerged from Swindon in February 1908, failing by less than a year to be the first Pacific in Europe but leading the next British 4-6-2 by 14 years. It was numbered 111 and named *The Great Bear* and its contribution to Great Western publicity was probably greater than its contribution to moving traffic.

The designer's intentions in building this giant engine have been the subject for much conjecture by writers. It has been suggested that pressure had been placed on Churchward by one of the GWR

Directors to build a super engine, while others have concluded that the engine was purely experimental, built to probe the unknown hazards of adapting a large, wide-firebox boiler, approaching American proportions, to the restricted British loading gauge. One thing that can be said with certainty is that the engine was not built because the 4-6-0 'Stars' and 'Saints' were inadequate for the job, for never during its 16 years as a Pacific was *The Great Bear* ever called upon to work a passenger train beyond the capacity of the smaller engines. By virtue of its unique position as Britain's largest locomotive and Britain's only Pacific, *The Great Bear* was prominent in the public eye. There is little doubt that its design and performance were discussed fully by GWR locomotive engineers, including W. A. Stanier, and it must have contributed to his standards of values.

As an exercise in the building of Pacifics, *The Great Bear* pointed the way to future practice, both in the sense of what could safely be done but also in design features wiser to avoid. The heart of a steam locomotive was always its boiler, in fact the main justification for replacing a 4-6-0 with a Pacific was that a larger boiler became possible. A larger boiler was only effective with a larger firebox and the grate area of *The Great Bear* was 41.9sq ft, a considerable advance on the 27sq ft of the 4-6-0s. On a hand-fired Pacific this did not automatically mean that the 4-6-2 would surpass the power output of the 4-6-0 by the ratio of 41 to 27, because the 27sq ft grate of the smaller engine could extend a fireman to his physical limit. The advantage of the larger boiler lay mainly in its capacity for thermal storage, which permitted the engine to be run for a period at a higher rate of steam consumption than could be expected in sustained working. There is no evidence that *The Great Bear* was ever called upon demonstrate this quality in service, but it was shown by Pacifics on other railways, including those of the LMS.

The Great Bear was a pioneer, so it is no sense of criticism that leads to the conclusion that some aspects of its design could have been better. The grate area was 41.9sq ft, but the firebox heating surface was little more than that of the Swindon No 1 standard boiler used on the 'Star' and 'Saint' class 4-6-0s. The comparative significance of grate areas and firebox heating surfaces has been debated, but let us observe that the remarkable steam-raising capacity of the LNWR 'George the Fifth' class 4-4-0s was obtained with a grate area of only 22sq ft, yet with a firebox heating surface comparable with that of the GWR Pacific. The firebox heating surface could have been increased by adding a combustion chamber to the front of the firebox and this became almost a standard feature of later Pacific designs; but in 1908 there was little world experience in the building of correctly-proportioned Pacific fireboxes and Churchward used a simple shape. This meant that the tubes had to be long and although the driving wheels were placed as close together as possible to minimise engine length, the tubes were 23ft long. In the light of later practice such tubes would be considered too long. Britain's last Pacific had tubes 6ft shorter than those of Britain's first 4-6-2. The ill-effects of long tubes could be reduced by correct proportions. Even at this early date Churchward realised this and made his tubes of 2½in diameter on his Pacific against 2in on his 4-6-0. There are no surviving test figures by which the maximum evaporation rates of *The Great Bear* can be compared with those of the 4-6-0s, in fact it is doubtful if the engine ever was fully extended.

The engine part of the locomotive was similar to the later 'Star' class 4-6-0s, with the same cylinder sizes and arrangement. The rear pair of trailing wheels under the firebox had inside bearings, which are reputed to have given trouble with heating. In this connection it is reported that when the well-known locomotive historian, the late E. L. Ahrons, was first shown a picture of a Raven Pacific of the North Eastern Railway he at once pointed to the trailing wheels with inside bearings similar to those on the GWR Pacific and predicted that they would turn out to be a point of weakness. The last three NER Pacifics had outside bearings. Against this the Chapelon compound Pacifics in France inherited this feature from the original PO engines, but when new engines of the same type were built for the Reseau du Nord the inside bearings were repeated. These engines were regularly worked harder than any British Pacifics in terms of power output, although their annual mileages were not excessive. There were German Pacifics which compared more closely with the low average power outputs typical of British Pacifics, but which worked high mileages with apparently no trouble from their inside trailing bearings.

The size and weight of *The Great Bear* limited its normal activities to the London-Bristol route, where it usually worked on the less exacting passenger duties and on fast goods trains. On one special occasion it hauled a freight train weighing 2300 tons from Swindon to Acton at an average speed of 24mph. The reputation of *The Great Bear* was such as to raise it almost to the position of a national institution. If it is judged as it was intended, as the first experimental Pacific, it emerges with more honour than in comparison with 4-6-2s built a generation later. The effect that this engine had on attitudes of GWR engineers is difficult to judge, but it could not have been without its influence. Holding its unique position as Britain's only Pacific for so many years meant that the words *"Great Bear"* and "Pacific" were synonymous. The building of the 'Castle' class 4-6-0s and their subsequent success made the end of *The Great Bear* inevitable; some parts of Britain's first Pacific were used in the 4-6-0 which replaced it, but it gained more immortality by its influence on the design of the first West Coast Pacifics.

After World War I the railways found themselves in a much less favourable position. The conditions under which they had prospered in pre-war days had gone, never to return. The general prosperity of the nation had received a grievous blow and the railways had to share the available traffic with a virile, growing road transport industry which had been stimulated by the advance in internal combustion engine practice that was the inevitable result of its extensive use for military purposes. Road transport was not then in a position to inflict the mortal damage that followed World War II, but in 1920 it was taking away much of the short-distance traffic. Bankruptcy lay ahead for some of the railway companies, yet the nation had not yet developed the depraved notion that it could do without its railways. The solution proposed was that the companies should be amalgamated into four large groups so that the weaker companies could be shielded by the strength of the more prosperous. In 1923 the West Coast Companies all found themselves part of the huge London, Midland and Scottish complex. Amalgamations of this sort allow for economies, but they bring the miseries of conflicting loyalties and thwarted ambitions. It might have been expected that the two West Coast Route companies, the LNWR and the Caledonian, would dominate the LMS, but this was far from being the case. The eclipse of Crewe as the nerve centre of mechanical engineering was an unexpected inversion of pre-war values. In 1920 C. J. Bowen Cooke, the designer of the 'Claughtons', died and following the preliminary amalgamation of the LNWR and the L&Y railways, the post of CME went, by seniority, to George Hughes of Horwich.

The ascendency of the smaller partner seemed inexplicable to the generation that had been taught that the LNWR was "The Premier Line", but Hughes was an able, broad-minded engineer who might, had he been allowed to carry through his ideas to fruition, have made a most favourable impact on the LMS locomotive scene. Many of the senior posts on the LMS went to Midland men and the operating department fell completely under Midland influence. The inner warfare which followed was unhappy and one of the first battle casualties was progress in locomotive design. The policy of a frequent service of light express trains, each with its 4-4-0 engine, had worked well enough on the Midland, which gained much of its passenger revenue from the intermediate stations, but it was not suitable for the LNWR, where the traffic pattern was different with the prizes situated at the end of the track. There was, as far as could be seen into the future in 1923, the need for long heavy trains on the LNWR and these trains demanded large locomotives to haul them at competitive speeds. Mr Hughes recognised this and started the preliminary planning for a Pacific locomotive.

The LMS needed a new powerful design, even in the early 1920s, because none of their large 4-6-0s had fully come up to expectations. The LNWR 'Claughtons' had started their lives with a number of encouraging test performances and with a number of first-class runs in ordinary service, but in average everyday running they rarely improved on the performance of the smaller 4-6-0s of the 'Prince of Wales' class or the 4-4-0 'George the Fifths'. Hughes had reinforced the 'Claughtons' by building some of the superheated version of his own four-cylinder 4-6-0, nicknamed the "Dreadnoughts", for service on the LNWR, especially between Crewe and Carlisle. There were some good design features in these engines, but they never promised to be more than a standby until a Pacific or a larger 4-6-0 could be developed. The "Dreadnoughts" had been built for use on services which required high power outputs for short periods only and the relatively small grate area of 27sq ft compared with 30sq ft of the 'Claughtons'. The driving wheels, 6ft 3in in diameter were admirably suited for the L&Y main line, but although it is generally believed that smaller driving wheels were better on the banks, the lessons of history prove no such thing. The relatively small driving wheels meant more rapid piston strokes in the four cylinders and this increased the drain of steam when the engine was running hard and fast.

The original, saturated, flat valve, four-cylinder L&Y 4-6-0s had been dreadful engines, but the superheated piston-valve rebuilds had some elements of advanced design by 1923 LMS standards. The new cylinders had outside Walschaerts gear, straight ports and generously proportioned piston valves with a long travel of $6\frac{3}{8}$in, but with a more moderate steam lap of $1\frac{3}{16}$in. It is not claimed that Hughes had absorbed the Churchward doctrine in full, but he was moving in the right direction. The effectiveness of his valves and cylinders was, however, reduced by leakage past the ball compression release valves. By the time this deficiency was realised and corrected it was too late, for the Stanier Black Fives were waiting in the wings and no one was interested in the Hughes "Dreadnoughts". In the early 1920s, however, the Hughes 4-6-0s were doing quite a lot of the Crewe-Carlisle running and they were appearing on LMS posters, where they looked well in the LMS red, making a picture as appealing to the non-technical as a GWR 'Castle' or an SR 'King Arthur', even if they lacked the size and presence of a Gresley Pacific.

Through the kindness of E. S. Cox, the only man who saw the development of the LMS Pacific through from start to finish from a responsible position, we are able to tell the story in some detail. Although he was only 23 years old at the time Mr Cox was given the job of doing all the preliminary schemes and diagrams. A start was made on the proposed Pacific on 22 February 1923 in the Horwich drawing office and the work was undertaken with enthusiasm — the words "We are going to lick creation with this" appeared in Mr Cox's diary. Had they been allowed to proceed they might very well have done so, and the largest British railway company would not have suffered criticism for working its expresses with the smallest locomotives. The Horwich Pacific design was based on a diagram dated 2 March 1923, in which the engine chassis was identical with that of the Hughes four-cylinder 4-6-0s except for the provision of 6ft 9in driving wheels. Three months later more detailed drawings were prepared and these showed a taper boiler with Belpaire firebox and a combustion chamber. This boiler was 6ft 3in diameter at the firebox end and 5ft 9in at the smokebox, with a moderate tube length of 19ft. The footplating in front of the cylinders was curved top and bottom in the same way as that of the "Dreadnoughts". Between the first diagram and this more detailed drawing the series of proposed standard engines was sketched out. These are the engines shown on the end papers of *British Railways Standard Steam Locomotives* by E. S. Cox (Ian Allan 1966). The fact that the Pacific has a parallel boiler in this series has no significance, as the drawings were only intended to show the general scheme of things.

The definitive drawing for the Hughes Pacific was Diagram No 17560, dated 9 October 1924, first published in *Locomotive Panorama* Vol 1 by E. S. Cox (Ian Allan 1965) and repeated in this book. This retained the taper boiler but differed in having the footplating immediately in front of the cylinders at a right angle instead of curved like the 4-6-0s. There was no further development between October 1924 and July 1925 while Hughes argued the case for his Pacific. The Euston management, left to itself, could hardly have avoided accepting the logic of the fact that the West Coast needed a big engine, but by this time the Midland lobby, led by J. E. Anderson, the Chief Operating Officer, who had the backing of J. H. Follows, by then appointed Vice President in charge of operations, was able to point out that the Midland Compound had performed very well in comparative trials against various 4-6-0s. With hindsight we can see through the flimsy nature of this argument, which was based on comparative rather than on absolute values. The Midland Compound only appeared to be good because the LNWR, L&Y and Caledonian 4-6-0s had performed so badly. If the Compound had been compared with a GWR 4-6-0 the results would have been very different, but the published results of the test running of *Caldicot Castle* in 1924 were so good as only to inspire disbelief in LMS circles. Anderson however, was able to present such a case for the Compounds and the Midland "small engine policy" that further progress on the Hughes Pacific was halted.

Had the engine been built its success would have depended on the cylinder and valve design. If the valve dimensions of the Hughes Mogul, which was being developed at the same time, or the experimental work on 4-6-0 No 1656 been used as the basis for improved valve events on the Pacific, and had the problem of steam leakage past piston valves been solved, the Horwich Pacific might have proved to be at least the equal of the Gresley design; and like the LNER engine, it could have been the basis of further progress. As things were the LMS struggled on with new 4-4-0s and aging 4-6-0s.

Side by side with the Pacific a 2-8-2 freight engine, using the same cylinders and boiler, was also being designed and this project received more sympathy from the Midland lobby because its main use would have been in solving a Midland problem, that of the Toton-Brent mineral trains which were needing pairs of 0-6-0s. The disadvantages of regular double-heading were obvious to Midland engineers, although it is possible to quote amateur partisan writings in the 1970s where the double-heading, even with 4-2-2 singles, was described as being very efficient. Anderson asked for three cylinders instead of the proposed four for the 2-8-2 and some work was done towards adapting the three-cylinder layout to the Pacific also. This was the last phase of the Horwich Pacific, as Hughes retired on 30 September 1925.

Hughes was followed by Sir Henry Fowler, the former Midland CME, and it appeared that the Midland victory was complete. Sir Henry was a man of high intellect whose main contributions to the company had been in administration, workshop organisation and in metallurgy. He does not seem to have possessed the driving force of emotional involvement in locomotive design which characterised a Churchward, a Gresley or a Chapelon. This need not have adversely affected the progress of the LMS if the chief had been allowed to channel the enthusiasm of younger men in the right direction. At first this might have happened. Less than a month after the retirement of George Hughes the leading draughtsman at Horwich drawing office, Edward Gass, was put in charge of the task of producing a compound version of the Hughes Pacific. The drawing office work was split between Derby, Horwich and Crewe. E. S. Cox was again given the job of producing the first diagrams and his last job before leaving Horwich for Derby was to produce the definitive diagram dated 14 November 1925. Whilst the work was in progress there had been a scare that the Civil Engineer would not accept the weight and a cut-down version was schemed out. This would have been only 12ft 11in high to chimney top and the tube length would have been 14ft 8in, which is very short for a Pacific. The objections to the original design were, however, withdrawn and the design reverted to the first scheme. The published drawing is No 18620 of 14 November 1925.

Derby drawing office was not to blame for the small engine policy. A four-cylinder compound 4-6-0 had been designed by Deeley in 1907, while in 1924 a larger three-cylinder 4-6-0 compound design took shape. This engine was really an enlargement of the 4-4-0 compound but it would have been a great asset to the LMS. It had little effect on the design for the compound Pacific which had its inspiration in France. At this time the Bréville four-cylinder compound "Super Pacifics" of the Nord were deservedly gaining a high reputation for energetic uphill work. A deputation led by Sir Henry Fowler visited all the French main line railways in October 1925. They found varied opinions about the efficacy of compounding and the best means for building such engines, as the Chapelon researches still lay in the future, but Fowler returned willing to press on with the LMS compound Pacific.

The design which emerged had the wheel spacing of the Hughes Pacific but the 180lb taper boiler was replaced with a parallel boiler of smaller diameter with a Belpaire firebox and a larger combustion chamber. The higher pressure of 240lb/sq in doubtless made this smaller diameter essential to keep the engine within the weight limits. The tube length was reduced to 17ft, which was reasonable, but the free gas area was unsatisfactory by later standards. The circumferencial riveted seam round the copper inner firebox at the point of attachment of the combustion chamber and the small radius at the throat are thought by Mr E. S. Cox to be possible sources of trouble.

The high-pressure cylinders were outside, set at an angle similar to the Horwich Moguls. They were slightly smaller than those of the Nord "Super Pacifics", as were the inside low-pressure cylinders. In order to leave room for larger journals on the crank axle the wheels were dished. This same feature was to be found on the Caledonian 'Cardean' class 4-6-0s, but it is not known if the Scottish engines inspired this design feature or if it was decided upon independently. The operation of the LMS compound would have been much simpler than the Nord engines, with their specially trained regular crews, and the cut-offs for high and low pressure cylinders were linked. A starting valve operating automatically as cut-off was shortened was to be provided. Such a valve had been used on an L&Y 0-8-0 and on 4-6-0 No 10456, which was converted to a compound to act as a 'guinea pig' for the compound Pacifics. A corresponding 2-8-2 design was developed simultaneously.

There seemed every chance that this design would succeed in being built and it is believed that some parts were actually cast, but events outside the LMS strengthened the hand of the Midland small engine lobby. In 1925 there had been an exchange between the Gresley Pacific and the Collett 'Castle' class 4-6-0 from the GWR, and the smaller engine emerged with most of the honours. The Southern Railway was contemplating a larger engine and J. Clayton was sent to ride on a GWR 'Castle' and a Gresley Pacific in order to adivse Maunsell on whether to build a Pacific or a 4-6-0. He advised the 4-6-0 and the 'Lord Nelson' class design was started. The prestige of the GWR 4-6-0s was at its highest and even the diehard J. E. Anderson of the LMS Operating Department and his friend on the board, J. H. Follows, were impressed. The heavy trains during the 1926 coal strike had left the Midland compounds sadly wanting, while the Gresley Pacifics, on the rival line, had frisked away with 600 tons behind their tenders. Again, the LMS wanted to introduce a prestige train on the Anglo-Scottish services in the summer of 1927 to counter successful East Coast propaganda and they realised that such a job was far beyond a single-handed Midland Compound. They realised also that, even if the compound Pacific was destined ultimately to be a great success, there would inevitably be a long period of teething troubles with a design so different from anything known in LMS experience. Their new argument was not that a big engine was ruled out, but that it did not need to be quite as big; they pointed to the GWR 'Castle' as exactly the size they wanted.

In the autumn of 1926 No 5000 *Launceston Castle* appeared on the LMS main line for a series of trial runs, while as a face-saver a Midland Compound was sent to the GWR to try its hand at a few relatively light jobs. The story of what happened lies mainly outside the Pacific story, but it is well known that the 'Castle' gave every satisfaction. It led to the stoppage of work on the Fowler Pacific and production of a new design for a three-cylinder 4-6-0 of about the same size as the 'Castle' by cooperation between Derby and the North British Locomotive Company. So great was the need for a new powerful engine that 50 of the new 4-6-0s were ordered straight from the drawing board. Meanwhile the new prestige express, named "The Royal Scot" to counter the East Coast "Flying Scotsman", was worked by double-heading in the summer of 1927 until the new 'Royal Scot' 4-6-0s were ready to take over in the autumn. It has been fashionable to condemn strongly the Midland lobby of the 1920s, and perhaps there is every justification for doing so when they stopped the Horwich Pacific in favour of 4-4-0 compounds. But in citing the GWR 'Castle' as a better proposition than the Fowler compound Pacific and in building the 'Royal Scot' 4-6-0s, the logic of their argument has much to commend it. Mr Cox, who was in a position to know all the facts, is of the opinion that there were a number of design faults in the Pacifics which would have reduced reliability in service, while the success of the 'Royal Scots' in service is a matter of recorded history. In 1927 it looked as if the 4-6-0 had gained a resounding victory over the Pacific, with only the East Coast remaining faithful to the larger engine.

The success of the 'Castles' on LNER and LMS metals, the building of the SR 'Lord Nelsons' and the GWR 'Kings', seemed to suggest that the 4-6-0 was firmly established for many years to come. When even the LMS, with similar distances to the LNER, also chose the 4-6-0 it looked very much as if Gresley had the mistaken policy. We know now, however, that this was a premature belief; it was not the addition of an extra pair of wheels at the back, it was the lack of a few inches on the travel of the valves and a fraction of an inch on the steam lap which caused the defeat of the Gresley Pacific in 1925. The greater success of the Gresley Pacific in dealing with the low-quality coal in the 1926 strike was equally significant.

As the 1920s came to their close and the 1930s dawned the 'Royal

Scots' shed their teething troubles and under their influence LMS prestige rose, especially following the accelerations of 1932. In actual fact they were needing to be pressed rather hard on the heavier trains with the faster bookings and pilots were seen on the LNWR main line fairly frequently, whereas a double-headed Pacific on the GNR was regarded as an unforgiveable blasphemy.

In 1931 Sir Henry Fowler was promoted to research and E. J. H. Lemon was appointed in his place. Lemon's talents lay mainly in administration and it may well be that his appointment was only intended to be temporary. There had been changes in the higher command of the LMS and Sir Josiah Stamp, the eminent economist, who was now President of the Executive and Chairman of the LMS, realised that it was time that an end was put to the internal rivalries by appointing a man from outside to the position of Chief Mechanical Engineer. The lot fell upon W. A. Stanier, the second man at Swindon, who was invited to take up the chief position on the LMS from 1 January 1932. The task facing the new chief was a formidable one and among his aims was that of providing an express locomotive capable of working the heaviest trains from Euston to Glasgow unchanged. The 4-6-0 'Royal Scots' had performed this duty occasionally, but in normal running the narrow firebox had taken enough by the time Carlisle was reached. The new locomotive was perforce a Pacific and this time the engine really did get built. Its ancestry may be summarised thus:

Date	Event
1903	Development work on Churchward 2cyl 4-6-0s reaches fruition
1903	De Glehn compound *La France* introduced on to the GWR
1906	The first Churchward 4cyl locomotive *North Star*
1908	*The Great Bear* built
1922	The first Gresley Pacific built
1923	Formation of the LMS
2/3/23	First diagram of Horwich Pacific
8/6/24	Drawing No 17309, taper boilered 4cyl 4-6-2 (Also as 2-8-2)
9/10/24	Drawing No 17560, definitive diagram of above (Also as 2-8-2)
7/7/25	Drawing No 18478, as above but 3cyl (Also as 2-8-2)
30/9/25	George Hughes retired
23/10/25	Horwich 4-6-2 re-arranged as 4cyl compound (Also as 2-8-2)
28/10/25	Drawing No 18604, cut-down version (Also as 2-8-2)
14/11/25	Drawing No 18620, definitive compound diagram (Also as 2-8-2)
10/26	*Launceston Castle* loaned to LMS for trials
1927	Work on compound Pacific suspended, 'Royal Scot' 4-6-0s built
1/1/32	W. A. Stanier appointed Chief Mechanical Engineer

The story of development was not quite ended. Alternative schemes were considered in 1932 before work was started on the first Stanier Pacific. All the above events had their influence to a greater or less degree on the Pacific which was ultimately built.

CHAPTER FOUR

The First LMS Pacifics

One of the first tasks undertaken by the new CME was the building of the prototypes of a new design of express passenger engine larger than the 'Royal Scot' class 4-6-0s. In the summer of 1932 the LMS embarked on an extensive programme of acceleration of its main-line services as a counter blast against increasing road competition. The 'Royal Scots', by this time equipped with narrow ring piston valves, rose well to the occasion and some excellent work was recorded on the new timings in the summer, but the need for something larger and more powerful was obvious. The 'Royal Scots' were being worked very hard for their size. It is true that, on the GWR, loads just as heavy were worked on schedules even more exacting, but these heavy loads were seasonal or limited to a single crack train each day such as the down "Limited"; the LMS main line usually carried more trains loading to over 500 tons each day. The newer LMS coaches were heavier for a given passenger capacity and a train which in the late 1920s would have weighed 450 tons would, in 1932, be about 50 tons heavier. Even on the flatter gradients south of Crewe the 'Royal Scots' often took pilots and the proud regimental motto of *Nulli Secundus* had rather a hollow meaning.

Unlike Gresley on the LNER and the original ill-fated schemes of Hughes and Fowler, Stanier had no remit to build a 2-8-2 freight engine with the same boiler and cylinders as a Pacific. There were two reasons for this; the mineral traffic had not expanded as had been hoped, but had declined during the Depression; and the major freight problem, that of the Toton-Brent coal trains, had been answered by the building of the Garratts. These engines did not show the Garratt type at its best but their shortcomings were due to poor valve design and to undersized axleboxes rather than to any failure of the basic conception.

The idea of an express Garratt, based on two Midland compounds, had appealed to Anderson and Beyer Peacocks had schemed out two designs in 1930. One was for a Garratt which would have consisted of two Atlantics with Midland compound cylinders and an enlarged version which would have been, in effect two Pacifics. These designs were revived and presented to Stanier as the need for something bigger than the 'Royal Scots' arose. It was suggested that these could, with advantage, be built as four- or six-cylinder simple engines, but Stanier rejected the idea as he could see no need for anything more powerful than the Pacific he had in mind. Anderson had retired by this time, but it is ironical to think that the man who, for so long, had wanted to run the Anglo-Scottish services with Midland compounds, was, before he retired, associated with a scheme which involved a locomotive weighing over 200 tons.

It can well be imagined that the project for an LMS Pacific was received with enthusiasm by the younger and keener LMS engineers. It most certainly was a tonic to amateur LMS enthusiasts, who first heard that something was afoot in the early months of 1933. Schoolboy doodlings produced such alternatives as a King-sized LMS 4-6-0 with a taper boiler and Lentz poppet valves and a 'Royal Scot' lengthened into a Pacific. By midsummer it was generally known that the new LMS engine was to be a Pacific and that excellent source of information to the younger generation, the *Meccano Magazine*, revealed that it was to have a taper boiler and four cylinders of the same size as a GWR 'King'. The appearance of a small 0-4-0 tank engine with a stovepipe chimney as the first new design to appear under the name of the new CME caused some to wonder if the stovepipe was to be the new LMS standard. Mr Cox has since revealed that the stovepipe was carried forward from the brief interregnum of Lemon and Beames and that the first drawings of new Stanier engines were so adorned pending a decision on the future shape of chimney. It is rumoured that Stanier's old chief, G. J. Churchward, was asked for advice and replied: "Why not give them proper GWR chimneys?" Finally the Derby drawing office, after some consideration of the Caledonian chimney, produced the pattern which became famous when used on many standard Stanier locomotives.

A three-cylinder Pacific with cylinders arranged as on the 'Royal Scots' was, in fact, much more than a schoolboys' doodle; it might very easily have been built. It is generally believed that, from his experience on the GWR which never had a three cylinder-locomotive, Stanier was naturally hostile to three cylinders, but actually he had an open mind on the subject or he would never have retained the three cylinders of the 'Patriot' on his 'Jubilee' class 4-6-0s, nor would he have built three-cylinder 2-6-4 Tanks for the Tilbury section. A three-cylinder Pacific was seriously considered.

The first proposals were put forward on drawing No EU8, which allowed two alternative designs, both with 6ft 9in driving wheels and either three cylinders 19in in diameter and 28in stroke, arranged as in the 'Royal Scots'; or four cylinders of 16½in diameter and 28in stroke. A taper boiler with tubes 22ft long was proposed for either engine. Stanier shrank from the combustion chamber proposed for the Fowler four-cylinder compound with a riveted front right round its starting point, which could have given a lot of trouble. A flanged pressed throatplate wrapper more like that of the Gresley Pacifics was adopted and this allowed the 22ft tubes to be shortened to 20ft 3in. The final diagram was EU12 of 25 April 1932, when the four-cylinder 'King' front end with 'King'-sized 16¼in by 28in cylinders and 6ft 6in driving wheels was decided upon. There had been some resistance by the Civil Engineer to a new heavy express engine and it is probable that the case which could be made for the superior balancing of four cylinders had assisted in the choice of this arrangement. In the light of later practice it might have been possible to have built a three-cylinder engine with no hammer blow. The staggered cylinders and connecting rods of almost equal length followed the De Glehn layout used on the GWR.

In June 1933 the first LMS Pacific emerged from Crewe Works, over ten years since the first design of Hughes Pacific had been started with such high hopes. Mr E. S. Cox, who had seen the whole story through from start to finish, makes the comment that "I think it is fair to say that there was no time in this long period when the railway would not have benefited from an engine of this capacity."

Photographs of the new Pacific No 6200, un-named and in shop grey, appeared in the press in late June 1933 and the *News Chronicle* newspaper invited its readers to suggest suitable names for the new giant and sister engines to follow. This was probably an exercise by the newspaper with no blessing from the LMS as the suggestions, many of which were better than those actually chosen, were ignored. The first impression was of an engine of all the talents, combining the large cylinders and high tractive effort of the GWR 'Kings' with the boiler power of the Gresley Pacific. Its appearance was impressive and the main criticisms were directed against the small tender. This was bigger than the standard LMS tender used on the 'Royal Scots', but it was small for so long an engine. The proposed Hughes Pacific would have had an eight-wheeled tender, but this would have increased the already long wheelbase of No 6200 to something even more unmanageable. The first Pacific is recorded as being completed on 27 June 1933 and handed over to traffic on 1 July 1933. Photographs exist of the engine in shop grey un-named, named *Princess Royal* and re-named *The Princess Royal.* On 15 August, 1933, the engine, then painted in LMS red, made a press run to Crewe with an invited party of press representatives, and on 22 September it made its first through trip to Glasgow on the down "Royal Scot".

An examination of the early photographs and the leading dimensions of No 6200 showed that it was something more than the second GWR Pacific for, while hints of its GWR ancestry were obvious, the new machine was very much an engine in its own right, the first LMS Pacific. The taper boiler was an innovation for the LMS, but it was different from those of the GWR in that the taper was equally divided between the upper and lower boiler surfaces, whereas the GWR had all the taper at the top with the lower surface level. This had the optical effect of making the degree of taper on GWR locomotives more obvious. The great length of the Pacific boiler made the taper less apparent than that of the GWR engines or later Stanier locomotives with shorter boilers. The grate area was 45sq ft as against the 41sq ft of the Gresley Pacifics and the 34sq ft of the GWR 'Kings', and its very size must have been daunting to firemen used to nothing larger than the 31sq ft grates of the 'Royal Scots'. The boiler pressure was 250lb, the same as the 'Kings' and the 'Scots'. The boiler was domeless, with the regulator valve combined with the superheater header; a rudimentary casing resembling a small dome actually housed the top feed clacks. Top feed was a GWR feature destined to spread to the LMS. Four pop safety valves were mounted over the firebox, which was a combination of the wide and Belpaire types.

The tube length of 20ft 9in was more than that of the 19ft on the Gresley Pacifics, but it was less than the 21ft of the Raven Pacifics, the 23ft of *The Great Bear* or the 22ft originally intended. This tube length has latterly been a subject of criticism of the original design, but tube length is not fatal in itself; it is the ratio of length to internal diameter which is important. One of these long tube boiler, with later modifications, was destined to perform one of the greatest feats of sustained steaming in British locomotive history.

Nevertheless the tube length was a design feature which was later modified. When the design was being prepared Stanier was at first dubious about providing a combustion chamber partly, as mentioned earlier, because he considered that there were some risky design features in the proposed Fowler compound Pacific boiler with its short tubes and long combustion chamber; partly, perhaps, because Churchward rejected combustion chambers after unfortune experience with the 'Kruger' class 4-6-0s, and possibly he was influenced also by German thought, which had rejected them on several of the Reishbahn locomotives. He doubtless considered that the staying problems would be increased and perhaps he was not convinced that Crewe Works could carry out the difficult flanging operation. Swindon had retained the vertical firebox plate at the tube end. Any doubts were later proved to be unfounded as later Crewe showed its ability to build large Pacific boilers which were an advance on Swindon practice, but the first two engines evidently posed quite a few problems, especially as Stanier insisted on Swindon standards of workmanship for certain details, which did not always conform with the economy drive imposed by Sir Josiah Stamp.

The original boilers had 170 small tubes of 2¼in outside diameter and 16 flue tubes of 5⅛in. The first two engines had the very unfavourable A/S tube ratios of 1/495 and their firebox heating surface of 190sq ft compared with 160sq ft of the LNWR 4-4-0 'Georges', which had less than half the Pacific's grate area and were remarkable steam raisers. The 16 flue, two-row superheater with two single return loop elements per flue followed Swindon practice in its general conception of giving moderate superheat only, but the arrangement of fastening the elements to the header was pure Schmidt. This small superheater was the design feature which raised the greatest misgivings when the first LMS Pacific was discussed in the technical press. In its defence it could be claimed that the GWR 4-6-0s, at the height of their reputation in 1933, were performing admirably. The Churchward theory was that it was wasteful to raise steam temperature to a point higher than that at which it would be saturated at the point of exhaust. It was considered wasteful to throw useful heat away up the chimney. Under perfect conditions of operation the theory was sound and it was supported by the excellent results obtained from the Swindon locomotives. The great epics of GWR running had, however, been made by locomotives burning high-grade coal and with the boiler pressure kept near to the blowing-off point. GWR locomotives lost much of their sparkle when pressure fell and they had been unhappy with imported coal during the 1926 strike. The new LMS Pacifics were likely to face greater operational difficulties on longer continuous runs, with the risk that pressures would tend to fall before the end, while the quality of coal available for LMS engines was, in general, lower than that of the best Welsh steam coal used on the GWR crack working.

It is, however, illogical for critics to suggest that the low superheat was the cause of bad steaming. The degree of superheat had nothing to do with the steaming. It could be argued that heat used for raising the temperature of steam could not be used to evaporate water to make more steam, and examples could be quoted of excellent steaming by certain well-known classes of saturated engine such as the LNWR 'Precursors'. The steaming of the first LMS Pacifics was not always satisfactory, but the draughting was as likely to be to blame as the low superheat, since the free gas area was only 5.33sq ft, little greater than that of a 'King' and less than that of a 'Royal Scot'. The percentage of free gas area to grate area was only 11.6% and it is probable that this factor in conjunction with poor A/S ratios was as much to blame as the low superheat for the early troubles of the LMS Pacifics. Steam was collected by a perforated pipe over the firebox in the GWR manner and the regulator was on the saturated side of the superheater header. This did not prove to be very satisfactory due to cracks developing in the rather complicated header casting, which led later to a reversion to the more usual regulator placed in the dome.

The smokebox was a departure from the built-up type used on the 'Royal Scots', which in its turn was derived from Midland practice. The Pacifics had the GWR type of cylindrical smokebox resting on a saddle. This proved in practice to be a great improvement, as leaks developed with age and mileage on the locomotives with built-up smokeboxes, such as the 'Royal Scots' and 'Patriots', which justified starting a drastic rebuilding that was almost a replacement even under wartime restrictions. The smokebox was of the same external diameter as the rest of the boiler and this marked a reversion to the policy of Johnson, which had been altered by Deeley; but in this latest case the GWR influence was also at work. The boiler was fed by an exhaust steam injector below the right-hand footplate and a live steam injector on the left; feed water was carried to the top feed clacks by pipes outside the boiler casing.

The De Glehn layout was not ideal and the front-end framing was weak owing to lack of bracing between the outside cylinders as a result of the inside valve gear. Loosening of the cylinders was a frequent occurrence and keep plates were later welded to the frames. This was a congenital fault of engines built to the De Glehn pattern and the GWR 4-6-0s suffered in the same way. It was never cured on the LMS until a different cylinder pattern was adopted for later Pacifics. In post-war years the front-end framing was completely renewed and the 'Princesses', which had been very uncertain performers in the late 1940s and early 1950s, enjoyed a new lease of life in the late 1950s.

The GWR type of axleboxes were used with pressed-in brass and white metal crown. This proved a most valuable improvement compared with the previous LMS type and the use of similar boxes on the 'Royal Scots' caused a dramatic reduction in the incidence of hot boxes. The coupled wheelsprings were of the plate type underhung, but the original intention of trying compensated springing on one of the original three engines was not pursued. This is regrettable and we do not know to what extent slipping might have been reduced. The bogie was of the De Glehn type, owing its origin to the French compounds on the GWR. The trailing end was supported by spliced framing, which was originally designed for the proposed Fowler compound Pacific and 2-8-2. The trailing truck was pivoted just behind the rear coupled wheels and outside bearings were provided.

The driving wheels were fitted with the Gibson ring of triangular section to fasten the tyres. This proved to be a good feature of the Stanier engines and fractured tyres, which could be nerve-racking, became a thing of the past. The balance weights for the coupled wheels were built up by steel plates on both sides of the spokes and riveted; the requisite weight was provided by filling in between the plates with lead. The coupling rods and connecting rods were of high tensile molydenum steel, the outside connecting rods were fluted while the inside rods and the coupling rods were rectangular. The balancing was provided entirely on the wheels; the inside cranks had no balancing crank webs.

The cylinder layout followed GWR practice and was almost identical with that of the 'Kings'. The engine had staggered cylinders and connecting rods of almost equal length. An unusual feature was the spacing of the driving axles with 8ft between the first pair and 7ft 2in between the rear pair. This did not make the connecting rods exactly equal as the outside pair at 108in long were 5½in longer than the inside pair. This difference in length was not significant, but it was a departure from Churchward practice. The outside cylinders were inclined at an angle of 1 in 35, marking another departure from the 'King' layout while the inside pair were horizontal. This was most likely due to clearances on the LMS being more restrictive than those on the GWR.

There was some conjecture about the reasons for adopting four sets of valve gear instead of having a set of rocking gear and the reduced resistance of two sets of gear. The inside sets of gear added to complication, as they had to be located in a cramped position which made maintenance difficult because parts of the gear above the bogie were very inaccessible. The GWR arrangement, where the outside valves were driven by the inside gear, had the disadvantage of slightly uneven valve events aggravated by the short connecting rods. This was partly overcome by a cranked rocking lever, which in practice gave an acceptable solution. This was, however, rejected by the LMS. The alternative arrangement of rockers driving the inside valve from the outside was worse in that it introduced the effects of valve spindle expansion which may well have made the inside valve events some-what ragged. Purist thought must have prevailed at Derby and four separate sets of gear were thought to be justified to maintain precise valve events. The complication of four sets of gear was not unknown as there were four sets on the Southern Railway 'Lord Nelson' class 4-6-0s but in this case they were essential for their eight-beat crank arrangement.

The inside admission piston valves had 1¾in lap with ¼in lead and were 8in in diameter, which was 1in smaller than the valves of the GWR 'Kings'. This need have been no disadvantage since their optimum speed range was in the useful 40-80mph band. It could be argued that the 9in valves of the 'Kings' and the 'Duchesses' were too large for everyday running. The thermo-dynamic performance of the 'Princesses' was not inferior to that of the later LMS Pacifics, although these were faster and more powerful. The valves had six narrow rings of the type finally adopted for the 'Royal Scots'. These gave freedom from leakage from the start and the trouble that beset the 'Royal Scots' and the early LNER Pacifics was avoided.

The slide bars of the first two LMS Pacifics were a copy of the GWR 'rabbit ear' type. They lacked stiffness and apparently gave trouble with crossheads in their early days. When No 6200 was on its way to Euston for its first public unveiling there was trouble and even on the famous high-speed test run to Glasgow and back by No 6201 in 1936 the crosshead had to be hurriedly re-metalled at St Rollox before the return journey. It was only because of some heroic effort by R. A. Riddles that the journey could be made as scheduled.

The first two engines had a 16-feed mechanical lubricator feeding atomised oil to the front and back of each steam chest and to the bottom of each cylinder, and unatomised oil to each piston rod gland. There were many hand lubricating points on the original pair of engines closed by corks, which made their preparation somewhat more arduous than on later Pacifics, so much so that No 6201 rejoiced in the nickname of "Corky Liz".

The cab owed nothing to the GWR or the Midland; its nearest relative on the LMS was the later L&Y design. The Caledonian whistle was adopted and it was mounted in a horizontal position in front of the cab. The wide firebox imposed problems for the location of the reversing gear. The reach rod which passed outside the firebox was, of necessity close to the edge of the cab for the normal screw handle, so an intermediate reduction gear was fitted. The reach rod was in two sections, one from the cab to a position in front of the firebox and a second rod from there to the weigh bar just in front of the centre coupled wheels. Hand-operated trickle sanding was applied in front of the first and second pair of driving wheels and behind the second pair. A de-sander which washed the rails with hot water was fitted behind the rear pair of driving wheels to prevent the sand interfering with track circuits; it operated automatically in time with the forward sanding. This device was not perpetuated after the first pair of engines.

A steam brake cylinder located between the second and third pair of driving wheels applied pressure to brake blocks forward of each pair of coupled wheels. The bogie brakes used on the 'Royal Scots' were not used on the Pacifics. In this connection Stanier was following GWR practice, as the bogie brakes on the early 'Castles' were not continued on the later 'Castles' nor on the 'Kings'. A crosshead brake pump maintained the vacuum when running. The ejector was carried just below the driver's look-out window and its discharge pipe ran along the boiler side just below the handrail, entering the smokebox and discharging through the chimney.

The tender was criticised as being too small for the engine, but a larger one would have increased the total length to an undesirable figure. Later engines had higher tenders on the same wheelbase. The close proximity of the LNWR water troughs allowed a six-wheeled tender to have high coal capacity with 4000gall of water, against 5000gall of the eight-wheeled tenders of the Gresley Pacifics. The low water capacity was destined to prove a disadvantage on other railways such as the GWR, where various LMS Pacifics had to work during the 1948 Exchanges, and on other occasions in BR days. Three of the original type of tender were built; two were used on Pacifics and the third accompanied the 'Royal Scot' class 4-6-0 on its American tour.

Two of these tenders had roller bearings and the free-running qualities were demonstrated to a number of LMS VIPs when two men pushed the tender the length of the shop. These tenders looked like bigger Midland-type tenders but they looked small on the Pacifics. They were not completely satisfactory; it was hoped that they would be self-trimming, but in practice men had to go back and shovel coal forward as the end of a 400mile continuous working approached and this added to the burden of a fireman, who in the early days might also have been fighting against shy steaming.

The second Pacific, No 6201, was handed over to traffic in November 1933 and at about the same time there came the sensational announcement that the third engine would be delayed as "a simplified form of turbine drive" would be tried. This remarkable departure from the normal pattern of things deserves consideration in a separate chapter.

In 1934 No 6201 received a double chimney of repellent aspect in which the inside cylinders exhausted through the front nozzle and the outer pair through the rear. The performance seems to have been as unsatisfactory as the appearance and the engine speedily reverted to normal. Possibly this incident made the authorities shrink from ever using a double chimney on a 'Princess', which is a pity, for a properly-proportioned double exhaust, which need not have been ugly, might have benefitted the 'Princesses' just as it did the 'Duchesses' and the Rebuilt 'Royal Scots'.

During 1934 the first two Pacifics took their place in the LMS locomotive stock. Varying accounts, ranging from success to failure, enlivened discussion in railway society club rooms and on platform ends. While this was going on the professionals were conducting tests and seeking ways in which the production members of the class might, with advantage, differ from the prototypes. It became apparent quite early on that if the long continuous run to Glasgow was to be an all-the-year-round possibility, then there would have to be boiler changes which would improve steaming. It was also decided that the temperature of the superheated steam might also be raised. Temperature of steam did not automatically improve steaming, which depended mainly on boiler draughting and basic proportions.

Attention had been focused on the need for more superheat by the disappointing performance of the 5XP 4-6-0s of Stanier's design as compared with the 'Patriots' and the degree of superheat achieved on Nos 6200/1 was not considered to be satisfactory for the turbine engine. Plans were made to build a boiler with 32 elements for the turbine locomotive and also to test a similar boiler on an ordinary 'Princess'. Meanwhile it was thought that 24 elements would prove sufficient for the production batch of reciprocating Pacifics to be built in 1935. Before these engines were all in service it was decided to build some with 32 elements and it was the leading dimensions of these which were published when the first of the 1935 batch was illustrated. It has been suggested that some of these engines were first built with 32 element boilers and that they were later rebuilt with 24 elements, while other writers claim that the early examples were built with 24 elements. The first engine, No 6203, was illustrated in the technical press in July 1935 and the accompanying table of dimensions specified 32 elements. There is, however, one indisputable fact and that is that on 25-27 November 1935 No 6203 with 24 elements ran tests against No 6209 with 32 elements. The test report can hardly be in error and four months is a short time for a boiler change or major modification to be made on a new engine. It would certainly be too short a time for the engine to have reached its first planned boiler change. It would appear that Nos 6203-6206 received the 24 element boilers from the start, but that later the smaller superheaters alternated among a number of 'Princesses'.

The test running of November 1935 revealed a slight advantage to No 6209 with the larger superheater, but dogmatic conclusions cannot be based on a few variable speed tests. We are indebted to Mr E. S. Cox for the full story. It was mistakenly thought that superheat temperatures rose directly with the number of elements. Later it was found that temperature was powerfully affected by the resistance to the flow of gases along each individual tube. Nothing was done about lowering the resistance in the tubes when the 24-element superheater was introduced, with the result that the average and terminal temperatures were disappointing. The 32-element superheater gave a sufficient temperature, but this was nowhere near the temperature which should have been obtained with such a large superheater. If the large tubes had been increased from the existing 5⅛in to 5½in, the desired temperature might have been obtained with 24 elements. Some disappointment with the temperature continued even with the 40 elements.

A modified boiler was used on No 6200 from April 1935 onwards. This boiler retained its 20ft 9in tube length, but the number of small tubes was reduced to 110 of 2¼in outside diameter. The 32-element superheater had a heating surface of 594sq ft but the 5⅛in flues were retained. This boiler was on No 6200 when it ran its successful trial runs in June 1935. The original boiler from No 6200 was altered to 32 elements, but with 119 small tubes of 2⅜in outside diameter and retaining the short firebox and long tubes. In 1936 this boiler was fitted with a dome and separate top feeds and it was on No 6201 when the latter ran its high-speed trials to Glasgow and back in November 1936.

Soon after the news of the test runs by 6200 were published the Turbomotive No 6202 made its appearance, followed shortly by the first of the new batch of ten conventional Princesses. First sight of the latter revealed an obvious difference from the first two: the front of the firebox had moved forward and was now over the centre of the rear coupled wheels, while that of 6200/1 barely reached half way between the rim of the wheel and its centre. This was because the combustion chamber extended an additional 15in into the boiler, reducing the tube length to 19ft 3in. The first four of the batch had 141 small tubes of 2¼in diameter and 24 flues of 5⅛in outside diameter, with a superheating surface of 467sq ft, while the remainder had 112 small tubes and 32 flues of the same diameter, but with a superheating surface of 623sq ft. On test these engines showed a slight advantage, but the 24-element engines proved to be capable of better running than the original pair with 16 elements. The A/S ratios were improved, but the 1935 engines were only slightly better than the originals in the proportion of free gas area to grate area. In course of time the 24-element engines all received 32 elements and the long-tube boilers had the number of small tubes increased to 119, enlarged to 2⅜in which raised free gas area to 13% of grate area and the A/S tubes to 1/469.

The original Nos 6200/1 had small tubes in a horizontal diamond-pattern pitch layout similar to that used by the GWR and the LNER. Some authorities consider that this gave better water circulation. The later, more cramped layouts were of the vertical diamond pattern. Boiler design was always a compromise between sufficient free gas area and good circulation and design was often hampered by restricted space.

The domeless boiler continued on the 1935 batch up to the end of the LMS, but there were two domed boilers in the mid-1930s. One went to the Turbomotive at its first boiler change in 1936. The other went to the 1933 engine No 6201 and was on this engine for its record run to Glasgow in November 1936; later it was carried by 6200. During the 1950s under BR ownership there was a general conversion of 'Princess' boilers to the domed pattern. The reversion to domed regulator boilers has been the cause of some debate among enthusiasts, those with Swindon sympathies considering it to be a retrograde step; the real reason for the change was that cracks developed in the rather complicated header castings with smokebox regulators.

There were a number of small differences between the 1933 and the 1935 engines and a few small variations of individual locomotives. The LMS Pacifics broke away from Derby practice by having a central dart and locking handle on the smokebox door, but No 6212 ran for years with 11 lugs round the periphery. The pipes to the top feed clacks were carried under the outer boiler casing on the later engines, while the originals had these pipes outside the cleading plates. The GWR type slide bars of Nos 6200/1 were replaced on Nos 6203-12 by a stiffer design of motion bracket with shorter slidebars and a massive slidebar support bracket, which allowed platform-end observers to identify the engines as they approached. The rear section of the reversing rod was carried further forward from the cab to a position in front of the rear splasher, instead of to the rear of it as in the originals. Lubrication was altered and there was less drawing of corks while an engine was prepared. Nos 6203-12 had two 12-feed lubricators, one on each side, and Nos 6200/1 were later altered to conform, though they retained their corks. The coupled-wheel boxes of Nos 6203-12 were supplied by an eight-feed lubricator located further back on the right-hand side. The crosshead brake pump was continued on the 1935 engines, but from 1938 onwards they began to be removed from all LMS engines.

In 1938 No 6205 was modified to use derived gear for the inside cylinders. The inside sets of Walschaerts gear were replaced by rocking levers driven from the outside gear, the opposite to the arrangement on the GWR 'Kings'. This involved the use of a strengthened motion bracket in the form of an inverted triangle below the running plate, which made the engine easily identifiable.

Although 32-element superheaters were standardised, there were many small variations in the number and diameter of the small tubes and in the actual elements; these variations extended into BR ownership and they account for small differences in dimensional tables published by authors of repute. In LMS days the long-tube boilers were only used on Nos 6200/1, which were in the happy position of having three boilers to be shared by two engines, while one spare boiler had to be shared by the ten standard engines. In the early 1950s the frames of Nos 6200/1 were modified to take the standard boiler and it is a standard boiler which is on the preserved No 6201. Eight of the 'Princesses' received new front-end frames during the years 1952-54 with beneficial results to performance, but with the strange fact emerging that two of the engines which appear not to have been modified were among the best performers of the late 1950s. No 46209 achieved the highest mileage credited to a 'Princess', 1,589,045, at the time of withdrawal in September, 1962, while some excellent running by this engine and No 46208 from Edge Hill Shed is detailed in a later chapter.

Small variations were made to details during the 25-29 years the engines lasted. All the boilers were fitted with continuous blow-down equipment, which had the aim of removing scum from the boiler by discharging a quantity of water which, it was hoped, would take surface scum away with it. This was at first discharged on to the track, but was later diverted into the ashpan. At first sand guns were fitted to blast the tubes clean by blowing a jet of sand through them, but these were later discarded. The spark deflector plates in the smokebox were removed to improve steaming and there were numerous small modifications to springs, frame stretchers and axlebox guides. Hand-operated sanding was replaced by steam sanding.

The original tenders resembling Midland design were replaced by tenders of Stanier design, of similar length but with high sides and curved coping. These tenders held 9 tons of coal and 4000gall of water. The Turbomotive and the first standard Pacific of the 1935 batch entered service with the new tender which was running behind No 6200 before it ran its test trips in June 1935. Even this tender carried little enough coal for the 400mile continuous run in adverse weather conditions and a further modification allowed 10 tons to be carried. This could be raised to 12 tons by careful packing. A steam coal-pusher similar to those used on the later 'Coronation' class Pacifics was used on the tender attached to No 6206.

Although limited in numbers and overshadowed by later Pacifics the 'Princesses' made a vital impact on West Coast operating.

CHAPTER FIVE

The Turbine Experiment

It had originally been stated that three Pacifics were to be built in 1933, but when the second engine emerged from Crewe towards the end of the year, it was announced that there would be some delay before the third example joined the other two because "a new and simplified form of turbine drive was being adopted". This set locomotive enthusiasts guessing and a small railway-minded group in the sixth form of a Leicestershire grammar school — who formed an oasis of culture among a motor-minded majority — looked around for clues. They finally lighted on a news item in the April 1933 *Railway Magazine*. This was a photograph and brief description of a Swedish 2-8-0 freight engine which, apart from the substitution of a non-condensing turbine for the orthodox cylinders, differed little from the conventional locomotive. Subsequent events proved that the schoolboys' deduction had been well founded.

The basic conception of a turbine was as old as man's exploitation of steam power, having been employed in a crude form by Hero of Alexandria in 120BC. The basic advantages of a rotative engine, as compared with a reciprocating motion, were obvious and accepted but there were limitations of metallurgy and of metal-working tools which delayed the appearance of a practical form of steam turbine until the Hon. C. Parsons introduced a 6hp engine in 1884. The practical demonstration of future possibilities came in dramatic fashion at the 1897 Queen Victoria Diamond Jubilee Naval Review, when a steam launch named *Turbinia* shocked the solemnity of the occasion by dashing up and down the assembled lines of warships at an astounding 34½ knots. It was soon predicted that the days of the reciprocating engine were numbered on both land and sea, but it was in the larger installations of ocean-going ships and in power stations that the turbine found its true vocation. Only a decade after *Turbinia's* demonstration the *Dreadnought* of 1906 and the *Lusitania* and *Mauretania* of 1907 had taken the battleship and the ocean liner into new dimensions of size and power. This was made possible by the greater efficiency of the turbine at maximum power output and the fact that it needed less space.

Turbines functioned at their greatest efficiency with a condenser and they gave their greatest power at maximum revolutions. This meant that some form of reduction gearing was necessary between turbine and driving wheels on a locomotive. A turbine locomotive promised higher thermal efficiency, better balancing and reduced hammer blow on the track, but at the expense of higher initial cost. The turbine itself promised to show less deterioration with mileage than conventional cylinders and valves, but if a condenser was used there was an additional source of possible trouble.

The first British attempt at building a turbine locomotive was the Reid-Ramsey turbo-electric, first built in 1910 as a private venture by the North British Locomotive Company. It ran a few short trips on the NBR and Caledonian Railways and it was confidently predicted in the non-technical press that it marked the doom of the conventional steam locomotive. It made little impact in its original form, but was rebuilt with geared drive in 1924. It was exhibited at the 1924 British Empire Exhibition and was photographed hauling two bogie coaches. It looked a neat and workmanlike job. It was intended to send it to the 1925 Railway Centenery procession at Darlington, but various difficulties prevented its appearance and little more was ever heard of it.

Another private venture was the Ramsay turbo-electric locomotive built by Armstrong Whitworth and Co. This was of the 2-6-0, 0-6-2 wheel arrangement and some test running took place on the L&Y section in 1922. Even if it had fulfilled expectations a total hp of 1100 with overload provision for 1440 for a total weight of 156 tons did not promise a sensational advance on an orthodox contemporary 4-6-0. With electric drive, capital cost must have been considerably above that of a conventional steam locomotive and in actual fact performance never remotely approached the rating for its traction motors. It was cut up after about two years and a very modest mileage.

The next venture did at least manage some revenue-earning miles. This was built by Beyer Peacock in 1926 and it used the Swedish Ljungstrom turbine driving six coupled wheels through gears. This engine differed from normal practice in that the condenser was on the driving portion of the machine with the turbine reduction gearing and six-coupled wheels, while the boiler was carried on idle wheels. In 1927 this locomotive ran on the LMS Midland section on the Manchester-London service and on the Bristol main line. Between Derby and Manchester it showed its ability to climb the banks in a way never before recorded and it anticipated the impact of the Stanier 4-6-0s a few years later. Despite this promise of improved performance there was little prospect of any overall economy which would have ensured orders from the railway companies. The engine was returned to the makers, who kept it for a time in the hope of finding some overseas railway that was interested.

The condenser required air cooling fans and some provision had to be made for providing draught for the fire when steam was no longer exhausted through the blastpipe into the atmosphere. The non-condensing Swedish 2-8-0 locomotive was a compromise in that some potential scope for further economy was sacrificed for greater simplicity. The work done on the Grangesberg-Oxelösund Railway in Sweden was brought to the notice of Mr, later Sir William, Stanier with the suggestion by Dr Guy of Metropolitan-Vickers that he might be interested enough to go to Sweden to see the engine at work. Stanier accompanied Dr Guy to Sweden and what he saw there resulted in the LMS giving authority for the building of a locomotive on the same general principle. By eliminating the condenser it was possible to build a simple, robust locomotive retaining the advantages of blastpipe draught, but with the promise of economy due to the elimination of losses inherent in the reciprocating engine, such as throttling, leakage and heat transfer in the cylinders. The design was not the complete success that had been hoped and it did not start a revolution, but it came nearer to success than any other departure from the conventional Stephenson-type locomotive ever built in Britain.

Economy of initial construction cost was obtained by making the engine with many details similar to the standard reciprocating Pacifics, but some potential advantages of the turbine locomotive had to be abandoned. It would, for example, have been possible to have used smaller driving wheels because there was no need to limit rotational and piston speed as was the case with a high-speed reciprocating engine. Smaller wheels would have permitted a larger boiler or more room for the ashpan. One of the younger Derby engineers did indeed suggest 5ft driving wheels under a Garratt boiler. The economies of some degree of standardisation with the other Pacifics and the possibility of conducting a fair test of turbine vs reciprocating drive with the same boiler were over-riding.

Although No 6202 was intended originally to have been one of the 1933 batch, it was not until June 1935 that the first and only British turbine-driven Pacific emerged from Crewe Works. By this time the standard Pacifics were shedding their gremlins and the new batch which appeared only a few days after the turbine engine, had modified boilers with 24- or 32-element superheaters replacing the original 16 elements. The boiler originally intended for the third Pacific was never used on No 6202, but was fitted to No 6200 in April 1935; it was present on that engine when it ran its high-speed test runs in June 1935. The boiler first used on the Turbomotive was similar to those on the 1935 batch of standard Pacifics, but with a slightly different tube layout. This boiler was domeless, with 32 superheater flues containing bifurcated elements. It was later replaced by a non-typical boiler with 40 elements which was fitted with a dome. At first this boiler had the standard bifurcated elements in its 40 flues, but these were later replaced by triple elements giving a higher nominal superheating surface but yielding a comparable steam temperature.

Dynamometer car tests were run in May 1936 with the 32-element boiler which gave initial steam temperatures of approximately 575°F. in October 1936 the engine was tested with the 40 bifurcated elements and the steam temperature was around 685°F, while in June 1937 the 40-element boiler with trifurcated elements gave much the same initial steam temperature but with a 2.5% improvement in coal consumption due to better boiler efficiency. It must be realised that these variable speed dynamometer car tests of relatively short duration did not give as complete a picture as the post war tests on the Rugby or Swindon Test Plants. The knowledge gained by the use of the 40-element superheater on No 6202 was destined to be of considerable value when the larger 'Coronation'-type Pacifics were designed in 1937.

The turbines were designed by Dr (later Sir Henry) Guy of Metropolitan Vickers, while the rest of the engine was developed at Derby by the LMS engineers in collaboration with Dr Guy and his staff. There were two turbines. The main unit was permanently coupled to the leading coupled axle through reduction gearing and was intended for a normal power output of 2000hp, rising to 2600 at 90mph and at 13500rpm. A small reversing turbine could be connected or disconnected at will through a sliding dog clutch. This was intended for use when setting back, for shunting or light running. As first fitted this had insufficient power for the engine to set back against a steep grade with a heavy train. It might not have been easy, for example, for No 6202 to have propelled a 16-coach train back up Camden Bank after arrival at Euston. In normal circumstances an engine would have been sent in to remove the empty stock and this did not prove a severe practical problem, but there was always the fear that some abnormal circumstance might find the engine wanting and cause delay. There was some trouble with the clutch teeth mechanism and the reverse turbine had later to be redesigned. In retrospect it might have been better to have provided a combined ahead and reverse turbine on one shaft as is done in marine practice, but space was a problem for any locomotive designed for the restricted British loading gauge.

The main turbine could not be designed to fit a narrow band of optimum performance as was the case with a marine turbine matching the cruising speed of a liner, but it had to be suitable for slogging up Shap or Beattock at 30mph or for speeds of up to 85-90mph on the favourable grades south of Crewe. The blading was designed to give as high an efficiency as possible over a wide speed range but the test results suggested that the optimum efficiency was reached at 50mph, which was a little on the low side for pre-war LMS main line express service. Something nearer to 65mph would have been closer to the ideal figure. This did not mean that No 6202 could not run at high speeds, as maxima of 90mph were recorded.

The turbine was permanently coupled to the leading coupled axle by triple reduction gearing using double helical gear wheels. Steam was admitted to the turbine nozzles through six hand-controlled valves. The normal practice was to use the ordinary regulator as a stop valve; it would usually be wide open while the engine was moving, control being applied by the number of valves open. An easy job would only need one or two, but climbing Beattock Bank with a 500ton train might need all six valves open, while a more gentle ascent such as that to Tring might be made using four valves. There was less delicacy of control than with a piston-engined Pacific. A situation might arise where, for example, three valves would not do the job, while four would cause the engine to gain time. This was liable to cause patchy running, but in practice the Turbomotive was reasonably popular with the men. Driver L. A. Earl had a specially soft spot for No 6202 describing it in a letter to Cecil J. Allen in 1936 as "the best of the lot". Later there was some criticism of the soft blast causing smoke to drift down, making the engine rather dirty to work. In 1939 No 6202 was fitted with deflector sheets and when Professor E. S. Waterhouse rode on the engine in 1943 and described his experiences in *The Railway Magazine* he found that he got less dirty than on a conventional locomotive.

Lubrication is, of course, important to any locomotive, but it was even more so when a high-speed turbine replaced the cylinders and motion and when reduction gearing was in constant use. The transmission shafts were all enclosed in a suspended case with a closed forced-feed lubricating circuit. There were three pumps. Two were steam-driven and worked continuously even when the engine was standing, forcing oil through at a pressure of around 7lb per sq in. The third pump was of the reversible-gear type, worked from the motion, and became operative as soon as the engine moved, while at 60mph the oil pressure was boosted to 16lb/sq in. The pumps were submerged in the sump and oil was strained before use and cooled after use.

The two sides of the locomotive were different. A long casing ran down the left-hand side above the running plate, joining a larger, deeper casing which extended below the running plate abreast of the smokebox and which housed the main forward running turbine. The right-hand side had a similar but smaller casing housing the reverse turbine, but there was no backward extension. On this side a conventional running plate extended backwards to the cab. The tops of the driving wheels were covered by small splashers on the right-hand side; they were under the casing on the left side. The six driving wheels were fitted with the conventional coupling rods just as if they were the wheels of an inside-cylinder piston engine. The whole machine had a neat and pleasing appearance. Had turbine locomotives become the general practice there would have been little loss in the visual appeal, though the vocal effects were less impressive; on No 6202 a low hum replaced the beat of a conventional steam locomotive.

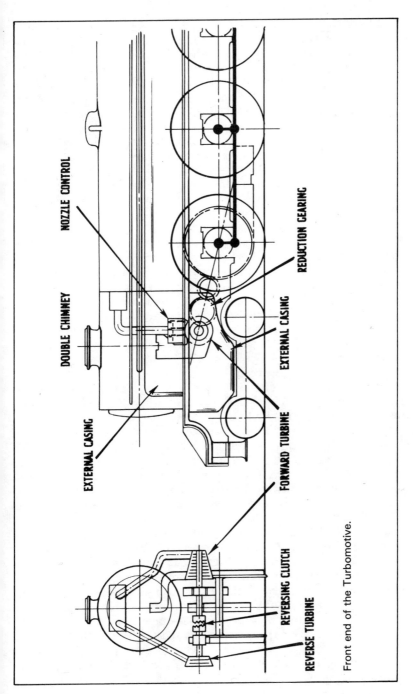

NOZZLE CONTROL

DOUBLE CHIMNEY

REDUCTION GEARING

EXTERNAL CASING

EXTERNAL CASING

FORWARD TURBINE

REVERSING CLUTCH

REVERSE TURBINE

Front end of the Turbomotive.

53

The effect of replacing cylinders with turbine and reduction gear caused a rise in the total weight of the engine, but the smooth turning movement as compared with the thrust of pistons made it possible for the Civil Engineer to accept 24 tons on each driving axle as against the 22½ tons allowed for a four-cylinder Pacific. This was an advantage when the turbine was starting a heavy train up Camden Bank or climbing Shap or Beattock. The smooth torque and the additional adhesion weight did not, however, eliminate slipping entirely.

There was a form of feed water heating by bleeding steam from the turbine cylinder. This was in addition to the exhaust steam injector and had the effect of raising the temperature of boiler feed to 275° F. Steam was taken from the turbine exhaust for train heating. At first there was a variable area choke in the double blastpipes which was linked with the number of turbine nozzles open. This was later found to be unnecessary and it was then set in the minimum position to ensure steaming. Originally a steam servo-motor assisted the engagement of the dog clutch for the reverse turbine, but this was later discarded in favour of a simple hand control from the cab. Had war not intervened Dr Guy would have introduced a form of interlocking control which would have made the operation of the forward and reverse turbines almost foolproof. The net result of all the additional refinements of design made the initial capital cost of the Turbomotive £20000 as against £12000 for the prototype piston-engined Pacific and £8500 for the production units of 1935. The fact that No 6202 was a one-off job increased its cost.

The record of No 6202 in service was by far the best of any unconventional steam locomotive to run in Britain. Up to the outbreak of war it had averaged 54000 miles per annum as compared with approximately 75000 by the 'Princesses'. This latter figure was exceptional for a British express locomotive and the 54000 of No 6202 was nearer to the average. The best year for No 6202 was 1936, when over 73000 miles were run. Yet there had been failures and the cost of providing inspectors or representatives of the CME's department, as a safeguard against mis-handling, could not be entertained for a whole class of locomotives.

During the first ten years of running there were 13 major failures, but none of these suggested a fundamental deficiency of design and it would have been possible by further modifications to have eliminated the source of trouble in each case. Six of the failures were due to the reverse turbine, four were caused by oil leakages and two were failures of the main forward turbine. The worst trouble of all was the failure of the flexible drive between the slow-speed gear wheel and the leading coupled axle. The most serious such failures all happened in wartime, including the breakage of the main forward turbine spindle when the engine was travelling at 60mph near Leighton Buzzard. In wartime repair was a lengthy business because of the delay in getting spares from Metropolitan-Vickers, who were fully extended with vital munitions of war. There was at times an over-cautious attitude among the operating staff, which resulted in the engine being stopped when the fault was not mortal. It may, however, be the case that excessive caution saved worse failures.

The appearance of the engine was changed, first in 1939 by the fitting of smoke deflector plates. The next alteration came after a withdrawal to store for almost two years following the outbreak of war. The engine had hardly got back into service before a failure of the reverse turbine in September 1941 caused another stoppage. When it re-emerged in 1942 the right-hand side had been altered in appearance by the extension of the casing backwards as far as the middle pair of driving wheels. This was to house a Worthington reciprocating oil pump to augment the supply of oil to the reverse turbine unit. The performance of No 6202 became more uncertain under wartime conditions, which of course adversely affected all engines. When peace returned the difficulties of the railways hardly abated and in the great snows of 1947 misery was unconfined. In such a world there was little hope for the development of an unconventional locomotive.

Finally it was decided that there was no justification for continuing the experiment when further heavy capital expenditure, including a new main turbine, would be needed. At that time No 6202 had run 440000 miles, a far greater mileage than any other unconventional British locomotive, but it was outlived by the Swedish freight engine which had inspired the project; this worked until the mid-1950s. The former LMS turbine engine was therefore rebuilt as a four-cylinder locomotive with 'Duchess'-type cylinders, but with a 'Princess' type boiler. This boiler was, however, non-typical, with a different superheating surface. The rebuilt engine No 46202 was given a name, *Princess Anne*, and recorders and photographers looked forward to an interesting variation from the standard 'Duchesses' or 'Princesses'. But alas, before anyone had logged a run worth publishing and before very many photographs had been taken, *Princess Anne* was damaged beyond economic repair in the terrible Harrow disaster of October 1952.

Opinions differ considerably about the wisdom of building No 6202. It is argued on the one side that turbine drive is fundamentally better than reciprocating propulsion and that the troubles which beset the Turbomotive were not fundamental and could all have been overcome. It is further argued that these problems would have been solved had war not intervened. On the other hand there is the argument than if steam relinquished its simplicity, then it could never hope to compete with diesel or electric traction. The LMS turbine project was an attempt to gain efficiency without undue complication. The economies realised in service were comparatively modest, with an economy in coal consumption of 5% or less, although a saving of 13% had been attained on an individual test comparison. This was equal to that which might have been expected by compounding, but the turbines could be accommodated within the restricted British loading gauge more easily than could the large low-pressure cylinders of a compound Pacific. If the turbine engine had shown a sensational improvement in running standards, then there might have been added justification for further development, but in practice the best that could be claimed was "as good as" rather than "much better than" the standard 'Princesses'. In 1937 further competition from the larger 'Coronation' class Pacifics reinforced the case for the piston-engined type. In 1946 tests on the New York Central between diesels and the 4-8-4 'Niagara' class steam engines showed an economy by the diesel of less than the 5% of No 6202 and yet the decision to introduce diesels in quantity was taken. This emphasised that technical revolutions usually have non-technical stimuli.

The writers recall posing the question of turbine locomotives to a distinguished member of the CME's Department at Derby who, alas, is no longer with us. His reply was that, had it been possible at the wave of a wand, to have re-tooled Crewe Works for the building of turbine engines, then it would have been wise to change over, but the economies actually promised by No 6202 would never have justified the capital expenditure. Again in 1960 Sir William Stanier himself admitted to one of us that he saw No 6202 in retrospect as an engine with much potential, one of the unfulfilled promises of the steam era.

CHAPTER SIX

The 'Princesses' on Test

The new LMS Pacific seemed to be an engine of all the talents and the younger enthusiasts confidently expected some remarkable running. Older and more experienced recorders, such as the late Cecil J. Allen, recalled the early days of the Gresley Pacifics and they realised that a period of trial with modifications and perhaps a few set-backs would be a more realistic expectation. The experienced viewpoint proved to be the correct one and two years were to pass before work worthy of the size of the engine appeared in print.

On 15 August 1933 No 6200 *The Princess Royal*, resplendent in LMS red, set out from Euston with a test load of 14 bogies, including the Horwich dynamometer car, which weighed 500 tons, tare and 505 tons gross, carrying specially invited press representatives. No banking assistance was given from Euston and the daily press the next day announced that No 6200 had accelerated to 42mph on Camden Bank! For steam such a start would indeed have been exceptional, but the true facts are that 42mph was reached at Primrose Hill Tunnel after a stretch of level track beyong the summit. The actual start was good enough as the sixth coach passed mp 1 in 3min 8sec from the start, which outclassed anything previously recorded with similar loads. It excelled even the starts of the visiting GWR engines *Polar Star* and *Launceston Castle*, although the GWR had the generally well-deserved reputation of being the finest starters in Britain. It was rare for a banked 'Royal Scot' to beat No 6200's time to the top of the bank, although this did occasionally happen. It was a tribute to skilful handling by Driver A. Parsons of Crewe, but it was not destined to be characteristic of LMS Pacifics, which themselves rarely if ever repeated No 6200's start and gained a reputation for being tricky engines to get away without slipping.

The start was the end of exceptional performance on No 6200's first press run. The intention was to run fairly gently down to Crewe keeping the normal Special Limit timing and to run more smartly on the return journey. Actually the engine never made the return journey as, after some undistinguished running, barely reaching 'Royal Scot' standards, the engine failed with a hot driving axle box at Elmhurst Crossing, 118.8 miles from Euston, in 122min 42sec. The LMS tried to save the day by rushing the reporters back to Euston in a seven-coach train weighing 215 tons in a net time of 142min for the 158.1 miles behind a run-down 'Royal Scot' hastily pressed into service. The papers were kind to the LMS on the following morning, although one reported the overheating of the engine's "hot box". Generally speaking, the brisk start and some good photographs help the LMS image. No 6200 had run 5000 miles before the press run without giving any axlebox trouble and axlebox overheating was not destined to prove a congenital weakness of the class.

On 22 September *The Princess Royal* made her first through run from Euston to Glasgow and it was announced that when two Pacifics were available they would undertake the entire working, running through for 401½ miles unchanged and climbing the banks unaided. On the up journey the 299 miles from Carlisle to Euston were run non-stop. It was an arduous assignment, which made severe demands on the steaming qualities of the engine and on the fortitude of the fireman. Crews were changed at Carlisle. On the first trip no records were broken, but Shap was topped at 24½mph with a tare load of 431 tons, 460 tons gross, and Beattock at 25½mph. The outward sign of an engine working through from Glasgow was the Caledonian-type route indicator which aroused interest when seen at Euston. In everyday service all was not plain sailing in the early days and the nearly empty tenders, the black and obviously tired firemen and the sprinkling of late arrivals indicated that problems had to be faced and overcome before reliable operation could be claimed or further acceleration be contemplated.

On Friday 6 April 1934 *The Princess Royal* was given its first turn at a high-speed run over an easy road with a relatively light load. This was on the 5.25pm up Liverpool express, which had a booking of 142min for the 152.7 miles from Crewe to Willesden, the fastest start-to-stop booking on the LMS. It was known unofficially as "The Liverpool Flyer", but this was never given the blessing of authority. Driver A. Parsons of Crewe, who undertook much of the early test running of No 6200, was in charge and Cecil J. Allen was invited to ride and share the recording with D. S. Barrie, the official LMS representative. Whatever happened was destined to be accurately recorded, but alas there was nothing sensational to report. It was not a bad run in any sense, but it was undistinguished for so large an engine. The load was 380 tons gross and the 152.7 miles were run in 134min 37sec or in 132min net with a maximum speed of 85mph at Hademore. This gained good publicity in the daily press but serious students of locomotive performance were less impressed, despite a favourable presentation by Cecil J. Allen. When it was remembered that on 18 October 1932 the redoubtable Laurie Earl, with Patriot No 5959, brought the "Mancunian" from an emergency stop at Polesworth up to Euston, 106½ miles, in 92min with a pass-to-pass average of 80mph for 54½ miles from Rugby to Willesden, the performance of the much larger Pacific with only five tons more was hardly sensational.

The year 1933 had seen the publication of some exceptionally good work with heavy loads by the GWR 'Kings' and the LNER Pacifics. These included such epic runs as No 6028 *King Henry II* passing Westbury, 95.6 miles, in 91½min with 555 tons on the down "Limited", or No 6022 *King Edward III* with the up "Limited" and 575 tons coming up from Exeter, 173.5 miles, in 175½min net. With such ammunition the GWR supporters argued that the case for a British Pacific was "not proven". The East Coast enthusiasts could cite No 2544 *Lemberg* on the down "Scarborough Flier" weighing 570 tons reaching York in a net time of 192½min for the 188.2 miles and the 180lb Pacific No 2549 *Persimmon* with 19 bogies weighing 660 tons gross covering the 79.4 miles from Doncaster to Peterborough in 85min 11 sec, after which No 4476 *Royal Lancer* carried on the good work with 85min 51sec for the 76.4 miles up to Kings Cross. The LNER supporters were no more impressed by the early performances of the Stanier Pacifics than the Swindonians; they claimed that it was proved that only the master could build a successful British Pacific and "the other lot" had been foolish to try.

Such ideas were, of course, premature as was recognised by Cecil J. Allen when he wrote in June 1934 that he thought the bad steaming was just a passing phase which would be put right as minor adjustments were made. As things worked out the adjustments proved to be rather more than minor and quite a lot of money had to be spent of boiler modifications before the expected improvement took place. There was no lack of platform-end gossip to the effect that "the new big-uns won't steam", but it was in a more minor key than the criticism of the Stanier 5XP 4-6-0s, later to be known as the 'Jubilees'. The reason for this was, most probably, that towards the end of 1934 the various 5XP classes were given some very severe testing on the Birmingham trains. The two classes of 4-6-0 were worked much closer to their maximum on the test schedules than was the case with the larger Pacifics. The 'Royal Scot' called for considerable duration of steaming because of the distance, but it did not call for any exceptional power outputs from a Pacific. There were significant indications even on the disappointing runs that there was no lack of evidence of power and speed potential in the new engines.

In late 1934 and early 1935 a series of tests were made with both Pacifics and 'Royal Scots' between Euston and Carlisle with various grades of coal. The choice of the correct grades of coal for the long continuous runs was the main aim of the test exercise and the evidence of locomotive performance was incidental. The No 2 Dynamometer car of LNWR origin was used and Mr Cox, writing in *Locomotive Panorama* Vol 1, had scant respect for its value as compared with the better-equipped Horwich car, which at the same time was being used for the tests of Class 5XP 4-6-0s on the Birmingham services. In view of the limitations of the ex-LNWR car direct comparisons with the 5XP engines employed on a different type of duty are invalid.

'Royal Scots' Nos 6158 and 6117 were tested against Pacific No 6200 on the 10am from Euston to Carlisle and on the 12.10pm from Carlisle to Euston. There was considerable variation between the grades of coal and both Pacific and 'Royal Scot' varied between a best figure of 3.12lb/dbhp/hr on the excellent Grimethorpe coal to over 4lb/dbhp/hr with some of the inferior coals. The 'Royal Scots' had to be driven rather hard on some of the trips, but the capacity of the Pacific for time recovery was noted in the report. The conclusions which can be drawn from these tests are limited, but as the Pacific and the 'Scots' were used over the same route, with the same trains and with the same dynamometer car, and gave lb/dbhp/hr figures, which were not significantly different, it is safe to conclude that the 'Scot' and Pacific in its original low superheated form had a similar basic thermal efficiency. In this connection it has to be noted that some of the lowest coal/dbhp/hr figures ever recorded in Britain were to the credit of the low-superheat GWR 4-6-0s.

The LMS was a very interesting railway in late 1934 and early 1935, but attention was mainly centred on the various 4-6-0 classes. The most sensational happenings took place on the LNER with the introduction of the giant 2-8-2- No 2001 *Cock o' the North* in the summer of 1934, followed by the high-speed test runs to Leeds with No 4472 *Flying Scotsman* on 30 November 1934 and with No 2750 *Papyrus* to Newcastle on 5 March 1935, with its 108mph maximum on the return journey. Most enthusiasts expected that any reply would most likely come from the GWR, which for so long had been the leader in high-speed running in Britain. The LMS was regarded as being a restrained, very respectable, railway, not without merit but lacking the sporting spirit so characteristic of the East Coast. In the summer of 1935, however, the LMS served notice on all those who could read the signs that, if they decided to use it, they had the motive power to challenge the best that anyone else could provide.

In April 1935, as detailed in the previous chapter, No 6200 emerged from Crewe Works with a new boiler having twice as many superheater elements. The advantages of this boiler were the higher temperature of the steam, which meant that condensation was avoided at all normal conditions of working and the incidental advantage that the better draughting meant more reliable steaming. In the summer of 1935 a number of test runs were made to assess the potentiality of the modified engine. One of these runs in particular was given wide publicity. On 27 June the load of the very fast up "Liverpool Flyer" was increased from its usual 350 tons to a 15-coach formation weighing 456 tons tare and 475 tons full. With this load No 6200 *The*

Princess Royal arrived at Euston 13½min early, having covered the 152.7 miles in 129min 33sec at a start-to-stop of 70.7mph. The pass-to-pass average from Welton to Wembley, 67.2 miles, was 77.2mph and 80mph was exceeded at eight separate places with a maximum of 86.6mph. The net time of the previous best run on this train by No 6200 in its original condition in April 1934 had been improved on by three minutes, despite almost 100 tons more weight behind the tender. Possibly it was not a run that caught the imagination of the general public in the same way as the 100mph maxima of the LNER, but to the serious student of locomotive performance it was a run of great significance which even the best of the LNER A3s or the GWR 'Kings' would be unable to surpass and might have found difficult to equal. The A4s were, of course, still at an early stage of construction.

The fast run from Crewe to Willesden was only one of a series of test performances and although it was probably the most spectacular, the whole series of runs and a full consideration of the recorded power outputs and the coal per dbhp/hr figures is probably even more significant. The test programme started with a series of runs on the 'Royal Scot' with modifications to the blastpipe cap. The first three trips were made with the original diameter of $5\frac{11}{16}$in and the last three with it reduced to 5½in. No exceptional speed was demanded but loads were very heavy. On the down run the load was 493 tons tare until the train was divided at Symington, while the southbound trip on 1 June 1935 was with 574 tons after Symington. This must have been over 600 tons gross.

On 25-27 June No 6200 ran a series of trials between Euston and Crewe taking the 10.30 am down and returning on the fast 5.25pm. The 10.30 was normally a heavy train and the Horwich dynamometer car was added to this. The 5.25 was specially made up to 15 bogies; it would usually have totalled 10 or 11 bogies behind a 'Royal Scot'. The fast run which was widely published was only the culmination of a series of very fine performances. On the first day the 10.30 loaded to 502 tons, tare, 530 tons full and reached Crewe in 144min or at an average of 64.4mph start to stop. A fast run had been hoped for on the return trip, but a heavy thunderstorm raged from the Midlands to London which caused slower running and signal checks for fear of washouts causing damage to the track. The average speed from Crewe to Willesden was a net 60mph, but actual arrival at Euston was 20min late. The following day the 10.30 was even heavier, weighing 515 tons tare or 545 tons gross, which was taken down to Crewe at an average speed of 62mph. The return journey with 475 tons was run at a start-to-stop average of 68mph, which might in itself have been published as a notable run had not the next day's time been better still. On 27 June the 10.30 loaded to 502 tons tare and 530 tons full, which was worked down to Crewe at an average speed of 61.6mph, not so fast as on the previous two days but still a considerable gain on schedule. Then followed the very fast up run in 129min 33sec Crewe to Willesden. This last run was one of the classics of locomotive performance between the wars and it remained the criterion of 'Princess' performance at its best over the high-speed section of the former LNWR main line. The Principal Assistant to the Chief Mechanical Engineer, R. A. Riddles, rode on the footplate as did

5.25pm Up Liverpool Express, 27 June 1935
Loco: 4-6-2 No 6200 *The Princess Royal.*
Driver: H. P. Smith (Camden Shed). *Fireman:* T. B. Pile (Camden Shed)
Load: 15 bogies, 453 tons tare, 475 tons full.

Miles		Schedule	Min	Sec	Speeds
0.0	CREWE	0	00	00	—
1.1	Basford Wood Box		2	35	40
4.8	Betley Road		6	47	60
8.0	Madely		10	06	57.7 on 1 in 177
10.5	Whitmore		12	33	64.3
14.7	Standon Bridge		15	53	80.4 max
19.2	Norton Bridge		19	22	Slack
21.2	Gt Bridgeford		20	56	80.4 max
24.5	STAFFORD	26	23	34	Slack
28.6	Milford		28	10	69
33.8	Rugeley	36	32	29	77.6
37.1	Armitage		35	00	80/76
41.8	LICHFIELD	42	38	40	76.2
48.1	Tamworth		43	19	85.4*
	Colliery Subsidence				Slack
51.6	Bolesworth		46	57	45
55.8	Atherstone		51	05	65.2
61.0	NUNEATON	60	55	21	76.2 max
66.7	Shilton		60	00	73.5 min
70.0	Brinklow		62	30	81.8 max
75.5	RUGBY	73	67	09	Slack
77.8	Hillmorton Box		69	56	55
82.8	Welton		74	38	67.2 min
88.4	Weedon		78	47	85.4 max
95.3	Blisworth		84	02	75
98.2	ROADE	94	86	27	71.5 min
105.7	Wolverton		92	10	81.8 max†
111.4	BLETCHLEY	105	96	43	72/75
117.9	Leighton Buzzard		102	00	72/75
122.0	Cheddington		105	23	71.5
126.4	TRING	119	109	16	67.2 min
130.1	Berkhamsted		112	21	78.9
137.2	Kings Langley		117	25	86.6 max
140.7	Watford		119	55	81.8
144.8	Hatch End		123	03	75 min
146.7	Harrow		124	28	81.8
150.0	Wembley		126	52	85.4 max
152.7	WILLESDEN JUNCT.	142	129	33	—

(Recorded by D. S. Barrie)

* At Hademore
† At Castlethorpe

Locomotive Inspector S. E. Miller of Willesden. S. A. Fisher, Assistant Chief Operating Manager, and F. A. Pope, General Assistant to the Chief Operating Manager, rode in the dynamometer car.

The timing was carried out by an LMS Officer, D. S. M. Barrie, an experienced recorder, and his speeds, taken by split-second chronograph over half-miles, were checked against the dynamometer car speed recorder. In view of its historic importance as showing a 'Princess' at its best the run is, happily, fully authenticated. The real triumph of the engine lies more in the generally high standard of work achieved during the entire series. An average load of 480 tons, tare, 505 tons gross, had been worked for 932 miles in three days at a start-to-stop average of 64.4mph. This would have been even faster if the fine weather which favoured most of the test period had also blessed the LMS that afternoon. Had there been no violent thunderstorm the overall average would have been raised to over 65mph. This was a result of great commercial significance, showing that the new Pacifics could run at high speeds on the easier gradients with loads as heavy as could ordinarily be accommodated in the platforms. The work was performed with good economy, as the coal/dbhp/hr averaged 2.94lb which, under the circumstances, was as good as anything recorded by a British express locomotive. This running was, of course, carried out under the best test conditions, in summer weather, with the best Grimethorpe coal and with picked crews while the engine, just run in after its boiler modifications, was at its very best. Although such running could hardly be expected as a daily schedule there was scope for improved running when more Pacifics were built and the CME's department could be well satisfied with the improvements effected by the re-draughted boiler with higher superheat.

On the Sunday following the fast running south of Crewe No 6200 was given a test run from Crewe to Glasgow and back to investigate its performance over the northern banks. This was not on a scheduled passenger train but on a special made up of 20 vehicles, which included some lighter stock. It weighed 461 tons, but as only the testing staff was carried the gross load would be little more. The running resistance of 20 vehicles of light stock would be greater than that of a 460ton train of 14 or 15 heavier vehicles, but the Horwich dynamometer car ensured that the power output would be correctly measured. Between Crewe and Carlisle the driver was H. Wilkenson and the fireman W. E. Robinson from Crewe North Shed; in Scotland Driver Marshall and Fireman D. Crawford of Polmadie took over (Driver Marshall had already featured in some of the best 'Royal Scot' runs north of Carlisle published by Cecil J. Allen). Locomotive Inspector S. E. Miller of Willesden, who had ridden on No 6200 between Euston and Liverpool, rode on the engine throughout the 486.6 miles, recalling the feats of endurance of the famous Locomotive Inspector Flewellen of the GWR. Not only were the men of the LMS to prove themselves as tough as those found elsewhere, but so was the locomotive.

Interest centred mainly in the ascents of the famous banks. The test train started from Lancaster and passed Shap Summit, 37.7 miles

LMS Test Running, *Symington-Glasgow,* **30 June 1933**
Engine: No 6200 *The Princess Royal.*
Driver: Marshall (Polmadie). *Fireman:* Crawford (Polmadie).
Load: 20 vehicles, including light stock, 461 tons, tare, 465 tons gross.

Miles		Sched. min	Actual min	sec	Speeds mph
0.0	Symington		00	00	—
3.7	Lamington		5	14	67
9.1	Abington	-	10	13	63
11.6	Crawford		12	40	57
14.3	Elvanfoot		15	20	64
17.2	Summit	19	18	25	49 min
27.2	Beattock	29	26	30	82/76
32.4	Wamphray		30	25	83/75
38.2	Nethercleugh		34	48	83
41.1	Lockerbie	42	37	03	75
44.2	Castlemilk Sdg.		39	40	66
50.2	Kirtlebridge	50	44	27	82/75
53.9	Kirkpatrick		47	20	86
58.3	Gretna	58	50	30	83
62.8	Rockcliffe		53	57	72
66.9	Carlisle	67	59	41	

(Recorded by D. S. M. Barrie)

Down journey
Crewe-Glasgow: 243.3 miles
Normal schedule: 290 min
Test schedule: 260 min
Actual time: 249 min 12 sec
Lancaster start — Shap Summit pass, 37.7 miles; 41¾ min
   Speed: Grayrigg 43mph
   Speed: Tebay 69½mph
   Speed: Shap Summit 35mph
Beattock — Summit, 10 miles; 16½ min
   Speed at foot: 58mph
   Speed at Summit: 30mph

Up journey
Glasgow-Crewe: 243.3 miles
Normal schedule: 285 min
Test schedule: 268 min
Actual time: 256min 25sec
Carlisle-Shap Summit, 31.4 miles: 37min
   Minimum speed on 1 in 125: 49mph
Coal: 52.6lb/mile. Water: 392lb/mile
Coal per sq ft grate area: 67.9lb
Mean dbhp: 1049. Maximum dbhp at 53mph: 1770 near Lowthar
Coal/dbhp/hr: 2.88lb. Water/dbhp/hr: 21.45lb

away and almost 900ft higher, in 41¾min. The minimum at the top of Grayrigg Bank was 43mph, after which speed recovered to 69mph at Dillicar troughs, while the 5.5 miles from Tebay to the Summit were run in 7min exactly with a minimum of 35mph. Beattock Bank was climbed in a similar fashion, with the 10 miles from Beattock Station to the Summit Box taking 16min 24sec with a minimum of 30mph. This was a considerable advance on the normal work of the engine before its boiler modifications.

Coming south the same high standard of running continued. The 66.9 miles from Symington to Carlisle were covered in 59min 41sec with a minimum of 49mph at Beattock Summit and a maximum of 86.6mph between Kirkpatrick and Gretna. It was emphasised, however, that high maximum speeds were not included in the aims of the test, which were mainly to test the economy of the engine and its performance uphill. Leaving Carlisle, the 31.4 miles to Shap Summit were covered in 37min with a minimum speed of 49mph on the long 1 in 125 to Trimby Grange Box and a recovery to 51mph on the final 1 in 106-130 to the Summit.

A maximum dbhp of 1600 was recorded on the ascent to Shap on the down journey and 1500 on Beattock Bank, while on the return journey 1590 was recorded between Law Junction and Cleghorn and 1770dbhp at 53mph near the start of the 1 in 125 between Penrith and Lowther. These were the actual drawbar hps without the correction for gradient in which equivalent form hps on the banks are usually published. The correction for gradient would raise the actual dbhp of 1770 to an equivalent figure of 2160, with a corresponding ihp of about 2500, which was closely comparable with the hps of the LNER 2-8-2 No 2001 *Cock o' the North* on the ascent to Stoke during a test run made in 1934. The cut-offs were 35 to 45% on the steeper ascents, while on the more level sections the engine was worked between 25 and 15%. On the Up Liverpool express the ascent to Whitmore was made on 30% and to Tring it was 25%, while 15-18% sufficed for the fast running elsewhere. The coal consumption on the Crewe-Glasgow-Crewe test run was 52.6lb/mile and water consumption was 39.2gall per mile. The average dbhp was 1049 and the coal/dbhp/hr was 2.88lb which, in conjunction with the 2.94lb of the very fast running south of Crewe, was as good as anything recorded by any British express locomotive tested up till then.

The LMS authorities had every reason to be satisfied with the events of June 25-30. The standards had been set for the Pacifics and all that now remained was for the nearest possible approach to these standards to be realised in everyday commercial service. The building of a Pacific was amply justified, for no 4-6-0 could have been expected to equal the combination of power, speed and endurance shown by No 6200. Even so, satisfaction was tempered by thoughts of what was being accomplished elsewhere. Despite these LMS achievements and the promise of further high class performance, the autumn of 1935 was dominated by the LNER with the spectacular debut of "The Silver Jubilee". Not only did the new A4s show a hitherto unequalled capacity for high speed, but on the heavy trains such as 'The Flying Scotsman' they gave indications that the East Coast had an engine of slightly smaller basic dimensions that was at least the equal of the 'Princesses' in power output. Meanwhile in France the Chapelon compound Pacifics, admittedly built to a more generous loading gauge and for an entirely different operational policy from that of the LMS, were producing higher hps from much the same engine weight. The more progressive spirits in the LMS design office, while indulging in some quiet satisfaction over the 'Princesses', realised that there were possibilities for further progress.

In the summer and early autumn of 1935 eleven more Pacifics were built with modifications from the original design, as detailed in a previous chapter. These all had combustion chambers extended further forward and shortened tube lengths, but no final decision was made as to superheater size since some of the engines had 24-element boilers. In November 1935 tests were carried out between No 6203, then fitted with a boiler with 24 superheater elements, and No 6209 with 32 elements. The tests were run on ordinary service trains from Euston to Glasgow and back with loads south of Crewe of 17 bogies weighing 540 tons tare, or 570 tons gross, and 15 bogies of 480 tons tare, 505 tons gross, over the banks. A small advantage was shown by No 6209 and the 32-element boilers were in course of time standardised. On the best run coal/dbhp/hr was 2.94lb with No 6209, but the average was 3.08lb against an average of 3.23lb by No 6203. On some of the runs steaming was not satisfactory, but a recovery north of the Border suggested mismanagement. The through working from Euston to Carlisle made a much heavier demand on the fireman than the shorter Carlisle-Glasgow run and perhaps it would be more fair to suggest that it was mis-planning rather than any fault on the footplate.

The year 1936 saw a number of test runs between the turbine-driven No 6202 and standard Pacifics. In the course of these trials some of the most significant indications of the efficiency of the engines in ordinary service emerged. The high power outputs of No 6200 in 1935 were not exceeded, but valuable indications were given of the way that these criteria could be approached in service. The tests were made with the Horwich Dynamometer Car on the 10am 'Royal Scot' in May and October 1936 and again on accelerated timings in June 1937. The standard Pacifics used were Nos 6212 in May and 6210 in October, while the June 1937 trials involved No 6202 alone. No 6202 had the 32-element boiler during the May tests, but in October and June 1937 tests the special 40-element boiler was fitted. With the dynamometer car added to what was normally a very heavy train, some formidable loads were made up on occasions, the highest being 569 tons tare or

600 tons gross, presumably 18 bogies, behind No 6212 and 564 tons tare behind No 6202.

There were individual feats of brilliance, especially by No 6202, which on one occasion climbed from Beattock to the Summit, 10 miles, in 15min 15sec. Earlier in the same journey it had run from Tebay to Shap Summit in an equally notable 7min 10sec; both of these climbs were exceptional with a load of 486 tons, tare, 510 tons full. No 6212, with its 18-coach load of 569/600 tons, passed Tring in 38min 45sec, but No 6202's time of 36min with 536/565 tons was probably better. Four of the six nozzles controlling the inlet of steam to the main turbine were open on No 6202 for the climb to Tring, while No 6212 was worked on 25% cut-off once Camden Bank was cleared. On the ascent to Shap No 6202 was driven with four to six valves open and five to six on Beattock. On one climb, presumably the 15min 15sec occasion, six valves were used throughout. The standard Pacifics needed cut-offs gradually increased to a maximum of 45% on Shap and 50% on Beattock. A maximum ihp of 2336 was attained at 72mph by No 6202; this was very similar to the best figures for the standard engines. Two performances taken from the tests of 1936 were quoted by Sir William Stanier in his Presidential address to the Institution of Mechanical Engineers delivered on 24 October 1941. No 6210 ran to Glasgow and back with an average load of 522 tons tare at an average speed of 52mph on a coal consumption of 2.98lb/dbhp/hr, while No 6202 with a load of 485 tons tare, but a higher average speed of 55mph, burned 2.78lb/dbhp/hr. The latter figure was among the best ever reached in a variable-speed dynamometer car test on an ordinary scheduled train, but it was closely approached on one individual up journey by No 6212 when the figure was 2.83lb. This equalled the coal/dbhp/hr figure of the GWR *Caldicot Castle*, which was the average of the two best runs in a series of tests run in 1924. At that time the LMS engineers were quite incredulous of the GWR figures, but in 1936 they were equalling them in rather more arduous conditions of working. The merit of the two runs quoted by Sir William Stanier was enhanced by the high mileages run since the last major overhaul; No 6210 had run 98977 miles since major overhaul but only 1778 miles since its last piston and valve examination, while No 6202 was credited with 102915 miles. Mileage figures must be related to the repair policy of the railway concerned and the extent of the care and attention given at intermediate overhauls must be considered.

The final series of tests with No 6202 in 1937 were made after the 40-element superheater had been given triple elements, raising its heating surface to 852sq ft. Some of the best individual coal/dbhp/hr figures were attained during these trials, with a figure of 2.71 on one run. The more important figure was the average for the entire series of tests, which worked out at 4% saving of coal and 10% saving of water in favour of the turbine engine. This was a modest improvement when allowance was made for possible testing error, but there were probably enough runs to strike a significant average. In ordinary service running the turbine engine was rarely on the "Royal Scot" or "Mid-day Scot" through workings, but it did a good deal of work on the 10.30am down returning on the fast 5.25pm up Liverpool. The economies did not justify a change over to turbine propulsion.

Some of these test runs were logged by passengers and published by Cecil J. Allen. No 6202 with a load of 17 bogies, 537 tons tare, 560 tons gross started well from Euston, passing mp 1 in 3min 15sec without banking assistance. This was equal in merit to the first press run of No 6200 and above the general standard. The speeds were very uniform, high uphill and moderate downhill, and the net times of 85min to Rugby and 77¼min Rugby to Crewe were good with this load. A run by No 6212 with a load of 548 tons, tare, 580 tons full, was patchy with net times of 90min to Rugby and 80min Rugby to Crewe; better runs by this engine similarly loaded were recorded in ordinary service. A run by No 6202 in Scotland showed a comfortable mastery over the schedule of the southbound "Royal Scot" with a 16-coach load of 525 gross tons. As far as we know this is the only complete log of a run by the Turbomotive north of the border and it is

Symington-Carlisle 5 June 1936
Engine: No 6202 (Turbomotive).
Load: 16 vehicles, 500 tons tare, 525 tons gross.

Miles		Sched. Min	Actual Min Sec	Speeds mph
0.0	Symington	0	00 00	—
3.7	Lamington		6 10	55
			pws	
9.1	Abington		12 35	52
11.6	Crawford		15 33	54/57
14.3	Elvanfoot		18 43	55
17.2	Summit	22	22 28	39 min
27.2	Beattock	32	31 31	77/65
32.4	Wamphray		36 00	73/66
38.2	Nethercleugh		40 57	72
41.1	Lockerbie	45	43 33	65
44.2	Castlemilk Sdg.		46 37	53
50.2	Kirtlebridge		52 08	70/63
53.9	Kirkpatrick		55 25	70
58.3	Gretna	62	59 13	72/68
			eased	
62.8	Rockcliffe		63 24	60
64.9	Kingmoor		65 22	62
66.9	Carlisle Arrive	71	68 17	—

(Timed by D. S. M. Barrie.)

this, rather than any exceptional speed or power, that justifies full tabulation.

No 6202 continued southwards with a time of 45min 50sec to passing Shap Summit, after which the running was easy. The aim of these test runs was to examine the coal consumption at normal running speeds rather than to find the maximum capacity of the locomotive.

A sidelight on the tests was that there were worries at times with steaming, especially with No 6202, which had a variable area blastpipe, and both engines were affected by the severity of the load. Here it must be remembered that one fireman was expected to work through for 300 miles to Carlisle. It was suggested that a reasonable load limit for the Special Limit timings would be 500 tons tare south of Crewe and 475 tons over the banks. These loads were frequently exceeded in everyday service. The test results were, on the whole, a vindication of the building of Pacifics; it would have cost a lot more to have run these heavy trains with two Compounds. The Stanier Pacific design, as modified with larger superheaters, had proved itself capable of a level of performance unsurpassed by any other British express locomotives in heavy load haulage and hill-climbing, though seriously challenged in the higher speed ranges by the new LNER Class A4 Pacifics.

The 'Princesses' were by no means sluggish and during 1936 there was definite evidence that they could run very fast. On 3 May 1936, during a series of brake tests, No 6203 *Princess Margaret Rose* reached a speed of 102.5mph near mp 39 on the descent from Tring to Cheddington. The load was seven bogies weighing 210 tons. The run had little contemporary publicity, but a note to the effect that a 'Princess' had reached 102½mph did appear in *The Times* newspaper and a paragraph was published in *The LMS Magazine* for March 1937. The speed is authentic as it was recorded by the dynamometer car and confirmed by the stopwatch timings of the late W. Rowing Coleby, an experienced recorder. Possibly the LMS realised that 102.5mph would be compared unfavourably with the 108mph of the LNER A3 No 2570 *Papyrus*, but the assistance from gravity on the descent from Tring was less than that on the Stoke-Essendine racing ground. A 'Princess' would probably have attained a speed comparable with an A3 if given a run down from Stoke, but the engine to challenge the A4 in this category of performance had yet to be built by the LMS.

The success of the LNER with the 'Silver Jubilee' streamlined train was something the LMS could not ignore. The idea of the super-express was alien to the basic LMS philosophy of a steady advance of the entire train service, but when it became obvious that the LNER would shortly introduce a high-speed express on the 'Silver Jubilee' pattern between Kings Cross and Edinburgh, the LMS had to investigate the possibilities of high-speed travel with a light load between Euston and Glasgow. The engine chosen for this exercise was No 6201 *Princess Elizabeth*, which had the long tube boiler with tubes increased to 2⅜in O/D giving an A/S of 1/470 and a 32-element superheater. This particular boiler had once been on No 6200 before modification. In late 1936 it had been fitted with a steam dome containing the regulator and separate top feeds and was one of the most successful despite its long tubes.

During the earlier years No 6201 had been rather under a cloud and platform-end gossips used to say their "6200 is a much better engine". The reputation of No 6201 was perhaps tarnished by the unfortunate experiments with the installation of a double chimney of an ill-advised pattern. Whatever reputation No 6201 had before the events of 16/17 November 1936, no one called it a bad engine afterwards. Just why No 6201 with the long-tube boiler was chosen with No 6200 as standby, in preference to one of the newer engines with shorter tubes and combustion chamber, is not clear; but No 6201 was particularly suitable in that it was fitted with a Hasler speed recorder which was essential if the many speed restrictions were to be strictly observed.

The test train was given a schedule of six hours to Glasgow and on the down run consisted of seven vehicles including the Horwich dynamometer car. The total weight, with some invited passengers and the test staff, was 225tons tare, 230 tons gross or just the same as the LNER 'Silver Jubilee'. The driver was Tom Clarke of Crewe North Shed assisted by Fireman Fleet, with Passed Fireman Shaw as relief engineman able to drive or fire as required. Crewe men were chosen as they alone knew the road from Crewe both to Euston and Glasgow. The Camden drivers, such as the fire-eating Laurie Earl, were disappointed at not having a chance to emulate their Kings Cross rivals. R. A. Riddles, the Principal Assistant to the CME was in charge on the footplate, armed with a continuous diagram of all the speed restrictions to be observed. This was hung round his neck and unrolled as the journey progressed. The full story of the heroic efforts of Mr Riddles in preparing the engine and in re-metalling a crosshead at St Rollox has been told in detail by O. S. Nock in *William Stanier* (Ian Allan 1964) and in *The Last Steam Engineer* by Col. H. C. B. Rogers (George Allen & Unwin 1970).

The speed of the test train was to be so much higher than that of the ordinary service trains that there many speed restrictions were called for which would not be noticed on an ordinary train travelling at lower speeds. There were 50 of these restrictions to be observed, which shows that record runs were more difficult to arrange than merely telling a driver to run hard. The running over the Euston-Crewe section was mainly a matter of keeping the restrictions and working up the engine to 85-90mph in between. Only on the descent from Tring was there a brief spurt up to 95.7mph. The greatest interest lay in the ascents of the northern banks. Finally Glasgow was reached in 353min 38 sec against the 360min schedule.

On the return journey another coach was added, bringing the load up to 260 tons. Euston was reached in 344min 15sec with a start-to-stop average speed of 70mph for 401.4 miles, one of the greatest feats of sustained high-speed steaming ever recorded. The pattern of running was much as on the down journey with the restrictions carefully observed and with surges up to 85-90mph wherever possible. There was one brief but significant example of the speed capacity of the engine when an average speed of 90mph was held for 6 miles from Winsford Junction to Coppenhall Junction, all level or slightly against the engine. Speed reached a maximum of 95mph on dead level track without a vestige of downhill to help and no influence of any impetus gained from a previous down grade. This argued that speeds well up in the 100s would have been possible on a long steep down grade without any restrictions. It was the hill-climbing which was most significant and this deserves full tabulation.

Carnforth to Shap Summit
Load: 7 cars, 225 tons tare, 230 tons gross.

Miles		Min	Sec	mph
00.00	Euston	00	00	
236.3	Carforth	201	28	83½
240.8	Burton	204	47	74
243.6	Milnthorpe	206	45	85½
245.5	Hincaster Junction	208	18	62 braking
249.1	Oxenholme	211	38	68/60 braking
252.6	Hay Fell	214	51	65½
254.3	Lambrigg Crossing	216	22	68
256.2	Grayrigg	218	04	66½
257.9	Low Gill	219	34	65 braking
262.2	Tebay	223	05	78½
266.0	MP 36	226	28	61
267.7	Shap Summit	228	12	57

Tebay-Shap Summit: Cut offs 25-32%
Boiler pressure   : 240-245lb/sq in
Average dbhp   : 1187
Maximum dbhp   : 1251
Maximum ihp   : 2413 (calculated)
Carnforth-Shap Summit 31.4 miles: 26min 44sec, average speed 70.5mph

Beattock-Beattock Summit
Load: 7 cars, 225 tons tare, 230 tons gross.

Miles		Min	Sec	mph
00.00	Euston	00	00	—
299.1	Carlisle	255	24	—
338.8	Beattock	287	35	80
341.4	Auchencastle	289	34	68
344.5	Greskine	292	30	57½
346.9	Harthope	294	59	57
348.8	Summit	297	06	56

Beattock-Beattock Summit: Cut-offs 30-37 ½ %
Boiler pressure: 240-245lb/sq in
Average dbhp : 1241
Max dbhp   : 1350
Max ihp   : 2428 (calculated)
Beattock-Beattock Summit, 10 miles: 9min 31sec

Symington-Beattock Summit
Load: 8 cars, 255 tons tare, 260 gross.

Miles		Min	Sec	mph
0.0	Glasgow	00	00	—
35.4	Symington	40	35	71 ½
39.1	Lamington	43	17	86 ½ /65 (braking)
44.5	Abington	47	49	74
47.0	Crawford	49	49	77 ½ /72 ½
49.7	Elvanfoot	51	57	80
52.6	Summit	54	20	66 ½

Lamington-Beattock Summit: Cut-offs 20-28%
Boiler pressure : 240-245lb/sq in
Average dbhp : 1117
Maximum dbhp: 1260
Maximum ihp   : 2448 (calculated)
Symington-Beattock Summit, 17.2 miles: 13min 45sec 74.5mph

Carlisle-Shap Summit
Load: 8 cars, 255 tons, tare, 260 tons gross.

Miles		Min	Sec	mph
00.00	Glasgow	00	00	—
102.3	Carlisle	93	20	20
103.7	Carlisle No 13 Box	95	31	51
107.2	Wreay	99	12	65
109.7	Southwaite	101	18	71 ½
113.1	Calthwaite	103	57	78/74
115.4	Penrith	105	45	83 ½ /80
120.2	Penrith	109	15	85/75 (braking)
124.4	Clifton	113	00	55 (braking)
128.5	Thrimby Grange	117	05	63
131.7	Shap Station	120	03	64/67
133.7	Shap Summit	121	50	66

Carlisle-Shap Summit: Cut offs 30-35%
Boiler pressure : 240-245lb/sq in
Average dbhp : 1180
Maximum dbhp: 1260
Maximum ihp   : 2343 (calculated)
Carlisle-Shap Summit, 31.4 miles: 28min 30sec average speed 66 ½ mph

The drawbar hps are the actual values as measured by the dynamometer car; the equivalent values would be 1900-1950 at the maximum outputs with averages of 1800-1850. These power outputs were similar to the best figures attained on the tests of No 6200 with heavier loads at lower speeds in 1935. The coal and water consumptions were moderate:

Down journey
46.8lb coal per mile
3.68lb/dbhp/hr
34.5 gallons water per mile
7.36lb water evaporated per lb coal
Up journey
44.8lb coal per mile
3.48lb/dbhp/hr
30.2 gallons water per mile
6.70lb water evaporated per lb coal

These figures of 3.48/3.68lb/dbhp/hr are naturally higher than the 2.9-3.1 figures recorded on several tests with the same class of engine at lower average speeds with heavier loads, because at the higher speeds more hp is needed to move the engine so that less hp is available at the drawbar. The indicated hps were similar to those when 500-600 tons were moved at normal express speeds and the basic economy of the engine was much the same. It underlined, however, the cost of high speeds and justified the charging of a supplementary fare for travel by very fast light expresses.

The publicity value to the LMS of these high-speed runs was immense and after a year of almost unbroken triumph for the East Coast notice was served that a challenge could be expected from Crewe. The GWR, for so long the leaders in British rail speed, had rather a dull year in 1936. Driver Clarke became something of a national hero and the engine *Princess Elizabeth* was modelled in gauge 0 by at least two manufacturers; the 00 boom still lay in the future. Today, when speeds of 90-100mph over Shap or Beattock are commonplace, the 56-60mph of No 6201 seems pedestrian, but it was sensational in 1936 and no doubt today's publicity officers would be thankful for even a fraction of the enthusiasm which followed the events of that grey November some 40 years ago.

The more serious students of locomotive performance took stock of the record of the 'Princesses' with some satisfaction. The early troubles had been overcome and the LMS was in possession of an engine capable, on test, of working loads of 600 tons from Euston to Crewe at a 60mph average or nearly 500 tons at 70mph. Loads of over 500 tons could be taken over the northern banks, while in the realm of very high speeds, the steepest banks could be topped at 55mph or over with 250 tons. Speeds of 95mph had been recorded on the level with 260 tons and over 100mph with 210 tons down a relatively moderate grade. All this had been achieved with good economy, averaging 3lb of coal per dbhp/hr at normal speeds and 3.5lb at the highest speeds the road would allow. The through working from Euston to Glasgow presented no undue difficulties. On the other hand the Pacifics only gave of their best with the good Grimethorpe coal and steaming depended on skilled handling and a meticulous standard of maintenance. They could hold their own with most of the other British express engines, but the new A4 class Pacifics on the East Coast were a challenge. It would have been a rather bigoted LMS supporter who denied the possibility of an A4 equalling No 6201's record run to Glasgow and back, for the East Coast having been first in the field with their streamlined trains, were gaining experience of operating high-speed services, whereas the LMS plans were still being considered. In France engines no bigger than the LMS Pacifics were reaching ihps of 3500-4000, which took some of the gloss off the 2400ihp of No 6201, however good that was by British standards. Good as the 'Princesses' were it was cheering news early in 1937 to hear that an improved Pacific design was being prepared for a high-speed service to Glasgow.

CHAPTER SEVEN

The Everyday Running of the 'Princesses'

The potential of the 'Princesses' was established at a high level by the various test runs carried out during the years 1935-37. But such achievements had little commercial value if they remained isolated exploits never approached in normal daily running. There have been locomotives in British railway history which promised well in initial tests, but which later proved to be relative failures. A cross-section of timings made by ordinary passengers using the normal service trains, with drivers unaware that their efforts are being recorded, has greater commercial significance. In the case of the 'Princesses' during the years up to the outbreak of World War II there are sufficient runs of good quality on record under everyday conditions to form a gratifying confirmation of the test performances.

During the early years of Nos 6200 and 6201, with their small superheaters the pattern of running in ordinary service reflected that of the test running very faithfully. There was little that could be called exceptional for the size of the engine and certainly nothing seriously to challenge the best work of the GWR 'Kings' or the LNER A3s. There were several occasions when there was definite evidence of bad steaming apparent even to the passenger and doubtless many other occasions when skilled work on the footplate gave little hint to the passengers that all was not well at the front. Flashes of brilliance were recorded here and there in the course of a run which was undistinguished in its end-to-end times.

One of the best runs by a 'Princess' in its original condition was recorded by Cecil J. Allen in the summer of 1934 on the up 'Royal Scot' with a 15-coach load of 460 tons, tare, 490 tons gross, behind No 6200 *The Princess Royal*. The train was taken gently up to Shap Summit in 49min 40sec from Carlisle and undistinguished running followed as far as Crewe, which was passed on time. The 158.1 miles from Crewe to Euston were run in 164min 24sec despite a signal stop at Elmhurst Crossing, the scene of No 6200's failure on its first public run in August 1933, and a pw slack between Roade and Castlethorpe, where speed would normally have been high. The net time to Euston was 158min from Crewe, while the net time from Carlisle, 299.2 miles, was 324min. This was a good run by contemporary standards but in no sense exceptional, for on 12 June 1934, S. P. W. Corbett observed the arrival of the up "Royal Scot" at Euston in an actual time of 321min with the same 15-coach load hauled by the 'Royal Scot' class 4-6-0 No 6157. It may be claimed with some justification that nothing recorded behind a Pacific in its original condition could not be matched by an established 'Royal Scot' timing with the exception of the 400mile through run to Glasgow in regular service and the start from Euston on No 6200's first public outing. There is, of course, little doubt that the 'Scots' were pressed to their limit to do this.

The modifications to the boiler of No 6200 in the early summer of 1935 and the test runs of June raised the Pacifics to a new standard of running which even the GWR 'Kings' and the LNER A3s at their best could barely have matched. This new prowess was exploited in general service by the acceleration of the down "Mid-Day Scot" in the new timetable introduced on 4 May 1936. The train reverted to its old LNWR time of 2pm from Euston and reached Glasgow in 7hr 35min, the fastest time which had been scheduled up till then. Euston to Crewe, 158.1 miles, was booked to be covered in 163min, followed by 79min for the 71.9 miles to Lancaster, but then came an extraordinary booking of 59min for the 51.2 miles over Shap Summit to Penrith. This was described by Cecil J. Allen as the hardest task ever set to a West Coast train south of Carlisle. During the test running of the previous June No 6200 hauling 460 tons had passed the Summit in 41¾min from the Lancaster start, but now the "Mid-day Scot" was expected to cover the same distance everyday in 45min, with a load which varied from a minimum of 470 tons to a 16-coach formation of 530 gross tons. The daily schedule required a power output varying from 85 to 100% of that recorded on the test run. The booking of 19min for the 17.9 miles from Penrith to Carlisle did not appear difficult, as most of the distance is downhill, but the start from Penrith on a sharp curve was taxing and high maximum speeds were often needed for bare timekeeping. The load was reduced considerably after Carlisle, but the timing of 116min to Glasgow presented no difficulties, even though the engines had already covered 300 miles of hard running. Strangely enough in the July timetables this booking was eased to 120min and the total time to 7hr 40min, while the hard Lancaster-Penrith time remained unaltered.

On the very first day of the new booking No 6212 *Duchess of Kent* gained 22min of net time on the new schedule, but owing to easy running and adverse signals on the final downhill stretch after Beattock Summit had been passed and the hard work was over, the actual arrival was 4min late. The greatest interest centred inevitably on the Lancaster-Penrith section and here there was little in reserve. In the first selection of logs published by Cecil J. Allen exact time-keeping only took place on two runs, one with Pacific No 6203 *Princess Margaret Rose*, which covered the 51.2 miles in 57min 34sec against a booking of 59min, and one run when a 'Royal Scot' with a

Compound as pilot replaced the usual Pacific and completed the run in 56min 34sec. The Pacific was hauling 14 bogies weighing 443 tons tare and 470 gross and the double-headed train had 16 coaches weighing 530 tons gross. The best run by a Pacific with 16 vehicles was the inaugural trip of No 6212 with 520 tons, when there was a loss of 26sec on the timing. Only on the run by No 6203 with 470 tons and with the double-headed train was Shap Summit passed within the 45min booking. The worst run was one with No 6208 when 3½min were dropped with a 14-coach load. Here there has to be a sense of proportion. Had No 6208's time of 62½min with 470 tons been recorded a little over a year earlier behind Nos 6200 or 6201 with the small superheaters it would have been hailed as an epic performance; and had a 'Princess' equalled this time 20 years later, in the days when the 'Duchesses' dominated, then again the applause would have rung out. Mr Allen made the apt comment that "whether or no strict time had been kept on this series of runs they certainly form an impressive tribute to present-day motive power".

It was not long before better runs were timed. Mr Allen logged No 6209 with 14 bogies when Shap Summit was passed 1min 50sec under the very difficult 45min booking and Penrith was reached 2½min early. Barely had Mr Allen recovered his breath from this when a log from R. E. Charlewood, the most reliable of recorders, reached him telling how No 6208 *Princess Helena Victoria* had almost equalled the time of No 6209 with two additional coaches. A 16-coach train of 490 tons tare, 515 tons gross was taken from the Lancaster start to passing Shap Summit in 43min 30sec. While this was 20sec slower than No 6209 with two coaches less, the lighter train had made the faster start to Carnforth and the time of No 6208 with 16 bogies was only seven seconds more. The time of 35min 38sec from Carnforth to the Summit with 515 tons was destined rarely to be beaten by a 'Princess'.

North of Carlisle the load was reduced, but the locomotive had by then completed 300 miles of hard steaming. A new crew, however, had taken over and the booking to Glasgow presented few difficulties with a load which varied between eight bogies and a maximum of eleven. Net times for the 102.3 miles were often well under the 116min scheduled and a time of 108min net was recorded by the late R. E. Charlewood with No 6208 hauling 11 bogies weighing 339 tons tare and 360 tons gross. This booking was eased to 120min in the July timetable, but it was the Lancaster-Penrith booking which left little margin. When the "Coronation Scot" was put into service in the summer of 1937 it took much of the through Glasgow traffic from the "Mid-day Scot", which became a relatively easy job.

The southbound West Coast expresses had an easier task from Symington to Carlisle, as there was a substantial fall in altitude and the climb from Symington to Beattock Summit was nowhere steeper than the final 2¼ miles at 1 in 99. Engines could be extended on this climb in the knowledge that down the 10 miles from the Summit to Beattock high speeds could be attained by gravity alone, while the rest of the run to Carlisle could be made under easy steaming conditions and still delight a recorder. Loads were frequently quite heavy after the Glasgow and Edinburgh portions were combined at Symington. Some indication of these heavy loads is given by the test reports, but 17 bogies presented no difficulties in ordinary service. In March 1936 Cecil J. Allen published details of a run by No 6207 in his 'British Locomotive Practice and Performance' series in the *Railway Magazine*. The load was 541 tons, tare, 570 tons gross and the Summit was passed at 40mph in 22min 35sec from the start; this was a trivial 35sec loss on schedule, but without any excessive maximum speeds the train was 3¼min early at Carlisle.

The Princesses were able to take the 17 coach loads up to Shap Summit from Carlisle inside the 44min allowed and the rest of the journey to Crewe posed no problems. The road from Crewe to Euston was apparently easy, but with loads of over 550 tons and the engine approaching the end of a continuous 400-mile through working, the fireman was not to be envied. It was unreasonable to expect that an engine working through from Glasgow — and in the case of the up "Royal Scot," running non-stop from Carlisle — would equal the vigour of one on a Liverpool job. Yet some notable runs were recorded by Pacifics on the West Coast trains. For example on 27 August 1937 Driver Tom Clarke, famous for his handling of the test runs by Nos 6201 and 6220, brought No 6212 *Duchess of Kent*, reputedly one of the best of the class, up from Crewe to Euston, 158.1 miles, in 152min 26sec with the "Mid-day Scot" weighing 504 tons tare, 535 tons full. All the slacks had been observed with care and the downhill speeds were moderate. Bletchley to Tring, 15 miles, were run in 13min 8sec with a minimum of 61½mph.

One of the most colourful folk heroes of the West Coast was the Camden driver L. A. Earl, who was to the LNWR main line what Bill Sparshatt was to the GN and the Street brothers to the GWR. The railways were not averse to a little hero-worship of top link drivers by the younger generation at a time when the daily press resounded with the deeds of racing motorists and air pilots. Earl was short in stature but great in heart. In his off-duty hours he was a local preacher, but on the footplate he was a mighty pounder. Firing for Laurie Earl was a free slimming course for the strongest of men but, like Bill Hoole on the East Coast in post-war days, he was willing to do a spell of firing himself. He had corresponded with Cecil J. Allen in the days when he was on second-link main line duties and was doing his best with the aging LNWR express engines and the newly introduced Midland compounds. He welcomed the better engines of the 1930s and did great things with the 'Patriots'. He always spoke well of the 'Princesses' and never considered them inferior to the later 'Duchesses', but he had a shorter spell with the bigger engines before wartime restrictions limited speeds. He had an especially soft spot for No 6202, the Turbomotive.

One day early in 1937 Driver Earl and Fireman Abey were in charge of No 6206 on the down "Royal Scot" with a load of 15 bogies and a six-wheeled van weighing 492 tons, tare and 515 tons full. It was never the policy of Cecil J. Allen to solicit exceptional efforts from drivers, but on this occasion he was spotted among the passengers and one of the finest high-speed runs with a heavy load ever recorded behind a 'Princess' resulted. It was normally Earl's policy to start gently when the engine was running for 400 miles and he was driving for 300, and although he was banked to Camden the passing time of 10min 37sec at Willesden was nearly two minutes slower than the 8min 47sec of No 6200 on its first press outing in August 1933 when Camden Bank had been climbed unassisted with 505 tons. It was, of course, a wise policy to start gently and to let the engine find its own pace, especially as there was now power enough to climb to Tring 10mph faster than was the case in 1933. No 6206 was travelling at 60mph on the 1 in 335 when a pw slack brought speed down to 15mph. This gave Earl the opportunity to indulge in a spell of fast

---

Engine: 4-6-2 No 6206 *Princess Marie Louise.*
Driver: L. A. Earl. *Fireman:* Abey (Camden Shed).
Load: 16 coaches, 15 bogies + 1 six wheeled van, 492 tons tare, 515 tons gross.

Distance miles		Schedule Min	Actual Min Sec		Speeds mph
0.0	EUSTON	0	00	00	
5.4	WILLESDEN JUNCT.	10	10	37	
8.1	Wembley		13	22	59
11.4	Harrow		16	54	55
17.4	WATFORD JUNCTION	23	23	10	62½
20.9	Kings Langley		26	35	61
24.5	Hemel Hempsted		30	05	60
			pws		15
28.0	Berkhamsted		36	15	—
31.7	TRING	38	41	59	—
36.1	Cheddington		45	49	79
40.2	Leighton Buzzard		48	50	85/80½
46.7	BLETCHLEY	51	53	33	83½/79
52.4	Wolverton		57	46	85
54.8	Castlethorpe		59	31	—
59.9	ROADE	63	63	33	72½
62.8	BLISWORTH	66	65	55	76½
69.7	Weedon		71	12	79
75.3	Welton		75	36	70½
80.3	Hillmorton		79	45	75
82.6	RUGBY	87	83	14	—

Net time 79min *(Recorded by Cecil J. Allen)*

running. After a fast recovery beyond Tring, Cheddington was passed at 79mph and the engine was driven hard from there to the slowing for Rugby at Hillmorton; these 44.2 miles, with little difference in altitude from start to finish, were run at an average speed of 78mph. At the time Cecil J. Allen wrote that "as a feat of heavy load-cum-high speed performance I cannot recall having ever paralled this, whether on LMS, LNER or GW Railways". There were occasions when similar average speeds had been run on the East Coast main line with A3 class engines and over 500 tons, but there was a greater fall in altitude. Earl's performance has been estimated by Gp Capt Law to have involved an average edhp of 1280 and an average ihp of about 1930, which meant that No 6206 in ordinary service was matching the test running of 6200 in 1935.

The net time of 79min for so outstanding a run underlines the difficulty of the post-war 80min timing. On this pre-war occasion with the engine relatively new, the fast running from Tring to Hillmorton needed cut-offs normally 20%, but with 25% on the rises to Roade and to Kilsby Tunnel. For 40min the engine would be steaming at a rate above that which was, in the post-war age of scientific testing, considered to be a reasonable maximum for a single fireman.

After Rugby the running was easier until Stafford was passed, when No 6206 was again opened out to 25% cut-off and speed gradually accelerated from 22mph past Stafford to 67mph at Whitmore Summit. The running from Euston to Crewe would have been equivalent to a non-stop time of 152min. The load was reduced to 450 tons after Crewe, but the gain on scheduled time continued, with a net time of 150min against a booking of 159min. No 6206 was built in August 1935 and in mid-January 1937 it would almost certainly have the 24-element boiler.

A number of journeys published by Mr Allen in 1936 and 1938 show that while the very fast times of No 6206 remained the pre-war record with over 500 tons, they were approached on a number of occasions. These Euston-Rugby and Rugby-Crewe timings are summarised opposite.

The run by No 6212 *Duchess of Kent* with 537 tons tare, 570 tons gross, was a notable performance. Mr Allen estimated that the equivalent net time, had the run been made non-stop, would have been 156½-157min for the 158.1 miles from Euston to Crewe. The driver was Bowdler of Crewe and the engine was ably handled throughout. The estimate of a test optimum time of 158min to Crewe with 600 tons was closely approached on this run.

The other possibility suggested by the test running of No 6200 in 1935 was a start-to-stop average of 70mph with a load closely approaching 500 tons. This is based on the test run by No 6200, when 475 tons were worked from Crewe to Willesden in a time of 129½min, or at a start-to-stop average speed of 70.7mph. There would appear to

No 6201 *Princess Elizabeth* passing Edge Hill Goods station on an up Liverpool-Euston express./*Eric Treacy*

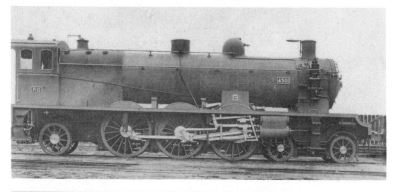

Top: No 4501 of the Paris-Orleans Railway, the first Pacific in Europe./Ian Allan Library

Above: No 111 *The Great Bear* of the Great Western Railway, the first Pacific in Britain./*Ian Allan Library*

Below: No 231 C12 of the Region du Nord of the SNCF at La Chapelle shed in 1954; this is an example of the narrow-firebox type of Pacific./*J. Cliffe*

Top: The first LMS Pacific No 6200 in shop grey and un-named at Crewe Works 1933./*LMS*

Above: The second LMS Pacific No 6201, un-named and fitted with shelter for indicating tests shortly after construction in November 1933./*W. H. Whitworth*

Below: No 6201 named *Princess Elizabeth*, fitted with oval buffers but retaining original tender, on the up 'Royal Scot' near Grayrigg in 1934./*H. Gordon Tidey*

Above: No 6200 *The Princess Royal* with long-tube, 32-element superheater boiler and high sided tender, photographed in January 1936./*Ian Allan Library*

Below: No 6201 *Princess Elizabeth* with high superheat, domed boiler as used on high-speed test run to Glasgow in November 1936./*LPC*

Bottom: No 6200 *The Princess Royal* with the boiler formerly carried by No 6201./*LMS*

Above: right: No 6202, the Turbomotive, on down Liverpool express on Bushey troughs. This shows the reverse turbine side./*Fox Photos Ltd*

Right: No 6202 seen from the main turbine side on down Liverpool express./*E. R. Wethersett*

Above: No 6209 *Princess Beatrice* of the 1935 batch on the down 'Royal Scot' on Bushey troughs on 13 October 1936./*Ian Allan Library.*

Above: *right*: No 6203 *Princess Margaret Rose* on a Euston-Liverpool express emerging from Northchurch Tunnel./*E. R. Wethersett.*

Right: No 6205 *Princess Victoria* climbs out of Liverpool Lime Street with a Euston express in the 1930s/*Cecil J. Allen collection.*

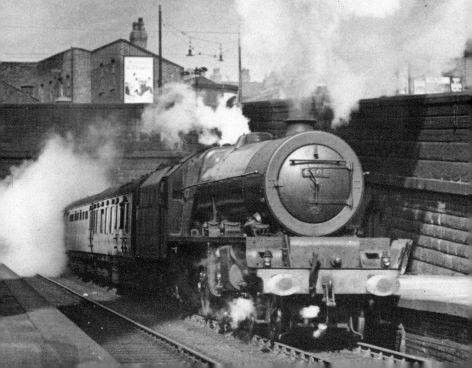

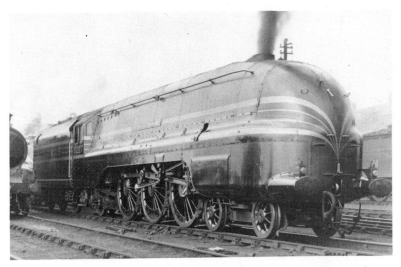

Above: Left: N0 6220 *Coronation* passing Carpenders Park on the high-speed press run prior to the introduction of the 'Coronation Scot', 29 June 1937./*E. R. Wethersett*

Left: No 6224 *Princess Alexandra* heads the up 'Coronation Scot' in ordinary service towards Shap Summit in August 1937./*Eric Treacy*

Above: No 6227 *Duchess of Devonshire,* one of the 1938 batch of red 'Coronations', at Polmadie Shed./*T. G. Hepburn*

Below: No 6231 *Duchess of Atholl,* one of the unstreamlined engines built in 1938, at Polmadie Shed./*T. G. Hepburn*

Above: 'Duchess' at war — No 6230 *Duchess of Buccleuch* ascends Shap with the wartime Euston-Glasgow day express./*Eric Treacy.*

Above: right: During the last few precarious days of peace the new streamlined Pacific No 6235 *City of Birmingham* leaves Liverpool with the 12 noon West of England train./*Eric Treacy.*

Right: Unstreamlined 'Duchess' class Pacific No 6232 *Duchess of Montrose* leaving Penrith with an up Anglo-Scottish express in the late 1930s./*Eric Treacy.*

Above: *left*: No 6229 painted red and re-named No 6220 *Coronation*, with the train prepared for the American Tour, on exhibition at Hartford, Conn., USA, in 1939./*Cecil J. Allen collection*

Left: The 'Coronation Scot' alongside the Baltimore & Ohio RR 'Royal Blue' express on Relay Viaduct near Baltimore. Britain's largest Pacific is completely dwarfed by a relatively small American express locomotive./*W. R. Osborne.*

Top: Streamlined Pacific No 6247 *City of Liverpool* in wartime unlined black./*BR.*

Centre: Unstreamlined Pacific No 6251 *City of Nottingham* in unlined black with streamlined tender./*BR.*

Bottom: the last Stanier Pacific built, No 46257 *City of Salford*, in LMS style lined black with BR lettering. The side openings to the ashpan differ from those on the engines above./*BR.*

Top: No 46246 *City of Manchester*, with streamlined casing removed, in BR black with LNWR-style lining at Crewe North Shed./*T. G. Hepburn.*

Centre: the record-breaking No 46234 *Duchess of Abercorn* in BR black with LNWR-style lining at Crewe North Shed./*T. G. Hepburn.*

Bottom: No 46205 *Princess Victoria*, with two sets of valve gear for four cylinders and modified motion bracket, in LNWR-style black at Nuneaton on an up Liverpool express in August 1950./*J. F. Clay.*

Above: No 46236 *City of Bradford* on the up 'Atlantic Coast Express' at Waterloo station during the 1948 Loco Exchanges, 17 June 1948. A 5000gal 'Austerity'-type tender is temporarily attached./*R. F. Roberts.*

Below: No 46236 *City of Bradford* leaving Kings Cross on the 13.10 Leeds express on 6 May 1948./*R. F. Roberts*

Above: No 46241 *City of Edinburgh* in experimental dark blue livery climbing to Shap Summit./*Eric Treacy*

Below: No 46225 *Duchess of Gloucester* in standard BR blue livery at Crewe North Shed./*T. G. Hepburn*

Bottom: No 46253 *City of St Albans* in Brunswick green livery at Crewe station in May 1953,/*J. F. Clay*

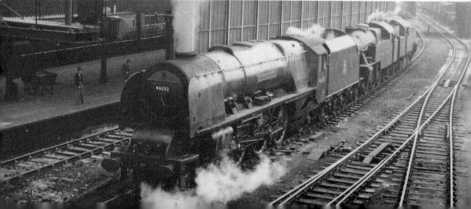

be no run on record in the down direction when a similar average speed was attained, but the down road to Crewe was considered to be slightly harder than the up road. The 5.25pm from Liverpool, known unofficially as "The Liverpool Flyer", had a 64.4mph booking from Crewe to Willesden. When this was first introduced it rarely weighed more than 300 tons and the 'Royal Scots' were given an XL limit of 380 tons for this train. The popularity of the train increased, a sure proof of the market value of high speed, and one of the first allocations of the extra Pacifics available after 1935 was for this train and for the very heavy down "Merseyside Express."

In April 1939 Cecil J. Allen described a number of runs on this train with Pacific haulage with loads up to and slightly over 500 tons. The official XL limit for a Pacific was 420 tons, but this was a cautious figure as it was proved that a 'Princess' had up to 10 minutes in hand on the schedule with 50 tons over this. The best run ever recorded on this train under ordinary service conditions took place after the Willesden stop had been discontinued and the booked time to Euston was 148min. The train alternated between Camden and Edge Hill men and on this occasion No 6200 *The Princess Royal* was in the charge of Driver L. Walls of Edge Hill, ably supported by Fireman H. Foster. The load was 15 bogies of 466 tons tare, 500 tons gross.

Speed rose to 52mph at Betley Road, fell only to 51mph on the 1 in 177 to Madeley, then rose to 85½mph at Great Bridgford, an unusual maximum with 500 tons on such a gentle descent. After a slowing to

Euston-Rugby (82.6 miles)

Loco No	Name	No of coaches	Tons tare	Tons gross	Net time
6202	(turbine)	17	536	560	85min
6211	Queen Maud	17	539	565	84
6212	Duchess of Kent	17	537	570	82
6212	Duchess of Kent	17	548	580	90
?	(unidentified)	18	555	585	88 ½
6211	Queen Maud	16	512	545	85
6200	The Princess Royal	17	548	580	87

Rugby-Crewe (75.5 miles)

Loco No	Name	No of coaches	Tons tare	Tons gross	Net time
6202	(turbine)	17	536	560	77 ¼
6209	Princess Beatrice	18	589	615	81 ¼
6212	Duchess of Kent	17	537	570	78 ½
6212	Duchess of Kent	17	548	580	80
?	(unidentified)	18	555	585	83 ½
6211	Queen Maud	16	512	545	80 ½
6200	The Princess Royal	17	548	580	78 ¼

52mph through Stafford speed picked up to 78½mph between Armitage and Rugeley, fell to 74 before Lichfield and reached 85½mph at Hademore troughs. The brisk pace continued until, shortly after passing Tamworth at 80mph, signals were on and the train was brought to a stop at Polesworth because sheep were straying on to the line. The 51.6 miles from Crewe to Polesworth had been covered in 48min 38sec.

The train restarted in less than a minute, but was 2¾min late when Rugby was passed. Subsequent speeds were 56mph at Kilsby Tunnel, 80½mph at Weedon, 77½mph at Blisworth, and when Roade Summit was topped at 72mph all but a mere 13sec of lost time had been recovered. The hard running continued with 87½mph at Castlethorpe, 80mph through Bletchley, 71½mph at Cheddington and a minimum of 64½mph over Tring Summit. The time of 12min 19sec from Bletchley to Tring was less than the 12min 33sec of No 6200 on test in 1935, but the latter put up a higher initial speed of 80mph against 75 and a lower minimum of 64½ as compared with 67mph. This would cancel out the effect of the higher load of 500 tons against 475 tons and the ihps would be similar. After reaching 83½mph on the descent Driver Walls was well ahead of time, but ill-luck again intervened as there was a dead stop for 4¼min for signals near Hemel Hempstead. A final 80mph at Wembley was unable to prevent a 7¾min late arrival at Euston, but had this excellent run been made without hindrance to the stop at Willesden the time would have been 132min, a start-to-stop average of 69.4mph, which was very close to the target of a 70mph average with 500 tons.

This run was exceptional, but there were several recordings of times of between 135 and 140min to Willesden with loads of from 470 to 510 tons. On one occasion a 'Princess' topped Tring Summit at 75mph with 420 tons and there was that classical bogey time for drivers of 9½min from Bletchley to Tring, which the great Laurie Earl is alleged to have made with a 'Princess' and eight bogies. It will never be known now just how close to the legend was the absolute truth, but the possibilities over this section were probed by Driver Starvis and No 46244 in 1957, as will be discussed in a later chapter.

The Pacifics were usually on the down evening "Merseyside Express," which loaded to 500-550 gross tons and was booked from Euston to Mossley Hill, 189.6 miles, in 200min. But they were not used on the fast Manchester 3¼hr, expresses the "Mancunian" and the "Lancastrian," until July 1939 and before they could have any impact, war had ended all LMS plans for progress. Among the engines used on the Liverpool trains the turbine Pacific No 6202 was a frequent performer. One of the fastest runs was when Driver L. A. Earl, on 10 September 1935, came up from Crewe to Willesden, 152.7 miles, in 131min covering the 77.2 miles from passing Rugby to stopping in Willesden in under an hour. The load was 11 bogies weighing 345 tons gross.

Later this was nearly equalled by the same engine with 14 bogies weighing 455 tons gross. On this run the passing times from Weedon to Wembley were a few seconds less than the classic test run of No 6200 in June 1935. As this run was perhaps the best example of combined speed and load haulage to the credit of No 6202 the relevant portion is best tabulated. Before Rugby there were checks and no running of any note.

5.25pm Liverpool-Euston
Engine: No 6202 (Turbomotive).
Load: 14 bogies, 429 tons tare, 455 tons gross.

Distance miles		Sched. Min	Actual Min Sec		Speeds mph
0.0	Crewe	0	00.00		—
75.5	Rugby	72	75	30	slack
82.8	Welton		85	50	20 sigs
88.4	Weedon		90	30	81½
95.3	Blisworth		95	48	—
98.2	Roade	93	98	15	70min
103.3	Castlethorpe		102	08	83½
105.7	Wolverton		103	53	—
111.4	Bletchley	104	108	23	76
117.9	Leighton		113	37	72/75
122.0	Cheddington		116	59	71½
126.4	Tring		120	48	68min
130.2	Berkhamsted		123	51	80½
137.2	Kings Langley		128	48	86½
140.7	Watford		131	17	78
146.7	Harrow		135	46	80
150.0	Wembley		138	08	86
152.7	Willesden Jc		141	23	

Net time: Crewe-Willesden 136¼min start to stop
Weedon-Wembley (61.6 miles): 47min 38sec pass to pass, average 77.6mph

In 1938 the "Royal Scot" was given a 7hr booking to Glasgow and it became an XL timing on which Pacifics were allowed 420 tons. This was probably a wise limitation for an all-weather timing and it was certainly a humane measure for the fireman, but there was evidence from time regaining on the earlier bookings that heavier loads might have been managed on individual occasions. In the winter of 1938 the stops at Rugby and Crewe were reimposed and the down 'Royal Scot' was given the same 7hr 20min to Glasgow that the East Coast 'Flying Scotsman' was taking to Edinburgh. This meant a booking of 80min for the 82.6 miles from Euston to Rugby.

On the previous timing of 320min to Carlisle in the summer of 1937 Driver Earl had No 6212 *Duchess of Kent*, one of the best engines in the class, at the head of a 16-coach train weighing 493 tons tare and 520 tons full. This was brought into Carlisle 4¾min early after checks which made the net time 304min for the 299.1 miles. Earl followed his usual practice on a 299mile non-stop run by starting easily, but such minimum speeds as 58½mph at Tring, 63mph at Roade, 64mph beyond Lichfield and 66mph at Whitmore meant good work with 520 tons. Grayrigg Bank was taken very easily with speed dropping to 22½mph, but this was the prelude to a vigorous climb from Tebay to Shap Summit, where speed fell from 64mph at Tebay to 35¼mph, held steadily over the last mile. This needed 40% cut off and full regulator and was another example of the best test performance standards being repeated in regular service. A speed of 87½mph was reached on the descent to Carlisle.

An example of a 'Princess' at its best on the winter booking with the intermediate stops again featured Driver Earl, but it is unfortunate that as on so many of these pre-war epics the name of the fireman, the real hero of the occasion, has not survived. This time the engine was No 6211 *Queen Maud* and the load out of Euston was 16 bogies of 512 tons, tare, 545 tons gross. The running was within schedule but not exceptional as far as Crewe, with times of 84min 59sec to Rugby and 80min 53sec thence to Crewe. At Crewe one coach was dropped and a most exceptional journey to Carlisle followed with a net time of 145¾min for the 141 miles, which was destined to remain the fastest on record with over 500 tons and a 'Princess' type locomotive. The climb from passing Carnforth to Shap Summit was 33min 36sec, which was 1½min under the booking for the 300 ton 'Coronation Scot' and 8½min under the schedule for the 'Royal Scot'. This was slightly better than the best climbs recorded by the 'Princesses' on the 'Mid-day Scot' in 1936.

Carnforth-Shap Summit (31.4 miles, 887ft vertical rise)

Locomotive:	6209	6208	6211
Train:	'Mid-day Scot'	'Mid-day Scot'	'Royal Scot'
Load:	14 coaches	16 coaches	15 coaches
	448/470 tons	490/515 tons	483/510 tons
Speed (mph) at:			
Carnforth	70 ½	71	76 ½
Grayrigg	40 ½	42 ¼	41
Tebay	71 ½	66 ½	71
Shap Summit	27 ½	28 ½	32 ½
Time	35min 31sec	35min 38sec	33min 36sec
Actual dbhp	1110	1205	1320
Equiv. dbhp	1345	1475	1540
Ihp	1720	1850	1940

These hps are, of course, the average figures for the whole of the climb in each case there would be peak maximum figures higher but less significant. The run by No 6212, which made a leisurely ascent of

Grayrigg Bank, would not show a very high average hp for the entire climb, but the short burst from Tebay to Shap Summit with a lower initial speed but a higher minimum at the top would involve a higher output.

These runs represent the cream of the recordings during the 1935-39 period. Such work could not be expected every day, but there are sufficient runs of the highest quality to leave the capacity of the 'Princesses' in no doubt. A run which was less spectacular and had less appeal to the amateur student of performance would be appreciated by the professional railway operating officer. It was timed by D. S. Barrie on the up 'Mid-day Scot', when No 6209 *Princess Beatrice* was at the head of a 13-coach load of 420 tons tare, 440 tons gross. A late start of 22min from Carlisle was converted into a 2min early arrival at Euston, with no maximum speed higher than 79mph, but with brisk uphill work. Here was the operating man's ideal of an engine, master of its load, gaining time without any undue strain on man nor machine.

The 'Princesses' had shown their ability to handle loads of up to 600 tons on schedules of 58-60mph and up to 500 tons on 64mph schedules south of Crewe and to work over 500 tons over the northern banks. They were able to average 1900-2000 ihp for half-hour periods with peaks of up to 2500 ihp. This could be done on a coal consumption just over or under 3lb/dbhp/hr. There were few if any British rivals to such work. The GWR 'Kings', in their pre-war condition, could reach the 2000 ihp mark for short periods on the Birmingham line, but it would have been unreasonable to have expected them to perform any better than any other 4-6-0 if faced with a continuous 400mile run. The A3 Pacifics of the LNER had a much more impressive array of 90mph maximum speeds to their credit, but their road lent itself to this. The 'Princesses' would doubtless have had more high maxima had they been running over such ideal galloping grounds as Stoke to Warrington, or Stevenage to Offord. The LNER record of high speeds on the level was also more impressive because of the opportunity given by the Darlington-York section. The comparable LMS section was Lancaster to Preston, which was shorter. Again, high speeds downhill and on the level were in the GNR tradition. The evidence suggests that the 'Princesses' were stronger on the banks, as would have been expected from their dimensions. The only engine from another railway which might have matched the 'Princess' under all conditions was the Gresley A4. The P2 2-8-2s could, of course, have equalled the LMS Pacifics on the banks and would have been better at keeping their feet in misty weather or for recovering from a slack, but would hardly have been suitable for high-speed running on easier grades as a regular practice.

The LMS had every reason for some qualified satisfaction with the 'Princesses'. They had raised the prestige of the railway and their best work could hardly have been matched by the 'Royal Scots'. They had saved money by reducing double-heading and banking assistance. On the other hand, there were design features which could have been improved, and their success came only from the very careful maintenance which was possible while they remained a small elite corps with good coal, skilled driving and firing and careful attention at the sheds. When a special effort was possible performance on the road was good and they ran high annual mileages, but they were destined later to prove very sensitive to reduced standards in the wartime and post-war worlds. While it is right for the 'Princesses' to be honoured for the work they performed during the years 1935-39, it is also true that the LMS was wise to have developed an improved Pacific from 1937 onwards.

CHAPTER EIGHT

'Coronations' and 'Duchesses'

The operating ideal of the professional railway officer is for the railway to be as much as possible like an enormous conveyor belt with the trains moving like equidistant parcels. The high-speed, super-express offends this ideal and there has always been enough resistance to prevent it becoming a popular feature of British railway operation. Basic LMS philosophy favoured a gradual improvement of the whole train service, but this laudable aim was destined not to be fully realised until electrification. The case for the light high-speed express had been strongly advocated by railway journalists. Following the fast run to Plymouth by the GWR *City of Bath* with the Royal Special in 1903, Charles Rous Marten and the Rev. W. J. Scott suggested possible timings of 2hr 45min from Euston to Liverpool as being reasonable for a 'Precursor' with a suitably light train. This may have been unduly optimistic, but the suggestions of Cecil J. Allen in 1919 for schedules of 6½hr from London to Glasgow and Edinburgh with loads of 200-250 tons, as soon as track could be returned to pre-war condition, had greater reality. Mr Allen saw his dreams fulfilled in the 1935-39 period.

The mid-1930's saw a stirring in railway offices all over the world towards higher speeds as a counter-move against increasing road and air competition. Its most sensational translation from aim to fact was the German streamlined twin diesel unit *The Flying Hamburger*, which streaked across the flat North German Plain at an average speed of 77.4mph with maximum speeds of 100mph. The line from Berlin to Hamburg was straight and level, but the lesson was there and, in course of time, other railways had to look to their own image. The first tentative experiments with diesel power for high-speed trains were made in the US at about the same time.

The early diesels had a high power/weight ratio, but a limited capacity and it was soon obvious that more passengers would have to be carried in more comfort if the railways were to be really competitive. This set steam engineers on their mettle and high-speed steam locomotives appeared in Germany and the US. The Germans built a large 4-6-4 streamlined steam locomotive with 7ft 6in driving wheels and in 1936 they reached 124½mph with this highly specialised design. The most significant American project was that of the Chicago,

Milwaukee, St Paul and Pacific RR, which introduced streamlined Atlantic class engines on their 'Hiawatha' express between Chicago and the twin cities of St Paul and Mineapolis. These trains had to run at speeds of up to and sometimes over 100mph to keep time. A speed of 112½mph was recorded under test conditions, while less well authenticated claims of over two miles a minute were made during the acceptance trials.

The advocates of the high-speed train found a powerful ally in H. N. (later Sir Nigel) Gresley of the LNER, who ran trials with conventional Pacifics in November 1934 and in March 1935 and built his 'Silver Jubilee' streamlined train with its A4 class Pacifics in the autumn of 1935. The impact was sensational, for on its first serious trial the 'Silver Jubilee' covered 43 miles at an average of 100mph with a twice-attained maximum of 112½mph. A few days later it entered regular service on a four hour booking to Newcastle. The 'Silver Jubilee' fulfilled the most optimistic expectations of the publicity department; everyone on or near the railway from the merest platform-end urchin to the commuting stockbroker raised his eyes as the new silver-grey apparition dashed past. It was no good insisting that under the casing there was an ordinary Pacific only slightly modified; to the general public the steam locomotive had stepped from a respectable maturity, which it shared with the traction engine, the tramcar and the paddle steamer, into the streamlined age of the racing car and the aeroplane.

The LMS realised that the East Coast was stealing the thunder. The more technically minded knew that the test running of No 6200 in June 1935, with reasonably high speeds with heavy loads and stout hill-climbing over the northern banks, was just as significant a display of good locomotive design, but its impact on the public was much less than the joyous high speed romps of the Gresley Pacifics. The success of the 4hr express to Newcastle made a high-speed run to Edinburgh only a matter of time and this was something the LMS had to match.

So it was that in November 1936 No 6201 *Princess Elizabeth* set out on its high-speed test runs to Glasgow and back. It was by then common knowledge that the LNER intended to introduce a six-hour service to Edinburgh in the summer of 1937 and the results of the test run by No 6201 suggested that something not much slower would be running on the LMS to Glasgow. Those who liked to see a locomotive shaped like one had rejoiced in the success of the conventional non-streamlined LMS Pacific and they hoped that the high-speed West Coast train would be hauled by an ordinary Pacific without any concession to the prevailing fashion. Early in 1937, however, it was announced that this hope was not to be fulfilled: the new 6½hr express to Glasgow would be worked by an enlarged version of the 'Princess' with 6ft 9in driving wheels — and fully streamlined.

There had been a number of suggestions in the Derby design office before the project was finalised. At first it appeared probable that a further five 'Princesses', Nos 6213-6217, would have been built, but there were progressive spirits who craved for something bigger and better. The leading force in this group was T. F. Coleman, a strong personality who had his origins on the North Staffordshire Railway and so had no undue reverence for the ideas of Derby, Crewe or Horwich. It was soon to be shown that he did not shrink from altering some features of Swindon origin and it is a tribute to the broad-minded attitude of W. A. Stanier that Coleman was given authority to go ahead with his ideas for enlarging the boiler and improving the cylinder layout. One scheme was for an enlarged 'Princess' which would have retained the De Glehn cylinder layout and an obvious relationship to the GWR 'King'. The other scheme was for a modified layout which was more like that proposed in 1924 for the Hughes Pacific which was never built. Had the Horwich Pacific really been built in 1924 and the normal processes of modification and development continued on the LMS, as it had with the Gresley Pacifics on the LNER, it is easy to envisage the 180lb pressure Pacific of 1924 evolving by 1937 into a 250lb Pacific not greatly different from the one which the LMS built under the influence of an entirely different chain of events.

The two schemes for an enlarged Pacific were intended for either streamlined or unstreamlined form. Derby drawing office was officially neutral but privately many of the engineers hoped that the unfrocked version would prevail. There were those who expected that the first scheme with fewer departures from the 'Princess' would win the day, but when Coleman took the two designs to Euston, Stanier accepted the second scheme with the Swindon theme somewhat muted. The publicity people had their way and the new engines were to be streamlined. As the design had been altered, a new class had been created and the numbers started at 6220; thus any ill-luck that might have been thought to follow the use of '13' in the number was avoided. In this connection it may be mentioned that with a number of excellent runs to the credit of A4 No 60013 and King No 6013; there is no reason to think that an LMS No 6213 would have done otherwise!)

At the end of May 1937 the first of the new enlarged LMS Pacifics was given its public unveiling. The first thing apparent to all was the shape of the streamlined casing which, with its bulbous front, was different from that of the LNER A4. The LMS streamlining had been decided upon after wind tunnel tests with models by the LMS Research Department at Derby and it was probably aerodynamically superior to the LNER pattern, but the wedge-shaped rising front of the A4 was of considerable help in keeping the cab windows clear of smoke and steam when the engine was running easily. The LMS pattern was less satisfactory in this respect and the size of the locomotive and the relatively easy schedule to which it was to work led to some trouble with drifting smoke and steam.

The bulbous front was built up on a specially prepared wooden jig which ensured the proper fitting of the casings when mounted on the engine. Before painting and lining there were large unbroken surfaces which detracted from the appearance of the casing, but when painted in the new blue with the horizontal lines running from a point in front to the rear of the tender and continued along the sides of the nine coaches the effect was striking. The bands were officially silver, but they weathered into white. There were broad bands at the top and bottom with narrow lines in between. The casing was raised over the driving wheels, allowing full access to the outside motion. This was an improvement over the fairing which covered much of the A4 motion and was unpopular with the enginemen. During the war this part of the A4 casing was removed and never replaced. The LMS engines had easy access to the outside motion, but the inside motion was less easily reached. There were removable plates to give access to the unseen portions of the engine, but it is doubtful if they were sufficient for easy maintenance. The appearance of the locomotive and train had been carefully considered and the side plates of the tender were extended backwards a little, making the relatively short six-wheeled vehicle look as long as possible. The appearance was striking and the publicity people were justified in expecting a favourable reaction. Even those who did not like streamlining had to admit that the worst excesses of some foreign air-smoothed locomotives had been avoided.

Those whose interest in locomotives was a little more than skin-deep were interested less in a photograph of the outside than in a line drawing of the internal features of the engine. When this was examined a locomotive of truly noble proportions emerged. The boiler was larger than that of the 'Princess' — in fact, it was difficult to see how anything much bigger could ever be accommodated within our restricted loading gauge. The firegrate area was increased to 50sq ft against the 45sq ft of the earlier Pacifics. This promised more potential power and a better capacity for dealing with low-grade fuels, but in practice such very large grates proved to be rather beyond the capacity of one man to fire and engines so fitted lived up to the promise of their grates on rare occasions only. The firebox was fitted with a combustion chamber and the firebox heating surface was increased to 230sq ft. The firebox was built of copper and the boiler shell of nickel steel. The firebox stays were of steel with the exception of the outer and top few rows, which were of Monel metal. The firebox door was of the sliding type, designed to direct the secondary air down on to the fire.

The boiler barrel was rolled in two rings only. The diameter at the front was the same as that of the 'Princesses', but it was 2½in greater in diameter at the rear. The tube length was the same as the earlier engines, 19ft 3in, and the longer combustion chamber and the shorter wheelbase meant that the smokebox was now directly above the bogie instead of being some way to the rear as in the 'Princesses'. A 40-element superheater with triple flow Wagner-type elements was provided; this had a superheating surface of 856sq ft against the earlier engines' 653sq ft. The experience gained with the modified boiler of the Turbomotive was of value in the development of the new enlarged boiler. Even so, this very large superheater gave a disappointing steam temperature owing mainly to the poor A/S ratio of 1/560 and the adoption of tubes of only 5⅛in diameter. To provide an increased free area in proportion to the large grate the number of small tubes was increased to 129. The layout of these perforce resulted in a relatively cramped vertical diamond pitch, which offended purist thoughts on optimum boiler proportions, but there was little room for anything else within the limitations of maximum diameter of the boiler and the loading gauge. Disappointing steam temperatures were features of the test results of other British Pacific designs with very large boilers and grates of 48-50sq ft.

The ashpan design was simplified as compared with the 'Princesses'. The side doors were abandoned in favour of dampers at front and rear, but this proved to be less than satisfactory and the 1938 batch had modifications with bottom hopper doors. Later a section of the grate was made removable to assist in fire dropping and later still Hulson firebars and a few examples of rocking grates were tried. The upper portion of the smokebox was cut away to conform with the streamlined shape and this looked most curious after the war when the streamlining was removed. Those engines built without streamlining had normal smokeboxes and eventually all engines were altered to this pattern. The floor of the smokebox was kept commendably clear of obstructions to facilitate cleaning.

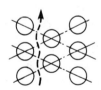

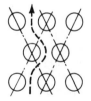

HORIZONTAL DIAMOND
GWR, LNER, SR BULLEID, CHAPELON

VERTICAL DIAMOND
LATER 'PRINCESS', 'DUCHESS'
BR STANDARD, LMS TAPER BOILER, SR
LORD NELSON

BOILER TUBE PITCH & WATER CIRCULATION

Boiler tube pitch layout.

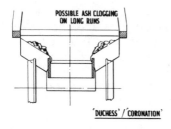

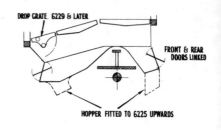

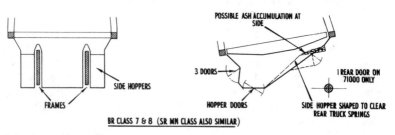

Ashpan arrangements.

The regulator was placed in the steam dome, which was situated further forward than that on the domed boilers of some earlier Pacifics. There was a Davies and Metcalfe exhaust steam injector with 13mm cones on the fireman's side and a live steam injector with 13mm cones on the driver's side. These delivered the water to the boiler through top feed clacks set much further forward than those on the 'Princesses'. The water was discharged into trays within the steam space in order to de-aerate the water before it was finally discharged through pipes below the water level.

The boiler was fitted with four pop safety valves 2½in in diameter mounted over the firebox. These showed a certain reluctance to re-seat themselves after blowing off, which caused a waste of steam that tended to negative any beneficial effects from the allegedly precise blowing-off of such valves. Many of the 'Duchesses' worked in ordinary service with valves blowing at 230-240lb against the official 250lb. Steam for the various cab fittings was taken from a manifold on the top of the firebox backplate. The fittings were of the standard LMS pattern, except that the carriage warming reducing valve was made with increased capacity to deal with the long trains that would be put behind such powerful engines. A sand gun was fitted to clear the tubes, but this was later removed.

When the engines were first introduced *The Railway Gazette* described the boiler as "an excellent example of high-powered design in all respects". As the engines progressed through lives of varied difficulty there were details which, in the light of later knowledge, might with advantage have been modified, but by comparative standards the boiler justified *The Railway Gazette's* description admirably.

The frames were 1⅛in thick and were constructed of high tensile steel which, it was claimed, permitted some saving of weight. The abandonment of the De Glehn layout permitted better bracing at the front end. At the rear two separate frame plates were spliced to the main frames and carried through to the rear-end buffer beam. This feature was the one remaining memory of the proposed Derby four cylinder compound design of 1925. The outer frames were splayed outwards and the inner frames inwards to take the side bearers for the two-wheeled trailing truck.

The new cylinder arrangement was generally similar to that of the Horwich 4-6-0 and the proposed Horwich Pacific of 1924. There were rocking levers behind the outside cylinders with long link rods to the inside cylinders. This avoided the errors due to valve spindle expansion, and apart from the effect of the slightly different connecting rod lengths gave equal valve events. The 16½in x 28in cylinders had enlarged valves of 9in diameter with 1¾in lap, ¼in lead and .060in exhaust clearance. This promised good high-speed capability — in fact, the optimum speed range was 55-110mph which, in the event, proved higher than most of work which the engines were called upon to perform, but it had the disadvantage of giving the comparatively large clearance volume of 12.5%. There was also the need for large steam lead settings, giving a low lap to lead ratio. At normal speeds this might be expected to give a relatively low cylinder efficiency and this seems to have been shown on the test plant. It must, however, be emphasised that such a criticism is concerned with relative values and the effects were marginal. The new cylinder arrangement was mechanically much better than that of the 'Princesses' and the problem of loosening cylinders was avoided. A stronger slide bar arrangement was possible.

The whole arrangement was specially designed to allow the removal of the valves for examination with the minimum of trouble. The valves and pistons followed standard LMS design, but by using lighter webs there was some saving of weight. The piston valves were fitted with six narrow rings to ensure steam tightness. The exhaust passages were carefully designed to give a free exit for steam and the blastpipe was a simple straight pipe without the Churchward jumper blastpipe top, which had been used on the earlier members of the 'Princess' class. In this connection it is of interest that a Churchward top was at first used on the Gresley A4s, but was later abandoned.

The pistons were of the box type provided with three narrow rings. Mechanical lubrication was provided for the cylinders. Atomised oil formed by mixing oil with a jet of saturated steam from an independent supply from the boiler was applied to the piston valve liners continuously while the engine was running, whether the regulator was open or shut. There were also feeds to each piston packing and two feeds to each cylinder barrel, one at the top and one at the bottom.

The crossheads were of the two-bar type, consisting of steel castings with bronze slippers with the portions in contact with the slide bars white-metalled. The gudgeon pin was prevented from turning in the crosshead by two keys and was secured by a split cone and nut. The coupling and connecting rods were of Vibrac steel specially designed to withstand the inertia stresses while running at high speeds. The tyres were secured by Gibson rings and the wheel rims were of triangular section. The whole of the revolving parts were balanced on each wheel and 50% of the reciprocating masses were balanced equally divided between each pair of coupled wheels. The class enjoyed a reputation for good riding.

The axleboxes were steel castings with pressed-in brasses completely lined with white metal on the bearing surface. There were no oil grooves to break the continuity of the oil film. Oil from mechanical lubricators was introduced through a row of holes on the horizontal centre line of the axle. The axles were hollow; this, it was claimed, saved weight with no loss of strength. The bogie wheels had 2in holes, the trailing axle and the leading coupled axle which carried the cranks for the inside cylinders were 3in and the second and third coupled axles had 4½in holes. In addition to mechanical lubrication every axle box underkeep was fitted with an oil pad which could be withdrawn for examination. A dust shield protected the inside faces of the middle and rear coupled axleboxes. The supply of oil from the mechanical lubricators was taken to the top of each axlebox through a spring loaded back pressure valve intended to keep the oil pipes full while the engine was standing and to ensure prompt delivery of oil the moment the engine moved. The sides of the axleboxes were fitted with bronze slippers making contact with the faces of the axlebox guides. The bogie and the trailing truck were of similar pattern to these on the 'Princesses'.

The 6ft 9in driving wheels were equally spaced at 7ft 3in and this meant that the coupled wheelbase was actually shorter than that of the 'Princesses'. The springs on both engine and tender were of the laminated pattern made of silico-manganese steel. The spring plates were of ribbed section with cotter-type fixing in the buckle. The spring links were adjustable by screws. There were rubber damper springs between the spring link heads and the frame brackets of the coupled wheels. A steam brake was provided on the engine, actuating brake blocks at the front of each pair of driving wheels. The brake gear was compensated to give equal pressure on each brake block. The driver's brake valve controlled the steam brake on the engine and the vacuum brake on the train and there were separate valves for the steam passing to the large and small ejectors. A crosshead vacuum pump was provided on the first batch of the class, but it was abandoned later.

The cab had double side windows and small glass wind deflectors. The front windows were hinged for easy cleaning and, being placed at an angle, gave no reflection. The crew had tip-up seats and gangway doors were fitted between engine cab and tender panel plates. Steam sand was provided in front of the leading and middle coupled wheels and behind the middle pair. Oil gun lubrication was provided for certain parts, such as the brake gear spring gear, reversing gear in cab and at other points. No steps were provided on the engine, but access was easy from the tender steps. The whistle was the standard Stanier pattern based on Caledonian practice.

The tenders carried 10tons of coal and 4000gal of water and they were shaped to match the streamlined casing on the engine. The side plates were carried back to a position level with the buffers. This was a slight improvement to the appearance in side elevation, as the short tender was a point of criticism of the looks of the LMS Pacifics. The rear fairing carried the horizontal lines along the side back to a position close to the front of the train and thus a gap in the end-to-end streamlining was avoided.

The main innovation was the coal pusher, which was probably inspired by the use of a similar device in Germany on the Wolff/Wagner high-speed 05 class 4-6-4s. The coal pusher was worked by a steam cylinder and it was of great value in pushing the coal forward towards the end of a long through run. Passengers in the leading coaches of trains hauled by these Pacifics were at times mystified by the explosive bursts of exhaust steam from this device. The tender was provided with the standard water pick-up apparatus.

The original set of coaches for the 'Coronation Scot' consisted of nine vehicles, which were similar to LMS standard stock but had the Thermo Reg system of pressure ventilation. The horizontal lines were continued to the rear of the train.

The general appearance of engine and train was striking and it attracted much attention from the lineside, which must have been gratifying to the publicity people. The LMS enthusiasts realised that here was an express locomotive which could meet the challenge of anything else in Britain. The LMS could claim to have 'Britain's Mightiest Passenger Locomotive' on sounder grounds than other British companies who had, in the past, claimed this title on the slender basis of tractive effort. There was, however, some regret over the cautious schedule of 6½hr to Glasgow, which was unlikely to extend such a large and powerful locomotive.

After a dramatic press outing in June 1937 the new Pacifics jogged their way gently along on the 'Coronation Scot' with no need for the fast running of the rival East Coast 'Coronation'. The new LMS Pacifics were seen very little on ordinary service trains in the winter of 1937 and early 1938.

In 1938 another ten were built, Nos 6225-6229 streamlined and Nos 6230-6234 unstreamlined. These were finished in standard LMS red with the bands on the streamlined engines in gold. Many thought the red and gold was better than the blue and silver and that the non-streamlined engines looked better than either. On the new engines small modifications were immediately obvious. There were additional ventilating louvres in the casing of the streamliners, the crosshead vacuum pump had vanished and there was a step below the drawhook. As first built, the single chimney was retained.

However, test running with No 6234 in February 1939 indicated that benefit was to be expected from the use of a double blastpipe and chimney. This was the simple double blastpipe where all the exhaust steam was combined before being discharged through twin 4.31in blast pipes. This device was simpler than the full Kylchap exhaust used on the LNER Pacifics, and it had the advantage of simplified smokebox cleaning. One Pacific, No 6245, built in 1943 had an experimental Kylchap double blastpipe and chimney, but it was soon altered to the standard layout. It would appear that there was some thermo-dynamic superiority in the French blastpipe, but it was more complicated and a lot depended on correct proportions. The LMS experience with the 'Jubilee' class No 5684 *Jutland*, which had been fitted with a Kylchap double blastpipe in 1936, had not been very satisfactory. Even if No 6245 had been better than the others any advantage would only have become apparent if the engine had been extended in the same way as No 6234 in February 1939. This could hardly have been possible in 1939, but the ease of smokebox cleaning had a practical reality in wartime and the simpler LMS double chimney was preferred.

Twenty more streamlined Pacifics with double chimneys were ordered by the LMS in 1939. These were to be painted red with gold lines and were to be named after cities. Five had been built before hostilities began and a start had been made on others. Five more appeared in 1940. The final engine of this batch, No 6244 *City of Leeds*, was re-named *King George VI* in April 1941. There was then a delay until 1943 when four more appeared, streamlined but painted wartime black. Another four followed in 1944, black but unstreamlined. These had streamlined tenders, which had already been completed. This meant that 18 of the original order for 20 Pacifics had been completed by the end of the war.

No more were built until 1946, when three more appeared. These were painted in the LMS post-war livery of black with maroon edging and straw-coloured lining. They had self-cleaning smokeboxes and rocking grates, evidence of the greater importance of availability in the post-war world. The foot-plating was broken in front of the cylinders instead of being continuous; this made it easier to remove the front covers of the steam chests and it was called "the utility front".

At about the same time the streamlining was removed from some of the engines and these also had "the utility front". The engines with streamlining removed had a cut-away portion at the top of the smoke-box showing where it originally fitted under the casing. These engines were readily recognised at a distance and the young members of the spotting fraternity called them "The Semis", considering them to be semi-streamlined.

Authority had been given in 1939 for the building of two experi-mental Pacifics of advanced design and had there been no war they would probably have taken the road in 1940. These were to take advantage of as many of the Chapelon features as possible with the exception of compounding. They would have had 300lb/sq in boiler pressure, a Houlet-type superheater giving 750°F steam temperature, separate headers for saturated and superheated steam, enlarged steam passages, steam chest volume, piston valve size and 1¾in steam lap. There would have been a Kylchap double blastpipe, more tubes of lesser diameter and a form of thermic syphon in the firebox. It was intended to build these after the war, but when peace came more limited aims were necessary.

In 1942 W. A. Stanier was appointed to the team of Scientific Advisers to the Ministry of Production, but he continued as the nominal CME of the LMS until his retirement in 1944, when the post went to C. E. Fairburn until the latter's sudden and unexpected death in October 1945, whereupon the rule passed to H. G. Ivatt, son of the former GNR chief H. A. Ivatt. Ivatt was responsible for the first experiments in main-line diesel traction with Nos 10000 and 10001 and it was decided to run tests between the new diesels and two improved Pacifics specially designed to give the best availability possible with steam. The specification had changed somewhat from the two experimental "Chapelonised" Pacifics projected in 1939, which it was hoped would raise performance on the road to new heights.

The new Pacifics, Nos 6256 and 6257, were intended to give the same performance on the road as the other Pacifics but to attain better mileage and to have lower repair charges. They were fitted with Timken tapered roller bearings except on the crank axle, where Skefco self-aligning boxes were used. The boiler had an enlarged superheater with Type 5P4 elements and a total heating surface of 979sq ft; the A/S ratios were, however, worse rather than better. This superheater was modified at the first boiler change. The new engines were fitted with side doors to the ashpan similar to those on the 'Princesses'. In order to provide room for a self-emptying ashpan a new back end was designed with a Delta-type cast steel pony truck. The reversing screw was brought forward out of the cab to an amidships position, while the cut-off positions were indicated on a drum close to the reversing hand wheel. These proved to be two very good locomotives, though they never attained the goal of 100000 miles per annum under the arduous postwar conditions.

In 1943 Stanier was honoured by King George VI with knighthood, partly for his services to the LMS and partly for his help to the nation in providing the munitions of war. In March 1944 Sir William Stanier was further honoured when he was given a Fellowship of the Royal Society. The only other locomotive engineer to have this honour was Robert Stephenson. It was fitting that one of the new Pacifics No 6256 was named *Sir William Stanier, F.R.S.* When the new locomotive testing station at Rugby was opened the LNER A4 class Pacific *Sir Nigel Gresley* gave a ceremonial twirl to the rollers while the new LMS Pacific *Sir William Stanier, F.R.S.* stood outside the Plant. These two Pacifics symbolised much of what was best in British steam locomotive practice, while the test plant pointed the way to further progress in the future.

CHAPTER NINE

High Speed and High Power

The first question which interested people asked about the new LMS Pacific was: "How will it compare with the Gresley A4?" The general expectation was that from its dimensions it could be expected to equal the East Coast Pacifics in high speed and could well be somewhat stronger on the banks. The A4s had, by mid-1937, proved themselves as not only very fast with light loads, but also capable performers with heavy loads, while No 2511, on test between Edinburgh and Newcastle, had climbed Cockburnspath Bank with an out-put of 2500-2600 ihp, which was at least as good as anything recorded by a 'Princess'. The new 'Coronation' class LMS Pacifics, however, promised to be more powerful and faster than anything so far seen on the LMS.

No 6220 *Coronation* left Crewe Works in early June 1937 and after running in was intended to run a press trip to Crewe and back on 29 June prior to starting regular service on "The Coronation Scot" on 5 July. As part of the working-up period the new engine was put on the up 'Liverpool Flyer' on 21 June, 1937 in the hands of Driver Tom Clarke of Crewe. The train was normally worked by Edge Hill and Camden men alternately, but this run was intended to allow Tom Clarke to take some measure of his engine before the press demonstration of the following week. The load was 11 bogies of 351 tons tare, 370 tons gross, and although the booking was the second fastest on the LMS the new Pacific could hardly be extended unless allowed to run ahead of time. The run became a succession of easings with a few openings out to test the uphill acceleration.

The initial start from Crewe was modest, but then the engine was opened out and speed rose from 61mph at Betley Road to 68mph at Madeley up three miles of 1 in 177. On the easier 1 in 348 there was a further rise to 71mph at Whitmore Summit. Then, after a period of easy running, it was decided to test the acceleration on a level road. Passing Weedon at 79mph the engine was opened out near mp 69 and a maximum of 93mph was reached between mps 65 and 64. This was attained on track shown as level on the published profile, but actually faintly rising at 1 in 2640. The minimum at Roade Summit was 86.6mph. After a further easing the engine was again given a run, passing Wolverton at 77mph, then falling to 74mph, speed picked up to 85mph at Bletchley, fell to 80mph at Leighton and was sustained at

99

79mph up to Tring. Easy downhill running then brought the train into Willesden 9½min before time. No record speeds or hps had been attained, nor had any been intended, but the crew had taken the measure of the new engine and there was evidence of plenty of speed and power available when the need came.

The LMS authorities were anxious that some of the favourable

5.25pm Liverpool-Euston 21 June 1937
Engine: No 6220 *Coronation*
Driver: T. J. Clarke, Crewe.
Load: 11 bogies, 331 tons tare, 370 tons gross.

Distance Miles		Sched min	Actual min sec		Speeds mph
0.0	Crewe		00	00	—
4.8	Betley Road		7	39	61
			opened out		
8.0	Madeley		10	38	68
10.5	Whitmore		12	50	71
			eased		
19.2	Norton Bridge		19	25	84
24.5	Stafford	26	24	05	40 slack
28.6	Milford		28	58	68
33.8	Rugeley	36	33	15	82/79
41.8	Lichfield	42	39	17	83
48.1	Tamworth		43	47	77
	Polesworth		pws		50
55.8	Atherstone		50	58	68
61.0	Nuneaton	60	55	08	79
66.7	Shilton		59	45	70/77
			eased		
75.5	Rugby	73	68	35	30 slack
82.8	Welton		78	02	49
			opened out		
88.4	Weedon		83	20	79
95.3	Blisworth		88	08	93
98.2	Roade	94	90	10	86.6min
			eased		
105.7	Wolverton		95	30	77/74
			opened out		
111.4	Bletchley	105	100	04	85
117.9	Leighton Buzzard		104	49	80
126.4	Tring	119	111	10	79min
			eased		
133.6	Boxmoor		116	35	80
140.7	Watford		122	07	74/72
146.7	Harrow		126	55	79
150.0	Wembley		129	28	82
152.7	Willesden Junct.	142	132	27	

(Timed by D. S. M. Barrie)

publicity that had been enjoyed by the East Coast following their high-speed attempts should now come their way. But the task of rivalling or beating the 112½ and 113mph maximum speeds of the A4s was not an easy one, however fast the new LMS engine promised to be. There was no stretch of road on the West Coast route as suitable for a high-speed attempt as the LNER main line between Stoke and Werrington or between Stevenage and Offord. The gentle ups and downs of 1 in 330 favoured higher uphill and lower downhill speeds. The 'Coronation' class Pacifics were bigger than the A4s, but it could hardly be hoped that they could reach a hp so much greater as to cancel out the more potent effect of gravity given by a 1 in 200 descent. The only down grade as steep as the East Coast high-speed descents was that from Whitmore to Crewe, which included 3 miles of 1 in 177, comparable with Stoke to Corby, but the complete descent was shorter than the LNER racing grounds and it was uncomfortably close to Crewe at the finish. If the LNER records were to be broken then *Coronation* would need to produce a short burst of high power to reach a high maximum speed in such a restricted space.

On 29 June 1937 *Coronation*, in the capable hands of Driver T. J. Clarke and Fireman J. Lewis of Crewe, set off with a load of specially invited guests and press representatives. One kitchen car had been cut out of the nine-coach 'Coronation Scot' set, leaving a tare load of 263 tons or 270 tons gross. There was no dynamometer car but so many expert recorders were carried that the events of the day can hardly be questioned. In one compartment there were Messrs C. J. Allen, D. S. M. Barrie and S. P. W. Corbett, while in the next there was O. S. Nock. The degree of agreement between these very experienced train timers was encouraging.

The initial start was gentle, but it was good work to accelerate to 82mph on the 1 in 339 to Carpenters Park and the indications were that the engine was still accelerating at the summit. Later 80½mph was sustained unvaryingly up the final few miles of 1 in 335 to Tring Summit, passed in a record 27min 45sec from Euston after 31.7 mainly rising miles. There was a maximum speed of 87½mph at Cheddington, near where No 6203 attained the previous LMS record speed of 102½mph, and running was moderate as far as Norton Bridge on the gentle ascent from Stafford to Whitmore. Here the engine was opened up and speed rose from 60 to 75½mph at Norton Bridge and further to 85mph at Whitmore Summit. Speed then climbed rapidly until the mile from mp 155 to mp 156 was covered in 32sec at an average of 112.5mph. The recorders all agreed that a maximum of 113mph had been attained which was an exact tie with the LNER record of *Silver Fox*. The LMS however, on the basis of the Hasler speed recorder, claimed 114mph and this was generally accepted as a new British record. The speed recorder alone was hardly convincing evidence, but it was generally realised that the maximum of 113 or 114 was not the limit of which the locomotive was capable, as it still seemed to be accelerating when steam was shut off and the brakes were applied near mp 156. Few people except the more ardent LNER supporters begrudged the LMS claim and this was especially so after *Mallard* raised the record to 125 or 126mph in July 1938. The LMS record of 114mph is non-proven, but at least 113mph seems well authenticated.

'Coronation Scot' Trial Trip 29 June 1937
Engine: No 6220 *Coronation.*
Load: 8 bogies, 263 tons tare, 270 tons gross.

Mileposts	Passing times	Differences	Speeds
148	123min 16.8sec	—	—
148 ½	123min 37.6sec	20.8sec	86.5mph
149	123min 58.0sec	20.4sec	88.2mph
149 ½	124min 7.8sec	19.8sec	90.9mph
150	124min 27.0sec	19.2sec	93.6mph
150 ½	124min 46.0sec	19.0sec	94.5mph
151	125min 4.6sec	18.6sec	96.8mph
151 ½	125min 22.8sec	18.2sec	98.9mph
152	125min 40.4sec	17.6sec	102.3mph
152 ½	125min 57.8sec	17.4sec	103.4mph
153	126min 14.8sec	17.0sec	105.9mph
153 ½	126min 31.4sec	16.8sec	107.1mph
154	126min 48.0sec	16.6sec	108.4mph
154 ½	127min 4.4sec	16.4sec	109.8mph
155	127min 20.6sec	16.2sec	111.1mph
155 ½	127min 36.6sec	16.0sec	112.5mph
156	127min 52.6sec	16.0sec	112.5mph
	steam off	brakes hard on.	

Milepost 156 was an uncomfortable 2.1 miles from Crewe station and the problem of stopping the train in time was the dominant thought in everyone's mind. At first the brakes seemed to make little difference and familiar landmarks such as Basford Sand Sidings and Crewe South Shed left vague images as they rapidly slid past. But at last speed began to fall and it was dropping quickly as the engine entered a succession of reverse curves through crossovers at 57mph before finally coming to rest at No 3 Platform in an unbelievable but true time of 6min 48sec for the 10.5 miles from passing Whitmore to the dead stand. The crockery in the kitchen car was sadly depleted and permanent way men pulled some wry faces when they examined some of the rail chairs, but some accounts of the incident have been exaggerated. It is unlikely that the engines of ambulances were started up as their drivers would hardly be in a position to judge what was happening to the south of the station. The last mile to the stop had take a mere 79sec, which hardly gave time for action or for lasting impressions to be formed. It was a tribute to the design of the locomotive and especially to the De Glehn bogie that nothing worse happened.

It had not been a wise piece of railway operation, but it had given some indication of the speed capacity of *Coronation* and we are grateful for the opportunity of making a comparison with other high-speed attempts by single-chimney Pacifics:

Rly	Loco	Load	From/To	Distance	Gradient (falling)
LNER	2509	230	90-112mph	9 miles	1 in 200
LNER	2512	270	85-113mph	11 miles	1 in 200/264
LMS	6220	270	85-113mph	7 miles	1 in 348/177/269

The LMS locomotive had made the most rapid acceleration and had, with little doubt, developed the highest hp at these very great speeds. It appeared in the summer of 1937 that somewhere around 115mph the possible ceiling for a single-chimney British locomotive would have been reached. This notion gained further strength from the high-speed attempt of A4 No 4489 on the day after *Coronation's* run. This was with a heavier 325ton train but the maximum reached was 109½mph. Later it emerged that there were difficulties with the steaming of No 4489 following its long wait at Barkston and it was suggested that other A4s were better, but there was no proof of what a single-chimney A4 might have done under more favourable conditions. The real advance came when the double-chimney *Mallard* made an all-out attempt in July 1938. This time *Mallard*, with 240 tons, in the course of its acceleration from 74mph to its sensational 125 or 126mph actually picked up from 85 near mp 99 to 115mph near mp 94. This was, for course, faster than the acceleration of *Coronation*, but *Mallard* was pulling a slightly lighter load, had the advantage of a double chimney, had a little more help from gravity and was certainly being pressed harder. Driver Clarke after the run said that *Coronation* was still rather new and stiff and he thought a few more mph could be added when the engine was more fully run in. Just what speed a double-chimney 'Coronation' class Pacific would have reached if driven hard down Stoke Bank without the worry of having to make a quick stop at the foot is conjecture. The chances are that it would have been a formidable rival to *Mallard*, but the A4 score is the one factually on board.

There was obviously no trouble with overheating of *Coronation* as the return trip was faster than the outward run and a much better example of good operating. Driver Clarke was given a free hand to gain on schedule and he made one of the fastest runs ever recorded in Britain by covering the 158.1 miles in 119min at a start-to-stop average of 79.7mph. This included a pass-to-pass average of 83.2mph over the 150 miles from Betley Road to Kilburn despite the Stafford and Rugby slowings and an average of 89mph over the 72.3 miles from Welton to Kilburn. There was a maximum of 100mph at Castlethorpe and 99mph at Kings Langley. Wherever the road allowed the speed hovered around the 90mph mark, with a drop to 86½mph at Tring Summit. Such a run deserves full tabulation.

The average speed of 89mph for 72 miles compared with the average of 91.8mph for 70 miles by *Silver Link* on its press run of 27 September 1935. The more undulating character of the East Coast main line made it essential for the A4 to reach higher maximum speeds of up to 112½mph to sustain this high average and the LNER run was more spectacular. The merit of the two performances was, however, similar, with little significant difference in the average hps. The new LMS Pacific had shown its ability to run as fast as the LNER A4s, but the most ardent of LMS enthusiasts would have been hard pressed to claim that there was a sensational improvement. It had to be admitted that an A4, extended from Crewe to Euston, could have matched the running of *Coronation*. Writing in August 1937 Cecil J. Allen said that the speed contest had reached the stage of "honours easy." Any advantage from the greater size of the LMS Pacific would be more likely to emerge if fully extended with a heavy load over the northern banks. This facet of their performance was not demonstrated until 1939.

The ordinary daily running of the 'Coronation Scot' was not difficult and little emerged as to the capacity of the new Pacifics. The five original blue 'Coronations' were not used a great deal on the ordinary express trains and nothing of any note was recorded.

No 6220's work on the 'Coronation Scot' was analysed in November 1937, when the addition of the dynamometer car to the nine coaches raised the load to 331 tons tare and 345-350 tons gross. The task did not prove unduly difficult, but ihps up to a calculated maximum of 2100-2200 were estimated from the recorded dbhps. The greatest interest centred on the banks; Shap Summit was passed at a minimum of 42mph and Beattock Summit at 39mph northbound, while coming south Beattock was topped at 57mph. Such speeds were typical of a normal timekeeping run. The engine was in good order, gave every satisfaction and performed its work without being pushed in any way. Cut-offs on the easier sections were 10-12% with 15-20% on the rising grades, while the normal working positions on the northern banks was 25% with 27% for very short distances near the summits. Coal consumption was moderate — 39.2lb/mile — and water consumption was 323lb/mile, while the firing rate was 47.3lb/sq ft of grate area per hr. The coal/dbhp/hr figure would not be expected to be comparable with that on a heavy train at a lower speed as a higher percentage of the total would be needed to move the engine on a fast booking, but the figure for the 'Coronation Scot' tests was 3.03lb which, under the circumstances, was very creditable. The calculated

Coronation Scot Trial Trip Crewe-Euston 29 June 1937
Loco: No 6220 *Coronation.*
Driver: T. J. Clarke. *Fireman:* J. Lewis (Crewe).
Load: 8 bogies, 263 tons tare, 270 tons full.

Distance miles		Schedule min	Actual min sec		Speeds mph
0.0	Crewe	0	00	00	—
4.8	Betley Road		6	06	71 ½
8.0	Madeley		8	44	74
10.5	Whitmore	11	10	42	80 ½
14.7	Standon Bridge		13	32	90
19.2	Norton Bridge	18	16	51	*74
21.2	Great Bridgford		18	25	82
24.5	Stafford	23	20	58	—
25.0	Stafford No 1		21	45	*30
28.6	Milford		25	13	75
30.9	Colwich		27	05	80/*71
33.8	Rugeley	31	29	18	90
37.1	Armitage		31	02	88
41.8	Lichfield	37	34	44	—
44.6	Hademore		36	36	92/89
48.1	Tamworth	42	38	55	90
51.6	Polesworth		41	27	*78
55.8	Atherstone		44	41	83/*71
61.0	Nuneaton	54	48	29	90
64.6	Bulkington		50	58	86
66.7	Shilton		52	29	93 ½
70.0	Brinklow		54	42	*85
74.9	Rugby No 7		58	25	88 ½/*40
75.5	Rugby	66	59	27	*40
77.8	Hillmorton		61	51	67 ½
79.9	Kilsby Tunnel Nth end		63	35	75
82.8	Welton		65	46	86
88.4	Weedon		69	41	92/*79
95.3	Blisworth	82	74	24	92
98.2	Roade	84	76	22	88 ½
103.3	Castlethorpe		79	36	100
105.7	Wolverton	88 ½	81	08	*83
111.4	Bletchley	93	85	10	89
117.9	Leighton		89	32	93/*85
122.0	Cheddington		92	21	89/87
126.4	Tring	107	95	23	86 ½
130.1	Berkhamsted		97	59	90/*85
133.6	Hemel Hempstead		100	16	93
137.2	Kings Langley		102	30	99
140.7	Watford Junct.	117 ½	104	53	*84
144.8	Hatch End		107	45	85
146.7	Harrow		109	00	96
150.0	Wembley		111	05	95
152.7	Willesden Jnct.	127	112	50	*85
155.1	Kilburn		114	33	*79
157.1	MP 1		116	57	—
158.1	Euston	135	119	00	—

* Service slack.
150.3 miles Betley Road-Kilburn 83.3mph pass-to-pass
72.3 miles Welton-Kilburn 89.0mph pass-to-pass

(Timed by Cecil J. Allen, D. S. M. Barrie and S. P. W. Corbett)

figure of 14.5lb of steam per ihp hr was prophetic in view of the tests on the Rugby Plant destined to take place in 1957/8. The engine was, of course, at its very best, being comparatively new yet fully run in, and the excellent Grimethorpe coal left little smokebox ash. It is understood that this high-quality coal was also used on the great occasions on the East Coast main line.

The decision was taken to build more of the 'Coronation' class Pacifics in 1938 and five of these were not streamlined. Still there was little in ordinary service which gave any indication of their potential power. While controversy raged during 1938 over the comparative uphill hps of the Gresley A4s and the Collett 'Kings', the LMS Pacifics were hardly mentioned until in December Cecil J. Allen suggested that the LMS Pacifics could with advantage be brought into the discussion as they incorporated the best features of Swindon design with the added advantage of high-temperature superheat. In February 1939 the opportunity was given for an unstreamlined Duchess class Pacific to show its full potential over the banks.

The engine chosen was No 6234 *Duchess of Abercorn*, the last of the 1938 batch, and it was given a test train of 20 bogies, including the dynamometer car, to haul from Crewe to Glasgow and back on a special test schedule on Sunday, 12 February. The bookings were based on those of the 7hr 'Royal Scot', which was usually worked by a 'Princess' with an XL limit of 420 tons tare. The test load was 604 tons tare and as no passengers were carried besides the staff, the total load would be under 610 tons. It was stated that the aim was to examine the possibility of combining some trains over the northern section as an economy measure, but the real reason was to examine the full power capacity of the engine. It was realised that running such as was being called for would not be practical as a daily performance.

On 12 February No 6234 was still fitted with single blast and its performance was patchy. There were some good features but also some disappointments. The test schedule of 39min, pass to pass, from Carnforth to the Summit was exceeded by 2min with dbhps little better than those of No 6200 in June 1935, but this was recovered by a fast descent to Carlisle. A stop for a banker was permitted on Beattock Bank, but the running out to Beattock was disappointing, mainly owing to indifferent steaming and the train had lost 9min before taking assistance. The return journey started better, with a good climb from Symington to Beattock Summit and a maximum dbhp of 2163, which was probably a British record up till then and is very possibly still a record for a British single-chimney engine. The figure of 2163 was the actual dbhp, not the equivalent form with the allowance for gravity on engine and tender. A full assessment of its significance would, however, need more information about the exact location and the relevant speeds. The climb from Symington to Beattock Summit was especially favourable for a maximum effort as restrained running down the other side and an easy road to Carlisle allowed for recovery. On this occasion No 6234 ran smartly from Beattock to Carlisle in a pass-to-stop time very similar to that of No 6200 in 1935. Maximum speeds were in the middle 80s, despite the 20-coach train.

The climb from Carlisle to Shap Summit again showed a loss of 2min on schedule. Although it could hardly be described as poor with 600 tons, faster climbs had been made by 'Princesses' only slightly more lightly loaded with 570 tons against No 6234's 610 tons. The day had fallen short of expectations with disappointment relieved only by the good climb from Symington to Beattock Summit and by the good coal/dbhp/hr figure of 3.08lb. Had these results been made public at the time the East Coast supporters would not have felt unduly worried.

A fortnight later the test was repeated, but in the meantime No 6234 had entered Crewe Works and emerged with double blastpipe and chimney. This was destined to make a big difference to the steaming, although it had aroused no anxiety on 26 February. This time the LMS really did have something to publish and to publish with justifiable pride. When the exceptional power outputs were known controversy between Doncaster and Swindon supporters was stilled; the Crewe creation had shaken them both.

The events of 26 February 1939 have become one of the classics of British steam locomotive history. In July 1938 the A4 class engine *Mallard* had applied a high transitory power output to a light train on a falling gradient and gained immortality by its maximum speed. In February 1939 *Duchess of Abercorn* applied an even greater power output to the less spectacular but potentially more valuable task of lifting a very heavy train up steep gradients. These two performances have become the twin peaks of British steam.

No 6234's achievements demand full tabulation with outline logs for the complete journeys and a more detailed consideration of the four climbs. The same 20-coach formation of a fortnight earlier was used and for the Crewe-Glasgow section the engine was in the hands of Driver G. Garrett of Crewe North Shed. Driver Garrett had appeared in some excellent runs published by Cecil J. Allen with 'Royal Scot' class engines, but the real honours must be given to Fireman S. Farringdon. It must be hoped that the inspector on the footplate gave the firemen a few spells in the course of the very strenuous running.

Soon after leaving Crewe the train was delayed by single-line working near Minshull Vernon, but after passing Winsford Junction the 132.3 miles to the stop at Carlisle were covered in 132min. The test schedule of 39min from Carnforth to the Summit, where 2min had been lost a fortnight before, were run in 33min 20sec despite a vertical rise of 887ft. This was not only a gain on the 'Royal Scot' booking, it was also less than the 35min allowed the 'Coronation Scot,' which had a load of less than half that of the test train. Indicated hps of up to and slightly over 3200 were officially estimated.

After Carlisle the engine was re-manned by Driver J. Marshall and Fireman D. Lynn of Polmadie Shed and the hardest continuous spell of the day had to be faced. The greater difficulty of Beattock Bank as compared with Shap is its greater length, with 10 miles averaging 1 in 75 without any break. There was an added operational difficulty in the wider spacing of the Caledonian water troughs as compared with those of the LNWR. This was recognised in the provisional test schedule, which allowed for a stop at Beattock for water and banking assistance. In the event No 6234 ran so well that it was decided to take the bank at a run and to stop at Symington for water. Beattock, at the foot of the bank after some lengthy stretches of 1 in 200, comparable with the climbs to Stoke or Stevenage on the East Coast, was passed in even time from Carlisle and the formidable bank itself was climbed in 16min 30sec with a minimum speed of 30mph. The downhill running to Glasgow calls for no special comment.

A relatively short turnround of two hours at Glasgow was the prelude to the most sensational time of the day. Now in the hands of Driver N. McLean and Fireman A. Smith, again from Polmadie Shed, the 105min booking of the 297ton 'Coronation Scot' was exceeded by a mere 1½min and an 8½min early arrival was achieved at Carlisle. The climb to Beattock from the north is much easier than that from the south, but nevertheless the continuous collar work between Motherwell and Law Junction was performed in good style with speeds of 44-47mph and dbhps of 1900-2000. The climb to Beattock Summit was followed by easy grades, which permitted a maximum effort just as the fall to the Trent Valley encouraged the East Coast drivers at times to run hard up to Stoke. Driver McLean pressed *Duchess of Abercorn* hard and in the teeth of a snowstorm the giant red Pacific went roaring over the summit without falling below 60mph. It would not have been a comfortable place for a photographer to have waited on this bleak Sunday afternoon, but had one done so his picture would have been historic. Tape recorders lay further in the future, but here the possibilities would have been even more dramatic. The actual dbhp recorded in the car was 2282 at 63mph and this corresponds with an equivalent figure of 2850-2900, something never before approached in Britain. The official calculated ihp was 3333. There was no indicating shelter and equipment on No 6234 and the figure was an estimate.

At Carlisle Driver Garrett and Fireman Farringdon again took over for the final stage of the return journey. Speed rose to 42mph on the 1 in 131 to Wreay and to 54mph on the easier grades through South-waite. On the "breather" near Penrith, where a few level sections broke the continuous climb, there was a further rise to 73mph before a reduction to 53mph round the curve through Penrith. On the continuous 1 in 125 speed fell to 38mph, but there was a final acceleration to 45mph as the grade eased towards the Summit. Shap Summit was passed in 40min 15sec for the 31.55 miles. The highest maximum hp figure of all was recorded on this section, with an actual dbhp of 2511, which again corresponded to an equivalent figure of about 2900 and a calculated ihp of 3348. Some doubts have been cast on the officially calculated ihp. The proportion of the engine's running resistance to the total hp when a heavy train is climbing these gradients is, however, very small and the drawbar hp was recorded by the dynamometer car, so it can be claimed with some confidence that *Duchess of Abercorn* had demonstrated its capacity to exceed 3000ihp for about five minutes and reach momentary peaks of around 3300ihp. Such figures have never been beaten by any other type of British express locomotive.

The LMS authorities had some real achievement to report after the events of Sunday 26 February, but the full story was not released to the public until April. There was rejoicing in the LMS camp over the knowledge that they now had a locomotive powerful enough to more than hold its own with any British competitors. Some of the enthusiasm was premature, in that it was not fully realised that such figures could not be expected in regular daily service. The coal/dbhp/hr figure of 3.12lb had shown that the economy of the engine was well maintained even at these high power outputs, but one fireman could not be expected to fire at the rate of 68.9lb/mile in ordinary working. There was also the question of slipping on the banks in bad weather. The weather had not been good on 26 February, but these were highly skilled crews and the engine was in good condition. Doubtless the sanders worked properly, but there was nevertheless a strange and sudden plunge of the dbhp curve halfway up Beattock Bank on the down journey. Was it a slip or an easing to prevent a slip by skilful anticipation? Mr R. C. Bond, who was in the dynamometer car, has subsequently told one of the writers that this was due to anxiety over water consumption. The British steam locomotive had been witnessed at its best on 26 February 1939, but by the time the results were published the world in which steam had risen to its zenith of achievement had only a few more months to run.

LMS Crewe-Glasgow Test Run 26 February 1939
Engine: 4-6-2 No 6234 *Duchess of Abercorn.*
Load: 20 bogies, 604 tons tare, 610 tons gross.

Distance Miles		Schedule min	Actual min sec
0.0	Crewe	0	00 00
2.85	Coppenhall Junct	5	5 45
			stop and single line working
8.80	Winsford Junct	11	33 30

Distance Miles		Schedule min	Actual min sec	
16.30	Weaver Junct †	18	40	40
24.15	Warrington †	25	47	35
27.65	Winwick Junct †	29	51	00
35.90	Wigan †	38	58	50
39.15	Standish Junct	42	63	20
45.55	Euston Junct †	49	69	50
51.0	Preston *	55	75	45
52.35	Oxheys	58	79	40
60.50	Garstang	66	88	00
				sigs
72.00	Lancaster †	76	98	15
78.25	Carnforth	81	104	05
91.10	Oxenholme	95	115	30
104.10	Tebay	111	130	20
109.55	Shap Summit	120	137	25
123.25	Penrith †	133	149	00
128.15	Plumpton	137	153	30
141.10	Carlisle	150	165	30

† moderate speed restriction
* severe speed restriction
Net time 142min

Carnforth-Shap Summit pass to pass (31.30 miles 887ft vertical rise):
    33min 20sec
Carnforth-Oxenholme (12.96 miles):
Average speed 68mph, Cut-offs 20-25%
Average dbhp 1870 (recorded),
Maximum dbhp 2120 (recorded), Boiler pressure 250lb
Maximum ihp 3209 (calculated)

Oxenholme-Tebay (13.08 miles):
Average speed 53mph, Cut-offs 25%
Average dbhp 1668 (recorded), Boiler pressure 245lb
Maximum dbhp 1934 (recorded),
Maximum ihp 2806 (calculated)

Tebay-Shap Summit (5.69 miles):
Average speed 47.9mph, Cut-offs 25-35%
Average dbhp 1830 (recorded), Boiler pressure 240lb
Maximum dbhp 2065 (recorded),
Maximum ihp 2963 (calculated)

Speeds:
Carnforth 75mph
Milnthorpe 74mph
Grayrigg 41mph
Tebay 75mph
Summit 30mph

LMS Crewe-Glasgow Test Run 26 February 1939
Engine: No 6234 *Duchess of Abercorn*.
Load: 20 bogies, 604 tons tare. 610 tons gross.

Distance Miles		Schedule min	Actual min	sec
0.0	Carlisle	0	00	00
8.60	Gretna Junct	11	10	40
25.65	Lockerbie	28	28	10
39.60	Beattock	41	39	40
49.60	Beattock Summit	61	56	10
66.80	Symington (stop)	76	74	00
66.80	Symington (restart)		78	25
102.25	Glasgow Central	118	118	25

The passing times from Beattock onwards are not comparable with the schedule as this assumed a stop for water and banking at Beattock and no stop at Symington. The downhill times from Symington to Glasgow are of little interest or significance and are not tabulated.

Carlisle-Beattock Summit (49.60 miles, 948ft vertical rise):
    56min 10sec start to pass

Gretna-Lockerbie (17.27 miles):
Average speed 59.3mph, Cut offs 20-25%
Average dbhp 1598 (recorded), Boiler pressure 250lb
Maximum dbhp 1733 (recorded)
Maximum ihp 2236 (calculated)

Lockerbie-Beattock (13.96 miles):
Average speed 72.5mph
Average dbhp 1609 (recorded), Cut offs 20-25%
Maximum dbhp 1823 (recorded), Boiler pressure 245lb
Maximum ihp 2556 (calculated)

Beattock-Summit (10.13 miles):
Average speed 36.8mph
Average dbhp 1724 (recorded), Cut offs 30-40%
Maximum dbhp 2081 (recorded), Boiler pressure 240lb
Maximum ihp 2761 (calculated)

Speeds:
Before Kirkpatrick 1 in 200 rising, 53mph
After Kirtlebridge level, 67mph
Before Castlemilk Sdg 1 in 200 rising 57mph
Nethercleugh 1 in 528 falling 80mph
Before Beattock 1 in 202 rising 61mph
Beattock Summit 1 in 75 rising 30mph minimum

LMS Glasgow-Crewe Test Run 26 February 1939
Engine: 4-6-2 No 6234 *Duchess of Abercorn*
Load: 20 bogies, 604 tons tare, 610 tons gross

Distance Miles		Schedule min	Actual min	sec
0.0	Glasgow Central	0	00	00
12.85	Motherwell ÷	19	19	45
18.25	Law Junction +	29	26	40
28.75	Carstairs *	43	39	30
35.45	Symington	51	48	15
39.15	Lamington		52	08
44.55	Abington		57	13
47.10	Crawford		59	36
49.75	Elvanfoot		62	03
52.65	Beattock Summit	69	64	40
62.65	Beattock	79	73	35
76.60	Lockerbie	91	84	25
93.65	Gretna	106	97	45
102.65	Carlisle	116	106	30

Motherwell-Law Junction (5.42 miles):
Average speed 46.7mph, Cut offs 20-30%
Average dbhp 1923 (recorded), Boiler pressure 250lb
Maximum dbhp 1998 (recorded)
Maximum ihp 2583 (calculated)

Carstairs-Symington (6.74 miles):
Average speed 46.1mph, Cut offs 20-25%
Average dbhp 1520 (recorded), Boiler pressure 245lb
Maximum dbhp 1638 (recorded)
Maximum ihp 2138 (calculated)

Symington-Summit (17.28 miles):
Average speed 63.4mph, Cut-offs 30-35%
Average dbhp 1860 (recorded)
Maximum dbhp 2282 (recorded)
Maximum edbhp 2900 (calculated)
Maximum ihp 3333 (calculated)

Speeds:
Law Junction 44mph 1 in 99 rising
Lamington 65mph 1 in 340 falling
Elvanfoot 68mph level
Summit 61mph 1 in 99 rising

112

LMS Glasgow-Crewe Test Run 26 February 1939
Engine: No 6234 *Duchess of Abercorn.*
Load: 20 bogies, 604 tons tare, 610 tons gross.

Distance Miles		Schedule min	Actual min	sec
0.0	Carlisle	0	00	00
4.80	Wreay		8	59
7.30	Southwaite		11	52
10.70	Calthwaite		15	11
12.95	Plumpton	19	17	45
17.85	Penrith +	24	21	50
31.55	Shap Summit	43	40	15
141.0	Crewe	153	153	05

+ moderate speed restriction   Easy running after Shap Summit.

Carlisle-Shap Summit: 31.55 miles, 848ft vertical rise

Carlisle-Plumpton (13.03 miles):
Average speed 43.9mph
Average dbhp 1822 (recorded),   Cut offs 30-35%
Maximum dbhp 2511 (recorded),   Boiler pressure 245lb
Maximum ihp   3348 (calculated)

Plumpton-Penrith (4.77 miles):
Average speed 71.4mph
Average dbhp 2000 (recorded),   Cut offs 20-30%
Maximum dbhp 2394 (recorded),
Maximum ihp   3241 (calculated), Boiler pressure 230lb

Penrith-Shap Summit (13.68 miles):
Average speed 44.4mph
Average dbhp 1560 (recorded),   Cut offs 30-40%
Maximum dbhp 2331 (recorded),   Boiler pressure 245lb
Maximum ihp   3021 (calculated)

Speeds:
Calthwaite   62mph, 1 in 172 rising
Plumpton   72mph, level
Penrith   74mph, 1 in 616 rising
Thrimby Grange 38mph, 1 in 125 rising
Shap   45mph, 1 in 142 rising
Summit   49mph, 1 in 130 rising/level

Summary of the day's running
Total mileage: 487. Average dbhp: 1214
Coal per mile: 68.7lb. Water per mile: 53 gallons
Coal per dbhp/hr: 3.12lb. Water per dbhp/hr: 242 lb
Evaporation per lb/coal: 7.74 lb
(Continuous blowdown in operation)
Coal consumption: 75.7lb per sq ft grate area
Maximum speed: 88mph
Weather: Some snow north of the Border, but moderating further south.

CHAPTER TEN

Plans and Frustrations

Had it not been for the high-speed press run of 1937 and the high-power test runs of 1939 little would have emerged as to the capacity of the larger LMS Pacifics up to the outbreak of war. The original five blue 'Coronations' did little main-line running beyond their employment on the 'Coronation Scot'. This was in contrast to the early days of the four grey A4s, which had regular workings on ordinary expresses at the weekends, notably on the up "Flying Scotsman" every Saturday afternoon. The mileage of the first five 'Coronations' suggests that a moderate figure was being accepted in the early years.

The schedule of 6½hr for the 'Coronation Scot' was a disappointment to LMS supporters, who had hoped for 6¼hr at the most. It was perhaps wise not to have attempted too much at first and it could possibly be argued that the LNER were running to an unduly close margin with the 6hr schedule of the 'Coronation'. This was especially true south of York. A very fast train is an operational problem on a busy main line and the West Coast route south of Crewe carried a heavier traffic than the East Coast.

The ordinary everyday booking of "The Coronation Scot" could be kept with the greatest of ease with no higher maximum speeds than 83-85mph, while the rival 'Coronation' needed 90mph speeds south of York for bare timekeeping and occasionally reached three-figure maxima. The hardest part of the West Coast booking was north of the Border and some quite smart running was sometimes recorded. After running 300 miles the engine was faced with a 948ft vertical rise to be made in 49.7 miles, booked to be covered in 50min.

On one run described by Cecil J. Allen No 6220 *Coronation* slowed to 65mph over Gretna Junction and then accelerated to 70mph up the 1 in 200 to Kirkpatrick and reached 81½mph on the short "breather" at Kirtlebridge. Up the second stretch of 1 in 200 to Castlemilk Siding the minimum was 75mph. This showed that the 70-75mph minimum speeds of the LNER streamliners at Stoke or Stevenage were well within the capacity of the LMS engines. The high speed of *Coronation* was cut short by a permanent way slack at Lockerbie, but a rapid acceleration took the train up to 85½mph at Wamphray and the impetus of this allowed Beattock Bank to be charged at 75mph. On the bank speed fell to 37mph, but recovered to 39mph before the summit. The net time for the 102.3 miles to Glasgow was 101min. Another run by No 6221 *Queen Elizabeth* had a similar net time to Glasgow, slightly slower on the 1 in 200 banks but faster on the 1 in 75 of Beattock Bank, where the 10 miles were covered in 12min 15 sec. In the easier southbound direction No 6224 *Princess Alexandra* ran to Carlisle in a net time of 97½min, but even this fast run did not involve a higher minimum speed over Beattock Summit than *Duchess of Abercorn* on test with its 20-coach train.

South of Crewe the timings were very easy and the engines could gain on schedule when required. On one run *Coronation* passed Tring in almost exactly even time in 31min 40sec for the 31.7 miles with a minimum speed of 67mph. Later in the same journey the 31.4 uphill miles from Carnforth to Shap Summit were run in 30min 27sec. One good up run was recorded when No 6220 cut the Crewe-Euston time to 135min for the 158.1 miles, but a similar 70.3mph average on the East Coast "Coronation" for its first 158 miles would have left it a few minutes behind time.

During the month of September 1937 it was reported that the 'Coronation Scot' never had a single late arrival at any of its stops. The record was not maintained in winter weather; as with the East Coast "Coronation", there were occasions when the coal did not last out, especially on bad days, and assistance had to be taken en route. The coal burnt on the test runs was about 7 tons for the through journey and the margin was normally ample, but a combination of stormy weather, and some deficiency in the condition of the engine or the quality of the coal, could use up the reserve. The average dbhp recorded on the 'Coronation Scot' test run with the addition of the dynamometer car was 825. This was more than the 600 average dbhp of the LNER 'Silver Jubilee', but was almost certainly less than that of the 'Coronation' south of York. There were rumours of exceptional speeds attained by the 'Coronation Scot' when regaining lost time, but enquiries have produced no solid facts in support. There is little doubt that the engines could have run faster if required.

In June 1938 a party of German locomotive engineers had been invited to join the British Institution of Locomotive Engineers on a trip to Glasgow. A special train of seven bogies was made up including the dynamometer car. This was hauled by No 6225 *Duchess of Gloucester,* a nearly-new red streamlined Pacific. The time of 6hr 50min to Glasgow called for no great effort with 232 tons, but the engine was extended slightly from Carlisle to Beattock Summit, which was passed in 44min 49sec for the 49.7 miles, while the bank itself was climbed in 10min 29sec with a minimum of 49mph. Had there been any last lingering embers of the Midland small engine policy remaining in the hearts of LMS officers then the events of this day should have banished them for ever. The argument that a large engine

115

is uneconomical on a light train was rudely shattered by No 6225's coal consumption of 28.2lb/mile. The Compound which worked through to Edinburgh in 1928 with a 180ton train burnt 35lb/mile and took over an hour longer. The coal/dbhp/hr rate of No 6225 was 3.32lb, which was, of course, heavier than the figure for hauling a normal load. It could be argued that to use a large engine on a light train was a misuse of capital equipment, but it was less wasteful of coal than the thrashing of a small engine which was overloaded.

The original coaches of the 'Coronation Scot', apart from a form of air-conditioning, were of the normal LMS pattern, but in 1939 it was proposed to introduce new 11-coach sets with articulated vehicles. LMS policy seemed to be moving towards heavier trains on the 6½hr schedules rather than further acceleration. The articulated trains would have not exceeded the total weight of the test train of the old 'Coronation Scot' set plus the dynamometer car, so they would still have been well within the capacity of the locomotive. Further ahead thoughts were turning towards a giant 4-6-4 engine with mechanical stoker capable of working 500 ton loads to Glasgow in 6½hr.

A few of the new articulated vehicles were ready for a 'Coronation Scot' train sent to tour the United States in 1939. A sleeping car, not part of the 'Coronation Scot', was added and the eight vehicles weighed 263 tons tare. The engine was No 6229, the original *Duchess of Hamilton,* which was painted red and became No 6220 from 1939 to 1942; later the original identities were restored. The train destined for America was given a brief run in this country on 9 January 1939. Starting from Blisworth it passed Weedon at 79mph, attained in 8min and over 6.9 miles of level track. Speed was maintained at 77½-79mph up the 1 in 350 to Kilsby tunnel and Rugby was reached in 19min 5sec for the 19.8 miles. This was another example of the mastery of a big engine over a light train, but again it gave little indication of the locomotive capacity.

The record of the new, larger Pacifics on the heavier loads was equally unrevealing. They slipped quietly into service, sharing with the 'Princesses' loads well within their capacity. Had peace been prolonged a few more years there would doubtless have been opportunities for something better to have been recorded. It is not suggested that the running was poor, but it was well within the capacity of the earlier 'Princess' class. During the winter of 1938 and 1939 the newer Pacifics were taking over much of the work. Observations on the 'Royal Scot' published in late 1938 showed that the 'Coronation' or 'Duchess' class Pacifics were used more frequently than the 'Princesses'. The additional number of Pacifics led to plans being made to extend their use to the Holyhead or the Manchester services, but war intervened before these plans came to fruition.

The introduction of the 'West Riding Limited' streamliner between Kings Cross and Leeds raised questions as to whether the LMS would run 'Coronation Scot'-type trains between Euston and Liverpool or Manchester in 3hr or something slightly less, but it is understood that no such plans were seriously contemplated. The aim was apparently to improve the entire service as far as possible. It would have caused considerable dislocation to have run a number of exceptionally fast expresses among the heavy traffic of the LNWR main line south of Rugby. It would perhaps make more sense to raise the average speed of a number of trains from 60 to 65mph rather than to try and thread a few 70mph flyers through with double blocking and the other operating essentials of very high speed. As things happened, the LMS had no time to put whatever plans they might have had into practice, as the tragedy which had seemed inevitable all through the summer of 1939 finally happened in September.

At a stroke all fast trains disappeared and a very rigid and restrictive war time plan was put into operation immediately. During World War I the main-line services had changed little during the first two years of war. In fact, much of the best work ever recorded by the LNWR 'George the Fifth' class 4-4-0s was timed during the first two years of war. In 1939 it was thought that bombing would be an immediate problem, but as the weeks of "phoney war" passed into months there was some relaxation of restrictions and a welcome improvement in schedules. These were still, of course, far slower than pre-war but they were fitted for the needs of the time. There were not enough Pacifics on the LMS for them to be used for the entire train service and loads had to be shaped to the possibility of 'Royal Scot' haulage at times. The 20 coaches or over seen on the LNER were not matched on the LMS, where 18 bogies were normally the limit. The 'Coronation' and 'Duchess' class engines handled the 17-18 coach loads with the greatest ease on the moderate gradients and usually climbed to Shap Summit without assistance, but a stop was normally made at Beattock for water and rear-end assistance up the bank. Where there was the chance to compare pre-war running with a section of a wartime run that was free from checks it often revealed little difference uphill, though of course downhill speeds were more strictly limited. In 1940 Cecil J. Allen published a run with No 6234 *Duchess of Abercorn*, hauling 17 bogies of 543 tons tare, 575 tons gross, when the 8.30 from Euston started from Watford and passed Tring, 14.3 miles, in 17min 50sec at a sustained 57mph on the 1 in 335. This was similar to the speeds up to Tring with 'Princess' class engines similarly loaded in the mid-1930s. No 6234 was stopped by signals outside Rugby, having covered 64.7 miles in 68min 34sec with no downhill speed over 66mph.

A better run on the 8.30 from Euston was described by Mr Allen in 1941, when No 6244 *King George VI*, streamlined and fitted with double chimney, was at the head of 17 bogies weighing 535 tons tare or 585 tons with passengers packed to standing. The start up to Tring was slower than No 6234 a year earlier, but less restrained running on the easier stretches, with 57½mph at Roade Summit, 76½mph on the level near Weedon and 61½mph at Kilsby Tunnel, took the train over the 65.2 miles from Watford to Rugby in a net start-to-stop time of 66min. An even better run was made from Rugby to Stafford with a maximum of 77½mph at Hademore troughs, a minimum of 66mph past Lichfield and a net time of 50min for the 51 miles from Rugby to the stop at Stafford. This trip showed that even time running over the easier stretches of the LNWR main line was easily possible with 17 bogies. The 'Princesses', of course, had shown their ability to do this, but the larger Pacifics did so with consumate ease.

No 6224 *Princess Alexandra,* with a 17-coach load of 530 tons, tare, 570 tons full, left Crewe 10min late and after signal checks reached Carlisle 5min early. The ascent to Shap was taken unaided and good progress was being made until Scout Green distant was sighted at danger. It came off before the train stopped, but not until speed had fallen to 25mph and this speed was maintained to the summit. A good start northwards from Carlisle was recorded when No 6232 *Duchess of Montrose* had a 17-coach load of 510 tons, tare, 560 tons full. This was taken to Beattock in a start-to-stop time of 41min 55sec for the 39.7 miles with one slight signal check at Lockerbie. There was a little disappointment in that the climb to Beattock Summit had not been taken unaided, but here the water could be a problem and the quality of the coal is unknown. The 'Duchesses' used a lot of water, not because they were inefficient but because they were big.

In 1943 Cecil J. Allen described two very good runs over the Crewe-Carlisle section. One was on the 10.00 from Euston, the wartime equivalent of the 'Royal Scot', with streamlined Pacific No 6221 *Queen Elizabeth,* by then fitted with double chimney, which had a 16 coach load of 480 tons, tare, 525 tons full. The ratio of gross to tare tonnage was greater on these wartime trains which were usually crowded. An actual time of 102min 42sec was achieved from Preston to Carlisle, or 98½min net. The outstanding features of this run were a very brisk climb of Boar's Head Bank with a minimum of 53mph up the 1 in 104 from Wigan, increased to 57½mph up the 1 in 366 past Coppull, and a final minimum of 55½mph up the 1 in 110 to the summit. The time of 5min 24sec for the 5.1 miles from Wigan to mp 11½ was unknown in Mr Allen's experience with such a load. Later the 31.4 miles from passing Carnforth to Shap Summit were covered in 37min 39sec with a minimum speed of 30mph. A second run by No 6234 *Duchess of Abercorn* had a more crowded train on the 13.00 from Euston and with 17 coaches of 499 tare tons the gross load was 560 tons. This was taken from Preston to Carlisle in about two min more than No 6221's run. Mr Allen wrote very enthusiastically about these runs after three years of war. The larger Pacifics almost casually had more than kept the timings of the pre-war 'Mid-day Scot' over the

118

Lancaster-Penrith section, a task which had fully extended the best of the 'Princesses' in 1936.

The most sensational wartime performance of an LMS Pacific was published in 1944 when C. M. Furst, a most experienced recorder, was on the 10.05 from Euston and No 6244 *King George VI* had a 15-coach load of 433 tons, tare, 475 tons full and had been all but stopped south of Oxenholme. This was a bad spot to be checked and a laborious recovery would normally have followed, but for some unknown reason the crew put No 6244 to an exceptional effort which recalled the *Duchess of Abercorn* trials. The train passed Oxenholme at 29mph and by Hay Fell, up 1 in 104-124-131, speed had risen to 54½mph, then on 2½ miles of 1 in 131 it rose further to 60mph and the final minimum on the 1 in 106 was 55mph. The 7.1 miles from passing Oxenholme at 29mph to Grayrigg Summit had been covered in 8min 20sec. Such a start would have been considered good in wartime if it had been on level track; it was really exceptional on gradients of 1 in 104 to 1 in 131. The hp has been calculated by Gp Capt J. N. C. Law, who has made a special study of train resistance, and he estimates an equivalent dbhp of 2375 and a corresponding ihp of 2815. This would suggest a steaming rate of over 40000lb/hr and during the eight minutes the ihp would probably have risen to a peak of about 3000, which was almost equal to the best recorded on test by No 6234 *Duchess of Abercorn* in 1939. The short duration of this effort put it within the capacity of one fireman, but there would probably have been some preliminary-build up. The reason for this exceptional effort is not known; it may have been a brief attempt to "see what she can do"; or it may have been an attempt at time regaining, but if so it was cut short because a freight train had been slipped in between the 10.00 and the 10.05 and the remainder of the climb to Shap Summit was made at freight train speeds.

This was typical of wartime operation. There was a poster of an express sidetracked to allow a freight train to be given the road with the words "Give your seat to a shell". The inference was that it was patriotic to delay passenger trains in favour of freight. The logic was unsound, as no attempt was made to assess the value to the nation of the time of military and businessmen who were delayed, and no explanation as to why a slow-moving freight train would have been delayed by a faster express train in front. There is more than a suspicion that it was considered by some that it was good for the souls of passengers to delay them. Making travel uncomfortable seemed to be undertaken with some relish, as though underlining the slogan "Is your journey really necessary?" It was also noticeable that when a really influential passenger was on board a clear path could always be found for an express. The unfortunate effect of all this was that there arose an attitude to punctuality that extended well into the post-war years and express trains were delayed in a way that must have taken the heart out of any driver anxious to regain time. The West Coast main lines were notorious for bad operating.

The immediate post-war years were a period of discomfort for travellers. At first petrol rationing limited road competition and trains continued to be very crowded. The East Coast made a valiant attempt to restore faster schedules when peace came but in the event it proved to be premature. The West Coast proceeded more cautiously. The track took some years to restore to a condition suitable for high speeds and during that period there were a few derailments of 'Duchess' class locomotives. There was, however, no suspicion of design faults in the engines, which at high speed on good track were among the best-riding express locomotives ever to have run in Britain. The situation became most depressing during the big snows of 1947, when travelling became as miserable as it ever had in wartime. Many people made up their minds to buy motor cars as soon as these became generally available and the birth of motor-car madness, though explicable, boded no good for the railways.

The post-war world was less sympathetic towards the railway industry and the true economic issues were clouded by political controversy, especially after nationalisation. The popular interest in trains such as the 'Coronation Scot' was not restored, though the enthusiast body grew considerably with the post-war boom in "spotting" among the younger generation. Many of the famous engines were unkempt and in poor condition and they had to carry on with a diet of coal of an inferior and variable quality. Many famous classes sunk to a much lower level of daily performance. On the West Coast the 'Princesses' during the late 1940s and early 1950s were hardly recognisable as the redoubtable performers they frequently were before the war. Generally speaking, the larger 'Duchesses' went through this difficult period better than most, because they had such a margin of potential power over timetable requirements. There were, of course, occasions when bad handling or poor condition brought bad runs from the 'Duchesses', but a critic writing to *Trains Illustrated* claimed that of all the British main-line locomotives the 'Duchesses' alone had, in his experience, no time booked against them. He had experienced much late running, but the lost time was not due to any deficiency of the locomotive.

As the 1950s progressed there was a slow improvement until in the later 1950s some of the best work ever recorded by the larger LMS Pacifics was recorded. The 'Princesses' also had a late-hour revival, but their performance was much more variable. The post-war world was not a happy one for steam locomotives, but during that period some of the best work of all was experienced.

CHAPTER ELEVEN

Post-War Problems

The LMS had only a short time left after the end of hostilities and those few years were years of tribulation. Enthusiasts who had hoped for a speedy return to pre-war speeds found that their hopes were unrealistic. The brightest spot on the LMS in those days was the success of the rebuilt 'Royal Scots', which ran very well, especially on the Leeds-Carlisle section. There was little hope of exploiting the power of Pacifics to any great advantage for several years and no large-scale building of the larger engines took place. This was in contrast to the policies of the LNER and Southern Railways. The LMS policy was to build just enough Pacifics to cover the harder duties and to work most of the mainline services by the rebuilt 'Royal Scots' and 'Patriots'. Without the Pacifics, however, the operation of the heavier West Coast expresses would have been more difficult.

In October and November 1945 some test runs were made with a 'Duchess' class locomotive No 6233 *Duchess of Sutherland* between Crewe and Carlisle and this was followed by similar tests of No 6252 *City of Leicester* in December. The loads varied between a minimum of 462 tons, tare and a maximum of 538 tons, tare, which probably meant 17 coaches, but the average speeds were low — 42-43mph as compared with the near 60mph averages of No 6234 in 1939. The coal used was Barnborough, which was of much inferior quality to the Grimethorpe coal fired on the pre-war tests. The engines showed their lack of appreciation by burning an average of 3.87lb/dbhp/hr as compared with 3.12lb/dbhp/hr of No 6234 when extended to record hps. Here alone was reason enough for the failure to repeat the 1939 test times in everyday 1945 service. Had a fireman found it possible to fire a 'Duchess' with Barnborough coal at the same rate as No 6234, at 68.9lb/mile and 75.7lb per sq ft of grate area, then there would only have emerged power enough at the drawbar to have worked a 480ton train at the same speeds as were attained in 1939 with over 600tons. The Barnborough coal was quite likely representative of the coal available in 1945. If high-speed steam trains were ever to run again in Britain better coal would be needed or severely limited loads would be essential.

The nationalisation of railways in 1948 did not bring joy to the amateur enthusiasts, who looked back with longing on the days of the pre-1923 companies. It was realised that drastic changes would be needed now that the railways were in such an unfriendly and competitive world, but there were fears that dull uniformity was the prospect before the industry. One event which came soon after the State had taken over was the exchange of locomotives in the early summer of 1948. Enthusiasts had hoped for something of the kind and they all had their own ideas of what would happen and the extent of the triumph which awaited their own favourite line. The hopes of the LMS enthusiasts were especially high; they had the largest Pacific and the results of the *Duchess of Abercorn* trials promised that little could be asked which would be beyond its powers.

In the event less new information as to the power and efficiency of the 'Duchess' emerged from the exchanges than was the case with any of the competitors. The tasks set to the competing locomotives were relatively light and they were naturally easiest of all to the largest locomotive. The Pacific chosen by the LMS was No 46236 *City of Bradford*. It was in the charge of Driver Byford, who had the reputation of being a very able engineman. He was criticised in some quarters for "coal dodging" — that is, driving more easily than the situation warranted merely to save coal — but there are doubts about the justice of this description. It was his policy to make one easy run on each test route and to be a little more brisk on the other; often recorders were there on the less energetic day.

The average dbhp for each run was included in the official report and the figures for *City of Bradford*, although not high, were much like those of the other competitors. The highest average dbhps for No 46236 were 867 on its own road and 866 on the ER main line. These average hps were exceeded three times by the A4 and once by the 'Merchant Navy', with a maximum of 917dbhp by the A4 on the Southern Region. These seem very low hps but they are comparable with those recorded when the Turbomotive was tested against ordinary Pacifics on the 'Royal Scot' and 'Mid-day Scot' in 1936/7. The frequent checks and the greater number of stops must have raised the power requirements of the rather pedestrian 1948 trains to an average figure comparable with the faster but less inhibited expresses of the mid-1930s.

There were a few flashes here and there of the kind of thing the 'Duchesses' could do. On 20 May 1948 *City of Bradford* was on the 13.30 from Paddington and was faced with the ascent of Dainton Bank with a load of 9 bogies weighing 327 tons tarc and 350 tons gross. From a start at Newton Abbot the summit was passed in 7min 22sec at a minimum speed of 27mph. Few if any better climbs to Dainton have ever been recorded by steam. The good work continued; after slowing to 45mph through Totnes the worst part of Rattery Bank was climbed at a minimum of 31½mph in the remarkable time of 4min 15sec, Totnes to Tigley. The remainder of the climb was taken more easily but Rattery was passed in 21min 55sec and the final net time of 46min from Newton to Plymouth was the fastest of any of the visiting engines.

When the official report was issued it emerged that on 20 May *City of Bradford* had recorded the highest edbhps of any of the competitors on both Dainton and Rattery Banks. On Dainton Bank at 32mph the 'Duchess' was exerting an actual dbhp of 1320 and an equivalent dbhp of 1865. This was matched on Rattery Bank at 32mph, when the figures were 1320 actual and 1817 equivalent dbhps. The cut-off was 30% at 44mph when the reading was taken on Dainton Bank and 35% at 32mph on Rattery Bank. The report gives the regulator as "just open" on Dainton Bank, but this must have special meaning for it needs more than a trickle of steam to produce 1865 edbhp even with an engine as big as a 'Duchess'. There must have been quite a high steam-chest pressure, but unlike the A4s the 'Duchesses' were not fitted with a steam chest pressure gauge. The boiler pressures 230lb on Dainton and 235lb on Rattery Banks.

On Hemerdon Bank the honours for the Exchanges rested with the A4 *Seagull*, which recovered so well from a pw check at the foot of the bank. There was no such incident to put No 46236 on its mettle, but it achieved the second highest hp on this bank with a figure of 1376 edbhp at 18mph. This needed 50% cut-off and full regulator. The large Pacifics are not at their best at such low speeds, but No 46236 did not slip at all on Hemerdon on this occasion. There was, however, an adverse comment in the official report to the effect that the No 46236 'slipped almost to a standstill' on Dainton Bank. Cecil J. Allen considered this to be unduly drastic for, although the engine did slip badly near Dainton Box, the speed dropped to 18mph which was more than a "standstill" and comparable with the pace of some engines that were not officially criticised. This was on the up journey; both climbs by No 46236 on the down run were excellent.

On 21 May *City of Bradford*, on the return journey from Plymouth to Paddington, attained an edbhp of 1825 on Bruton Bank. This was recorded near mp 125 while the train was travelling at 53mph on 35% cut-off and the regulator described as "just open". This was one of the occasions when the recorders had chosen the wrong day as the running on 19 May, when Cecil J. Allen was present, was much less energetic. The test report mentions an occasion on the Southern Region on 22 June when the speed was 51mph on the lower part of Seaton Bank and a momentary record of 2400edbhp was attained while the cut-off was 40% and the second valve of the regulator was just open. The boiler pressure and water level were, however, falling rapidly, so the effort was justly described as 'transitory'. Had it been required a 'Duchess' could, of course, have sustained such an effort for the entire climb, but it would have needed some preliminary build-up as the firing rate would have been well beyond the the capacity of one fireman. The task was within the reach of the engine as is proved by the 1939 trials of No 6234 and the Rugby test plant results of No 46225, which in 1948 lay in the unknown future. No special efforts were called for on the Eastern Region nor on No 46236's own main line. It was a matter for regret that speeds down the tempting Stoke Bank on the ER were limited to 75mph, which No 46236 slightly exceeded.

There were some higher downhill speeds on the SR up to a maximum of 85mph, but these were on steep falling gradients and would require little effort from the engine. The most exciting high speed sprint of the entire test period was timed by Norman Harvey on a pre-test run by *City of Bradford* between Salisbury and Waterloo. There was no dynamometer car and no record was being kept of the coal. The load was 450 gross tons, less than the loads of over 500 tons taken during the test period proper. The train had been delayed by a signal stop before Andover which put it 8¾min late. The SR pilotman said that had the engine been a 'Merchant Navy' he would expect to be right time at Waterloo and added that he was sure the LMR engine could do so equally well. With this encouragement Driver Byford gave No 46236 its head and 22.3 miles from Worting to Brookwood were reeled off at an average of 82.6mph with a maximum of 88mph near Hook. Despite another pw slack Waterloo was reached on time in a net time of 82min for the 83.8 miles. This was a very exciting experience for Mr Harvey, as speeds of 88mph were not common in 1948 though they were less rare on the SR than elsewhere. The road was easy and ten years later such speeds were commonplace with the 'Merchant Navy' class Pacifics, but in 1948 it was a highly creditable performance for a visiting engine.

The official report noted that *City of Bradford* rarely had its regulator opened fully during the test period. On the Eastern Region it was usually in the half-open position with the cut-off varied to suit the gradients, normally within the limits of 20-25%. On the level stretches the cut-off was usually 15% with the first valve. The one recorded use of full regulator was on Hemerdon Bank with 50% cut-off. This was, of course, more than even *Duchess of Abercorn* needed on Shap or Beattock in 1939, but the speed was much lower and the hp and drain of steam were less. On the Southern Region the first valve sufficed for most of the work with the main valve occasionally just open. On its own road No 46236 was notched up as short as 12% on the down grades, with 18-22% on the level and 20-26% uphill on regulator openings of from two-fifths to one-half. (However, without information as to the relevant steam-chest pressures these regulator positions mean very little).

The inspector who took *City of Bradford* on to the Western Region insisted on taking four tons, ten cwt of coal and no more on to his tender at Old Oak for a run to Plymouth and some WR men rubbed their hands in gleeful anticipation of a call for assistance at Newton Abbot. All was well, however, and the inspector was thereafter known as "Four Ton-ten Drury". Old Oak Common shed gave Camden something of a shock by returning *City of Bradford* cleaned as they had never seen an engine before or since. The LMR black used on No 46236 could look quite attractive when really clean.

The Report commended *City of Bradford* for very free steaming, a clear exhaust, free running and rapid accleration from rest, but it criticised the engine for bad slipping on the banks. In general the 'Duchesses' had a bad reputation for losing their feet, but it is doubtful if they really were any worse than other Pacifics. Cecil J. Allen in his book *The Locomotive Exchanges* (Ian Allan 1950) remarks on the strange fact that No 46236, which topped the western slope of Dainton at 18mph, was described as 'slipping almost to a standstil' while the 'Royal Scot', which really did slip badly on Hemerdon and dropped to 9½mph, was not criticised. In general, however, it is fair to say that 4-6-0s were less prone to slipping than Pacifics and the sure-footed GWR 'Kings' were particularly suitable for the short but very steep South Devon banks.

When the 1948 results were published in full the 'Duchess' was shown to be second only to the A4 in the moderation of its coal consumption.

Coal consumption, lbs per draw-bar hp/hr

Locomotive	Region				
	Western	Eastern	London/ Midland	Southern	**Average**
ER A4 4-6-2	3.19	2.92	3.00	3.20	3.06
LMR 'Duchess' 4-6-2	3.24	3.04	3.07	3.17	3.12
SR 'M.Navy' 4-6-2	3.61	3.73	3.57	3.52	3.60
LMR 'R. Scot' 4-6-0	3.64	3.26	3.37	3.24	3.38
WR 'King' 4-6-0	3.74	3.39	—	—	3.59

In the autumn of 1948 additional tests with Welsh coal were run on the WR with a standard 'King' and an experimentally-fitted King with high superheat. The Welsh coal was of a higher calorific value than the South Yorkshire coal used in the original 1948 tests and the comparison is more fairly made with the corrected figure, based on a common calorific value.

Locomotive	Coal	Actual	Corrected
6018 (low superheat)	S. Kirkby	3.74	3.74
6001 (low superheat)	Abergorki	3.33	3.52
6022 (high superheat)	Abergorki	3.10	3.25

The 1948 Exchanges were considered to be very important for a time, but as testing techniques improved following the opening of the Rugby Test Plant and the modernisation of the Swindon Plant, coupled with more scientific road tests, the value of the earlier trials was seen to be more limited. The number of checks and slacks which were inflicted on the test trains must have reduced their worth, too. Within the limitations, however, the A4 and the 'Duchess' stood out above the other contestants. The difference between 3.06lb/dbhp/hr and 3.12lb was hardly significant, it lay within the limits of testing error. The marginal advantage of the A4 in coal consumption was balanced by the failure of its middle big end on three occasions while *City of Bradford*, alone among the contestants, went through the entire series of tests without the need for the standby engine to take over. In 1937 Cecil J. Allen had pronounced a verdict of "honours easy" and the 1948 Exchanges did nothing to bring about a different verdict.

In May 1955 No 46237 *City of Bristol* was lent to the WR for a series of trials including dynamometer car tests on the Brimingham line and on the "Cornish Riviera" express. The engine was worked by WR crews and little fault could be found with its running in terms of times and speeds. When the coal/dbhp/hr figures were published however, there was some disappointment because the results were inferior to those of the 1948 Exchanges or those on the former LMS main line, both before the war and after. It may have been that lack of familiarity with the engine led to the coal consumption being higher than would have been expected. Published logs of the trial runs show that the steaming rates were rather erratic with short bursts followed by several miles of leisurely running. There was also some considerable day-to-day variation, with one run producing an exceptionally high coal/dbhp/hr figure that depressed the general average.

The trials did, however, demonstrate one definite weakness of the 'Duchess' design which had been there from the start but had not been shown up so vividly before. This was the relatively low superheat and correspondingly high water consumption. The distance between water troughs was greater on the WR main line than on the LMR south of the Border and on one run the 'Duchess' had to make an out-of-course stop to take on water. The WR engineers were, on the other hand, very favourably impressed by the free-running qualities of the visitor and this may have accelerated the experimental fitting of a double-chimney to 'King' No 6015 in 1955 and the subsequent fitting of all the 'Kings'. The results of tests may be viewed best in full perspective (see table opposite).

While No 46237 had not won a resounding victory on WR lines, as perhaps some LMR supporters had hoped, it returned without any loss of honour. The passing time of 162min (157min net) to Exeter with a load of 490 tons as far as Heywood Junction and 420 tons

Western Region

1948 Exchanges	lb/dbhp/hr		Coal
'King'	3.74		South Yorkshire
'Duchess'	3.24		South Yorkshire
'King' (low superheat)	3.33	(3.52)	Welsh
'King' (high superheat)	3.10	(3.25)	Welsh

1955 trials	lb/dbhp/hr		Coal
King (redraughted, single chimney)	3.60	(3.83)	Welsh
Duchess	3.62	(3.85)	Welsh
Duchess (one poor run eliminated)	3.44	(3.61)	Welsh

1956 trials			
King (double chimney)	3.41	(3.60)	Welsh

The figures in brackets are the corrected values assuming a common calorific value for the various coals.

afterwards was among the best ever recorded on the down 'Limited' and the minimum speed of 46mph at Whiteball Tunnel, although equalled by the the double-chimney 'King' in 1956, was as good as anything recorded by steam equally loaded. This was a tribute to the skill of the WR crew handling a strange engine. If a 5000gall tender had been borrowed for the trials there would have been more confidence to open up the Pacific. The larger boiler did not give the Pacific any more adhesion weight, nor any more short-time tractive effort on the South Devon Banks, and a pilot was taken from Newton Abbot. In January 1956 a number of WR 'Kings' were withdrawn for bogie modifications and some 'Princesses' and 'Duchesses' were lent to Old Oak Common shed and used on the Birmingham and West of England main lines. Performance appears to have been adequate, but not exceptional. Although these tests had revealed the 'Duchesses' as being capable of managing the hardest tasks set to WR locomotives without difficulty, it is only fair to add that the 'Kings' emerged as admirably suited to the needs of their own main line.

The real evidence of the capacity of the 'Duchess' class was revealed in full-scale scientific tests carried out in 1955/6 on the Rugby Test Plant and later on the Skipton-Carlisle line with the Mobile Testing Unit. By 1955 locomotive engineers had realised the limitations of the old-style variable speed dynamometer car tests. For example, in the tests on the WR in 1955 No 46237 had shown a 25% variation in coal/dbhp/hr figures on two successive days. It may be argued that this might be expected with a strange engine worked by crews of another Region, but a similar variation was observed with a Gresley Pacific tested on its own road with a regular Doncaster crew in 1928.

There were considerable variations in the day-to-day coal/dbhp/hr figures of some of the contestants in the 1948 Exchanges, though *City of Bradford* was fairly consistent. In 1957 the results of the 1948 Exchanges, although still a talking point among amateur enthusiasts, had already been cast aside by professional men as being of very limited value compared with the findings of the test plants.

The engine chosen to represent the 'Duchess' class in scientific testing was no 46225 *Duchess of Gloucester*. The highest sustained power outputs of steam in this country were developed by this engine on the Rugby Plant and these were confirmed in later tests on the road. The main limitation proved to be slipping and the true ultimate limit of the boiler was never reached. There was no need to seek redraughting modifications to raise the steaming rate as the slipping limit was reached with the unaltered boiler. For that reason the engine left the test plant as it went there, with its performance recorded but not improved. When tested with the best South Kirkby coal the front-end limit was never reached, but it was estimated as being well above anything actually attained. The highest evaporation reached was a maximum of 41500lb/hr, with the live steam injector which, although not necessarily the limit of the Duchess boiler, was never surpassed by any other locomotive tested in Britain.

The front-end limit is the point to which the draughting limits the combustion rate. If this rate was exceeded the exhaust got overloaded with smoke and pressure began to drop. The grate limit was the point at which further additions of coal brought no more steam, only more coal going to waste. Usually when an engine was given the full treatment at Rugby or Swindon these two figures were established, but in the case of the 'Duchess' they remain unknown. What they were is largely academic, because the slipping point was very real and a worry on the plant. If an engine slipped at maximum power output there was always a risk of twisted rods. The evaporation rates which were reached were, of course, well above anything that one could hope to sustain in service. Two firemen were required at maximum output, they had to work quite hard and the water consumption would have emptied the tender tank even on a line with the troughs as close together as the LMR. However, the maximum power outputs of various locomotives, even if obtained under artificial conditions, are of as much historic importance as maximum speeds.

Figures were established for a maximum output of 42000 which was chosen as a maximum, although 41500 was the highest actually obtained. At this maximum evaporation rate the sustained ihps were:

2910 ihp at 80mph   with 30% cut off
2860 ihp at 70mph   with 32% cut off
2810 ihp at 60mph   with 35% cut off
2775 ihp at 50mph   with 37% cut off

Although this was given as "sustained" it could not have been kept up for much over an hour because deterioration of the fire would have imposed a limit.

Some indication of what a steaming rate of 40000lb/hr meant on the road was given by a published test run with the mobile testing units coupled behind the dynamometer car and with resistance increased to the equivalent of a load of 900 tons. With this load and steaming at the rate of 40000lb/hr No 46225 showed its ability to sustain 30mph continuously on the 1 in 100 grades with no falling of the boiler pressure or the water level. On the easier undulations between Armathwaite and Culgaich 13.3 miles were covered in a passing time of 13min 48sec with speed rising to 74mph in one of the dips. The 'Duchess' was, however, close to its maximum practical power output, even if the boiler could have produced more steam, because there was slipping in the tunnels.

A boiler output of 40000lb/hr or over was only possible in perfect operating conditions, but the ability to do so made the engine more effective that a lesser machine at more moderate average outputs. There were occasions in ordinary service when the vast reserve power of a 'Duchess' was called for over a short distance. At a more moderate output of 34000lb/hr the 'Duchess' produced the following hps:

90mph	2415 ihp	60mph	2365 ihp
80mph	2410 ihp	50mph	2320 ihp
70mph	2390 ihp		

At a rate of 26000lb/hr the ihps varied between 1750 and 1800. There were occasions in ordinary service when an ihp of 2300-2400 was sustained for 15-20min. On the basis of the test-house figures this would not mean that the boiler needed to be mortgaged, though with one fireman there would be some very hard shoveling or some preliminary build-up in anticipation of a maximum effort. The economy of the engine was well maintained under sustained testing conditions. The figures for coal/dbhp/hr obtained during periods of steady steaming at constant speed on a test plant cannot, in fairness, be compared with the figures for a variable speed dynamometer car test on the road.

At a continuous 70mph and a steaming rate of 26000lb/hr No 46225 burnt coal at the rate of 2.5lb/dbhp/hr, with the live steam injector while when the steaming was stepped up to 40000 lb/hr the figure was 2.8lb. The lowest figure of all was established at a steaming rate of 20000lb/hr and at a speed of 30mph, when a figure of 1.99lb/dbhp/hr was obtained. This figure was of academic interest only; the economy of a high speed locomotive at 30mph was little use to practical operating officers wishing to know how to schedule fast express trains. The average consumption of steam per ihphr was 14.5lb, which was not a particularly good result as it was slightly inferior to the results from the 'King', the V2 and the 'Britannia'. In the 1948 Exchanges the difference between the 'Duchess' and the A4 was very small, with indications that the 'Duchess' was producing the better boiler performance but that the A4 was showing some advantage in the utilisation of its steam. If the results of the V2 on the Swindon Plant are a fair indication of the possible A4 results, then this might again have been the conclusion if an A4 had been on the Plant. In actual fact an A4 was on the Rugby Plant to give a ceremonial twirl to the rollers on opening day in honour of Sir Nigel Gresley, whose powerful advocacy of scientific testing had been instrumental in getting the Rugby testing station started. An A4 was never put through a proper series of tests.

One reason for this slight disappointment in cylinder performance is thought to be the large clearance volume of 12.5% as compared with the 7.9% of the ER A4 and the 5.5% of the WR 'King'. The steam temperature of No 46225 was also a cause of some disappointment. The steam temperature did not exceed 700°F until the evaporation rate reached the high figure of 37000lb/hr. There were, however, other compensations which brought the 'Duchess' up to a level of overall efficiency comparable with any locomotive tested at Rugby or Swindon. The time-honoured criterion of express locomotive capacity was stated by Churchward as a drawbar pull of 2 tons at 70mph. The WR single-chimney 'King' exceeded this figure with a maximum pull of 3.2 tons, but the 'Duchess' at maximum steaming rate could exert 5.1 tons.

The difference between the ihp and the dbhp of a 'Duchess' was very small for such a large and heavy locomotive. This low resistance hp has been the subject of discussion and doubts have been expressed in some quarters, especially when the 530hp needed to move the 'Duchess' at 70mph was compared with the corresponding figure of 830hp for the smaller GWR 'King'. Various attempts have been made to explain this disparity, but the possibility of some differences in the testing techniques of the various stations cannot be excluded. While it remains true that the test-house figures are still the most reliable single source of information about the performance of a locomotive, there are still some anomalies in the results, as emerged from a scholarly examination by D. H. Landau in the *Journal of the Stephenson Locomotive Society* for December 1970. This shows that considerable caution must be exercised in the quotation of figures from the official reports. The test figures from the Plant and from Controlled Road Tests should be studied in the light of the standard of running demonstrated daily on the road. In the case of the 'Duchesses' it is possible to produce a well supported summary of hps (see opposite).

Although the figures are based on official test results there is an element of approximation about them. There is some degree of

	ihp	dbhp at 60mph
Instantaneous all-out maxima beyond the capacity of the boiler to sustain. This has little commercial significance.	3300-3400	2800-2900
Short bursts of up to 5min beyond the sustained capacity.	3000-3100	2500-2600
Maximum continuous output on the test plant or on controlled road tests. Sustained for one hour under favourable conditions.	2800-2900	2300-2400
Sustained for 10-20min in ordinary service with one fireman.	2350-2450	1850-1950
Average continuous output possible in everyday service with one fireman at a coal rate of 3000lb/hr.	1600-1700	1100-1200

uncertainty in everything and for that reason ihps and dbhps are presented above in the form of a band of possible hps rather than as one single definite figure. No one ihp figure is claimed as having a firm association with any single dbhp figure, but somewhere in these bands of upper and lower hps there could be figures which represent the true ratios. No dogmatic claims are made for figures, which are intended to be indicative rather than specific. The figure of horsepower to be expected in ordinary everyday running with a single fireman and an acceptable firing rate seems very low for so large a locomotive. It is however, intended to be an average: and such an average on a through run from Euston to Glasgow might very well involve a high ihp of 2000-2100 on the northern banks, but counterbalanced by many miles without steam on the descent. The moderate average hp explains why it was possible to replace the 'Duchesses' with 2000hp diesels which could manage the average 'Duchess' job comfortably, though they never rivalled the *Duchess of Abercorn*-type maximum effort.

The horsepower figures for the 'Duchess' puts it in a leading position among British express locomotives. The figures recorded in the Test Plant and in actual running on the road were never beaten by any other British rivals, though they may have been closely approached in some instances. The 'Duchess' emerged as a very powerful, free-running machine.

In coal consumption the 'Duchess' did not surpass its rivals, though none of them could show any significant improvement. The minimum steam rate of 14.12lb of steam per ihp/hr was beaten by several other loco classes tested at Rugby or Swindon but good boiler perform-ance by the 'Duchess' seems largely to have redressed the balance. There was trouble on the Plant from the tendency of the cylinder relief valves to blow and the pop safety valves would tend to be slow to re-seat themselves once lifted. In some cases pressure had to fall to 210-215lb/sq in before the valves closed again and there have been observed cases in ordinary service when re-seating only happened at 185lb/sq in against a designed blowing-off point of 250lb. The 'Duchesses' were not alone in this; it afflicted other engines with pop safety valves, but this was a waste of steam which the GWR with its 'old-fashioned' safety valves largely avoided.

The main criticism of the "Duchess", however, was their tendency to slip, which at times reduced these very powerful locomotives to near impotence. The atmospheric conditions on the northern banks could be very trecherous and there was much day-to-day variation in running with, at times, climbs which involved a power output unequalled in Britain; but at other times the banker had to be called for a relatively moderate load. There is no evidence that any other Pacific type in Britain would have fared better if faced with mountain mists. Possibly a powerful 4-6-0 could have kept its feet a little better, but its smaller boiler and firebox would not have measured up very well to a through working from Euston to Glasgow. On balance there were more aspects of the test reports which justified satisfaction by the LMS and LMR authorities than there were points of criticism.

CHAPTER TWELVE

Some Notable Running in Ordinary Service

The records of the Test Plant did not tell the whole story of a locomotive. They gave a most detailed account of the running of one engine under conditions which were frequently far removed from everyday reality. The test results were indicative of what might be expected on the road, but there was no certainty that they would have any reality when compared with a random selection of runs timed on ordinary service trains. Running on the road was the product of design and operating and the latter was by far the most important. Clearly if the ability was not there, high-class performance was hardly to be expected, but the contrary was not true; a locomotive of ability was not automatically certain to produce its best in everyday running. The quality of the coal was a potent factor and the skill of the crew was even more important. On the West Coast Route trains were treated badly and much of the post-war running was a series of hops from signal to signal. This treatment must have taken the heart out of all but the most dedicated of engine crews.

As an example of the unsatisfactory conditions prevalent on the former LNWR main line it may be recalled that, even during the 1948 Exchanges when money was being spent on what should have been a scientific examination of locomotive performance, an RAF leave special with a 'Black Five' was allowed to take the fast road from Crewe in front of the up 'Royal Scot' behind a 'Merchant Navy' Pacific which had arrived slightly before time from Carlisle. The 'Royal Scot' was not allowed to overtake the special until it had reached Leighton Buzzard, 118 miles further south, by which time a whole series of checks had put the Pacific 40min late. Complaints brought the patronising comment that authority always knew best and there were good reasons for such practices, but this convinced no one. No reason other than someone's blunder could account for such acts of folly. The only thing that can be said in favour of LMR operating during this period was that it was not an act of spite against the visiting Southern Region engine, nor against the ER A4, which fared little better, for there were many occasions when the best LMR expresses were treated in a similar fashion including several in the personal experience of the writers. This bred a cynical attitude among the footplate staff and the will for punctual running must have been reduced. While it was probably true to say that other Regions were little better, the operating over the West Coast Route was worse than it ever need have been.

The remarkable thing was that there were occasions when first-class running did take place. If a selection of the best runs recorded in the 1950s is compared with a selection taken in the 1935-39 period then the post-war runs would be superior, but if a comparison was made on the basis of the average standard then the honours would go to the earlier period. It is sad fact that full appreciation of much of the post-war running depends on net times, as many of the best runs involved a late arrival although the engine had performed admirably. Many an excellent run would approach Rugby or Crewe in comfortable time for a punctual or early arrival, only to be kept waiting 5-10min a mile or so from the destination. Rugby rejoiced in the nickname of "Stop-all Junction" among the footplate staff.

In a comparison with running in the 1930s trains in the 1950s were mainly hauled by the larger and more powerful 'Duchess' class Pacific while the older 'Princesses' had deteriorated sadly in their running standards. In the 1930s these twelve engines were an elite corps — new, in excellent condition and fed with the best Grimethorpe coal. There was an official will to obtain punctual running. In the 1950s the 'Princesses' were outclassed by the larger Pacifics and much of their running was in sad contrast to their pre-war achievements. It is not, however, true to say that they never did well in the post-war world; later in this chapter details will be given of individual runs well above the general standard and comparable with the best pre-war epics. The 'Duchesses', on the other hand, had hardly had time to show their true worth in ordinary service before September 1939 and far more notable runs were timed behind these engines in the 1950s. It would probably be true to say that they made more consistently good net times than any of their British rivals though, thanks to the deplorable operating, actual punctuality was poor.

The heaviest loads to be found in Britain in the late 1940s and early 1950s were on the West Coast Route. Trains of 17 bogies were a common sight south of Crewe. On the easier bookings these could be handled with the greatest ease by a 'Duchess'. A cut-off of 15% and the first regulator valve would keep these trains moving at around 65mph on the gentle undulations of the LNWR with the steam lazily climbing out of the chimney and falling in characteristic fashion in front of the smokebox, to the discomfiture of lineside photographers. Such a run was timed personally in September 1951 when No 46239 *City of Chester* was at the head of a 17-coach train of 531 tons tare, 570 tons gross, on the 8.30 from Euston.

From Rugby, Nuneaton was passed in 16min 37sec at 69mph, and Stafford was reached in 55min 30sec or 53½min net after allowance for a 15mph check. After Stafford the engine was opened out a little more to 20% and full regulator, according to the driver, and this took the 17-coach train up to Whitmore with speed rising steadily to 61mph at the summit. After a maximum of 70mph Crewe was reached in 29min 30sec from Stafford. This was hardly an example of the full power of a 'Duchess', but it was an example of a heavy train handled with the greatest of ease on a road of gentle undulations.

A run timed by Norman Harvey displayed a little more energy. No 46228 *Duchess of Rutland* had a similar 17-coach load of 560 gross tons, but performed the start-to-stop run from Rugby to Stafford, 51 miles, in 51 min 18sec with a maximum speed of 78mph at Polesworth and a minimum of 60mph near Lichfield. This run was on the 14.00 Liverpool train and the crew comprised Driver J. Munslow and Fireman Freshwater of Camden shed.

These two runs showed the big-engine conception in successful operation, but although a nearly even-time run was achieved on the second occasion, neither of these runs showed a 'Duchess' at anywhere near its maximum. Cecil J. Allen published a run timed by V. W. Coles with No 46257 *City of Salford*, the last 'Duchess' to be built, on the 10.40 from Euston when a 16-coach load of heavier stock weighing 530 tons tare, 575 tons gross was taken from the Rugby start to passing Colwich 44.4 miles, in 41min 11sec, suggesting that a stop at Stafford in 48½min would have been possible had not signal checks intervened.

A run of exceptional merit happened on 17 March 1953, but was unfortunately not timed in detail. The down 'Mid-day Scot' had a load of 16 vehicles weighing 482 tons tare, 510 tons gross, behind No 46254 *City of Stoke-on-Trent* and Rugby was left 29min late owing to a late start from Euston and a signal failure at Tring. Crewe was reached in 66min start to stop for the 75.5 miles, a gain of 19min on schedule. Another exceptional run which was not recorded in detail happened when the up 'Red Rose' had left Crewe 18min late and was stopped on Camden Bank before entering Euston, which was reached only 4min behind time, or in a net time of under 140min for the 158.1 miles. The load was 15 bogies weighing 491 tons, tare, 540 tons gross and the engine No 46229 *Duchess of Hamilton*.

Another trip behind No 46229 *Duchess of Hamilton* on the up 'Red Rose' was recorded in detail by R. A. Vince on 11 April, 1954. The load was 16 bogies weighing 526 tons tare, 560 tons full and the 158.1 miles from Crewe to Euston were covered in 155min 45sec, or in 149½min net after allowing for one signal check and two pw slacks. This was an excellent example of heavy work being performed with no exceptional speed or power output. The maximum speed downhill was 77mph near Norton Bridge, but consistently good uphill work, including a minimum of 63mph at Tring, accumulated a steady gain on schedule. It was, however, significant of the operating standards of the time that although the recorder travelled on the same train every

Friday evening, this was the first time for six months that he had not been late at Euston. This was clearly not the fault of the 'Duchess' class locomotives, as this run showed that they could gain up to 15min on schedule with 560 tons and the previous run had gained 25min with 540 tons. A time of 150min from Crewe to Euston with 560 tons would require a continuous effort from the fireman, but it would not exceed the 3000lb/hr regarded by the testing engineers as reasonable for one man; the 140min effort may have required something slightly harder, which could not be expected with any regularity. The quality of the coal, the weather and the condition of the engine were of course important factors, but there was normally no job in the early 1950s which should have been beyond the capacity of a 'Duchess' even with over 550 tons.

Over the northern section there were of course more difficulties, yet much of the best work was recorded here especially in Scotland. In the August 1953 issue of *Trains Illustrated* a letter from W. J. Alcock gave details of a run on 28 December 1949, when No 46227 *Duchess of Devonshire* with a load of 525 tons accelerated from 58mph at Brock to 81mph at Galgate after nearly 10 miles of level or faintly rising road. This section from Preston to Lancaster was the nearest equivalent to the Darlington-York section of the East Coast route, but the near-level section was much shorter. Fewer sensational high-speed runs on level track were recorded on the West Coast, but this run showed that high speeds on the flat were easy enough for a heavily-loaded 'Duchess'. Later in the same run the climb from Carnforth to Shap Summit, 31.4 miles, took 35min 22sec.

The same recorder was on the 'Mid-day Scot' when No 46234 *Duchess of Abercorn* had a 17-coach load of 514 tons tare, 550 tons full and recovered 12¼min actual time and 14min net time between Lancaster and Carlisle, climbing from Lancaster to Shap Summit, 37.9 miles, in 44min 3sec. A number of recordings by reliable train-timers showed that loads of from 520 to 580 tons could be taken over Shap Summit by unassisted 'Duchesses' and the time from Carnforth to the Summit would vary between 35 and 40min. Nothing quite equal to the 33min 20sec of *Duchess of Abercorn* with 610 tons in 1939 was ever timed in the post-war world, but the 1939 epic was a definite attempt to find the maximum capacity of a locomotive which was nearly new and at the top of its form. There were, of course, occasions when the banker had to be taken, mainly in bad weather conditions. Slipping was the greatest fear.

A similar pattern of performance was demonstrated in the southbound direction. In December 1954 Cecil J. Allen, in 'British Locomotive Practice and Performance', published a series of runs southwards over Shap with loads of from 495 to 580 tons gross. The schedule at that time was 48min for the 31.4 miles from Carlisle to the Summit and the fastest climb was by No 46233 *Duchess of Sutherland* with 495 tons, when the summit was passed in 39min 2sec. The 580 ton train was worked by a 'Princess', No 46212 *Duchess of Kent*, which passed the summit in 48min 4sec. Relatively few notable runs over this section by the earlier Pacifics were published in post-war days. Although this work was reasonably good it was no better than that recorded behind the 'Princesses' in the years 1935-39, but the time of 40min 19sec by *Duchess of Abercorn* with 610 tons in 1939 shows that the 'Duchesses' were far from being fully extended. On two of the runs a net time of 72min was achieved over the 69 miles from Carlisle to Lancaster.

Some of the best work in Scotland was superior to anything recorded before the war in ordinary service. The run northwards from Carlisle was especially difficult, for Beattock Bank was more severe than Shap in that it extended for 10 miles at an average grade of 1 in 75 with no break of any kind. It was approached by 39.7 miles of generally rising gradients which, in contrast to the towering climb of the bank itself, were regarded as being almost level but in reality contained long stretches of 1 in 200 comparable with the climbs to Stoke and Stevenage on the East Coast route. Added to this there was a greater distance between water troughs than on the LNWR main line and worry over water could inhibit fast running, especially when trains were running in quick succession and the troughs were re-filling slowly. A number of runs timed by W. Robertson were published and these included some of great merit.

No 46220 *Coronation* was in charge of a 15-coach load of 505 tons tare, 540 tons full and a smart start from Carlisle was made with speed rising to 73mph at Floriston, only to be brought down to 12mph at Quintinshill. The acceleration up 1 in 200 was excellent with 540 tons as speed rose to 50mph at Kirkpatrick and the second stretch of 1 in 200 was taken at a minimum of 60mph at Castlemilk. Beattock was passed at 60mph and the bank was attacked unassisted. It was excellent work to pick up from 18mph after a pws to 23mph at the summit. The summit was passed in 59min 20sec from Carlisle, but had there been no checks or slacks perhaps two minutes could have been cut from these times. No 46233 *Duchess of Sutherland* had a similar 15-coach load of slightly lighter stock weighing 474 tons, tare, 510 tons full and ran even faster to Beattock, topping the first 1 in 200 stretch at 63½mph, the second at 66mph and reaching 79mph at Lockerbie. The start-to-stop run from Carlisle to Beattock over a road rising in its general tendency was completed in 38min 5sec for the 39.7 miles. A vigorous ascent was made with a 2-6-4 tank in the rear and speed rose to 37mph. Despite standing for 4½min waiting for the banker to come on and possibly taking water, the summit was passed before time and the train arrived at Symington 3¾min early.

The southbound runs over Beattock were more spectacular in speeds and times but were less demanding on the locomotives. Bookings of 75min for the 73.5 miles from Carstairs to Carlisle and 67min for the 66.9 miles from Symington were faster than pre-war and were very exciting in 1952/3. No 46231 *Duchess of Atholl* had a 16-coach load of 488 tons tare, 530 tons full and covered the 73.5 miles from Carstairs to Carlisle in an actual time of 69min 5sec. This required a minimum speed of 49½mph at the summit, a maximum of 84mph down the bank and 80mph near Quintinshill. No 46238 *City of Carlisle* had an even heavier 17-coach load of 532 tons tare, 570 tons full and covered the 66.9 miles from Symington in 73min 25sec after a signal stop at Kingmoor and a pws on the descent of the bank. This time the summit was topped at a minimum of 53mph, which with 570 tons was as near as any train in normal service appears to have got to the test run of No 6234 in 1939, when the summit was passed at over 60mph with 610 tons. Once over the top No 46238 ran easily and without checks would have kept the 67min booking. It would have been easy without extending the engine downhill to have cut several minutes from this time. The short climb to Beattock Summit from the north followed by easy downhill grades invited maximum efforts. The northbound journey was the greater test of locomotive capacity, but the 'Duchesses' were master of both up and down timings, subject only to the effect of mountain mists which could make them slip. Despite the occasional excellent unaided ascent the banker was taken more often than on Shap and under the circumstances this was probably wise.

In 1954 the 7.55 from Euston to Liverpool and Manchester was given a timing of 136min from Watford to Crewe, 140.7 miles. This was a heavy train rarely weighing less than 450 tons and often loading to 16 bogies. Later it was named the 'Lancastrian'. It was worked by 'Duchess' class engines from Camden Shed with Edge Hill crews. Much later Edge Hill had the job with their own 'Princess' class engines and it became one of the turns for the prototype 'Deltic' diesel when that engine was running test trips on the LMR.

There were some rare characters among the Edge Hill enginemen. One of these stalwarts was known at Lime Street as "The Ale-House Driver" — not, one hastens to add, because he was guilty of drinking on duty but because of his habit of making early arrivals and catching the casual porters in the pub. Some excellent running was performed by these men and Drivers Aitchison and Corbett had a very high reputation.

Like all trains on the former LNWR main line south of Crewe, the 7.55's running was subject to operating treatment on the day, but given a reasonably clear road there were some exciting runs. It has been possible to trace ten runs with heavy loads timed by reliable recorders and they make an interesting collection. Some are taken from the writings of the late Cecil J. Allen and others, which are here published for the first time, were recorded by P. J. Coster.

Watford-Crewe 140.7 miles

No 46239 *City of Chester*	469 tons tare	490 tons gross	135min 17sec	123 min net
No 46229 *Duchess of Hamilton*	487 tons tare	510 tons gross	138min 13sec	124 min net
No 46229 *Duchess of Hamilton*	500 tons tare	535 tons gross	136min 43sec	125½ min net
No 46257 *City of Salford*	483 tons tare	510 tons gross	130min 18sec	127 min net
No 46257 *City of Salford*	425 tons tare	460 tons gross	135min 52sec	127 min net
No 46237 *City of Bristol*	475 tons tare	515 tons gross	125min 35sec	122½ min net
No 46243 *City of Lancaster*	468 tons tare	505 tons gross	134min 10sec	127 min net
No 46245 *City of London*	445 tons tare	480 tons gross	131min 31sec	130 min net
No 46208 *Princess Helena Victoria*	418 tons tare	445 tons gross	136min 31sec	127 min net
No 46209 *Princess Beatrice*	443 tons tare	470 tons gross	145min 06sec	138 min net

This table is indicative of operating conditions in that no train had the same net time as actual time. Even the one which had the best road had lost three minutes by checks or pw slacks. On the evidence of these runs a 'Duchess', at its best, had over 13min in hand on this fast booking even with 500 tons. An examination of the details of the runs shows that on the fastest runs exceptional efforts were made over sections of the itinerary. The fastest net time of all was the result of an exceptionally fast Nuneaton to Stafford time, while two of the runs are notable for really outstanding climbs from Stafford to Whitmore Summit; another run had a quite exceptional maximum speed on moderate down gradients before Bletchley. The two runs by 'Princess' type engines were timed when Edge Hill engines took over the job. At that time Edge Hill had only one 'Duchess', which was not considered to be one of the best in the class at that time. Edge Hill men had been the most successful with the 'Princesses' and for many years they ran well on the "Merseyside Express" with these engines, always providing that they got the road. When faced with these engines instead of the

7.55 Euston-Liverpool and Manchester

Engine:	No 46239	No 46229
	City of Chester	*Duchess of Hamilton*
Load:	15 bogies, 469/490 tons	16 bogies, 500/535 tons
Crew:	Driver Corbett	Driver Aitchison,
	Fireman Burtt	Fireman Corfield

Distance		Actual min sec	Speed mph	Actual min sec	Speed mph
0.0	Watford Junct	00 00		00 00	
116.2	Stafford	113 22	63	110 01	54
121.5	Norton Bridge	118 05	72	115 02	66½
126.0	Standon Bridge	121 46	73½	119 01	71½
130.3	Whitmore	125 08	76½	112 36	74½
132.8	Madeley	127 08	79	124 35	79
135.9	Betley Road	129 18	92½	126 54	86
		sigs	10	sig stop	
140.7	Crewe	135 27		136 43	
	Net time	123min		Net time 125¼ min	

"Big Lizzies" P. J. Coster was filled with gloom, but after travelling to Mossley Hill for two days running he had to eat his words. The up runs on the 17.25 were even better than these down runs on the 7.55 and will be dealt with later.

A net time of under 125min with over 500 tons meant some hard running even for a 'Duchess'. Each of the very fast runs had one section of really exceptional effort. The first and third runs in the table were very fast from Stafford onwards.

In each case the good work done on the ascent was undone by the balked approach to Crewe station, but the credit to the Edge Hill crews remains. These runs were published in detail by the late Cecil J. Allen. The following two runs were timed by P. J. Coster and are here published for the first time. The first run has the lowest net time ever published and the second is the best run known to have been made by a 'Princess'-type locomotive.

The running between Nuneaton and Stafford was very fast on the first run. Normally the 'Duchesses' did not have the same opportunities for very high speed on the level and downhill as did the East Coast Pacifics, but here were speeds similar to those expected of the ER engines between Huntingdon and Hitchin, achieved with rather less help from gravity. The run by No 46243 *City of Lancaster* was rather slower overall than the one tabulated, but it was exceptionally fast after passing Tring in 17min 25sec at 62mph. Speed rose to 88mph near Cheddington and further to 92/93mph on the flatter gradients beyond Leighton Buzzard before the sight of an adverse distant signal brought the pace down to 70mph. The remainder of the journey was good, though not as fast as the run tabulated, but the high maximum speed reached on gentle down gradients was a tribute to the free running qualities of a 'Duchess'. The journey behind the 'Princess', No 46208, was not on the same level as the best runs by the larger engines, but it was outstandingly good for one of the older engines in August 1958. The fast spell between Cheddington and Wolverton recalled the style of the late Laurie Earl in pre-war days.

The official load limit for a Pacific on the fast booking of the down 'Lancastrian' was 510 tons tare and this was approached on some of the recorded fast runs. The train was observed with 17 bogies behind a 'Duchess' but no detailed logs with such a loading have come to light. Evidence that the timing would have been within 'Duchess' capacity with 17 or even 18 bogies is given by the net gains of 10-12min with 15 or 16 bogies. A run timed on the 10.40 down with a 16-coach load of 530 tons tare, 575 tons full, showed that the engine gained a total of seven minutes over sections where the running was comparable. The stop at Rugby would, of course, allow an opportunity to build up steam pressure or water level and the two trains are not completely comparable.

On his return journeys P. J. Coster used the 17.25 up 'Red Rose' and on this train two of the most outstanding post-war runs by 'Princess' class engines were recorded. Again the best pre-war standards were at least equalled and in both cases the usual practice of the great Laurie Earl was recalled in the way the maximum effort was made over the racing ground from Welton to Wembley. These

7.55 Euston-Liverpool and Manchester

Engine: Load:		Sched min	No 46237 City of Bristol 15, 475/515 tons		No 46208 Princess Helena Victoria 13, 418/445 tons	
Distance Miles		Sched min	Actual min sec	Speed mph	Actual min sec	Speed mph
0.0	Watford Junct	—	00 00	—	00 00	—
3.5	Kings Langley		6 12	54 ½	6 09	53
7.1	Hemel Hempstead		9 58	60	10 23	54
10.6	Berkhamsted		13 25	61	13 53	61
14.3	Tring	16	17 06	65	17 45	55
18.7	Cheddington		20 31	85	21 28	—
22.8	Leighton Buzzard		23 28	82	24 31	87/88
29.3	Bletchley	28	28 09	83/81	28 53	83/82
35.0	Wolverton		32 19	82	33 10	83
37.4	Castlethorpe		34 06	79	34 56	79
42.5	Roade	39	38 15	69min	39 08	68
45.4	Blisworth	42	40 47	72/76	41 41	—
			sigs	60	sigs	
52.3	Weedon	48	46 17	—	50 41	—
57.9	Welton		51 32	64	55 38	64/62
			sigs	30		
62.9	Hillmorton		57 49		60 00	76
65.2	Rugby	60	60 59	40	62 04	50
70.7	Brinklow		67 11	66/70	67 31	66
74.0	Shilton		70 01	68	70 09	68
76.6	Bulkington		71 56	—	74 01	67
79.7	Nuneaton	74	74 47	80	75 11	80/76
84.9	Atherstone		78 31	—	79 11	79/76
89.1	Polesworth		81 25	86/90	82 26	79
92.6	Tamworth	87	83 48	85/88	87 23 sigs	—
96.1	Hademore		86 12	83	92 29 sigs	
98.9	Lichfield	93	88 15	76 min	95 56 sigs	—
103.6	Armitage		92 00	77	100 54	65
106.9	Rugeley	100	94 28	80	103 44	72
109.7	Colwich		96 34	—	106 13	68/74
112.1	Milford	105	98 25	78	108 15	—
116.2	Stafford	110	101 40	60	111 55	52
119.5	Great Bridgford		— —	—	115 02	64
121.5	Norton Bridge	116	— —	—	116 58	60
130.3	Whitmore	125	114 13	68	125 28	60
132.8	Madeley		— —	76	127 43	70
135.9	Betley Road		— —	—	130 23	72
140.7	Crewe	136	125 35		136 31	
			Net time 122 ½ min		Net time 127min	

runs make an interesting comparison with the test trip made in June 1935 shortly after the larger superheater was fitted. The 1935 test run was a copybook example of sustained high speed steaming by an engine in the full flush of vigorous youth and in perfect condition. The 1958 occasions were examples of skilled crews getting the best possible work from engines which, in late middle age, had long since ceased to be the pride of the line. In 1958 full use had to be made of the down gradients which in 1935 had been used with some restraint.

No 46208 had a load of 429 tons, tare, 465 tons gross and Euston was reached in an actual time of 145min 36sec for the 158.1 miles, or in 140min net. This was an exceptionally good performance and the driver was not afraid to run fast downhill. No 46208 must have been in good order. The first sight of No 46209 on the following day was not re-assuring. In Mr Coster's own words: No 46209 was as black as an October Budget and had a bad blow on one inside cylinder gland. Appearances were deceptive, however, as No 46209 over long sections of the run did even better than No 46208. The start from Crewe was ominous as they wallowed up to Whitmore with clouds of black smoke and much noise but little speed. At the summit No 46209 was three minutes behind No 46208, but part of this may have been due to a more prolonged slack at Betley Road. The second run was nine minutes behind the first on passing Rugby, but a faster time up to Euston, 68min 50sec against 70min 4sec, made the net times from Crewe similar. Both were excellent runs and the times over the racing ground from Welton to Wembley make an interesting comparison with the 1935 test run with No 6200.

Welton-Wembley (67.25 miles, 230ft vertical fall)				
Year	Engine No	Load	time	Av speed
1935	6200	15/453 tons tare, 475 tons full	52min 14sec	77.2mph
1958	46208	13/429 tons tare, 465 tons full	52min 58sec	76.3mph
1958	46209	13/428 tons tare, 465 tons full	50min 30sec	79.8mph

The higher percentage of gross to tare weight in the case of the two 1958 runs was due to these trains being heavily loaded with passengers, while the 1935 train was made up to its test weight by the addition of empty stock. The two 1958 runs were much slower than the 1935 test trip in acceleration from the Rugby slack, but the minimum speeds at Roade Summit were similar on all three runs — 71mph by the 1935 engine and 72mph on both the 1958 occasions — but the 1958 engines reached higher speeds at Castlethorpe. The climb from Bletchley to Tring was slower by No 46208, which took 12min 45sec for the 15 miles with a minimum of 63mph against No 6200's time of 12min 33sec and a minimum of 67mph in 1935, but No 46209, with a roar from her chimney far louder than No 46208 on the previous day, stormed over the summit at 70mph after a time of 11min 50sec from Bletchley. On the descent No 46208 was slightly faster than No 6200, but No 46209 was driven hard downhill with a maximum of 96mph near Kings Langley. It will be recalled that the 'Duchess' class engine No 46229 had come up from Crewe in a net time of 140min but had not been timed in detail. The load was 540 tons and the difference between this and the 465 tons of the 'Princesses' is probably a fair measure of the comparative ability of the two classes.

One start-to-stop run from Rugby to Euston, timed by P. J. Coster, came quite close to the speeds of the two 'Princesses'.

Engine: No 46228 *Duchess of Rutland, Load:* 15, 482 tons tare, 525 tons gross

Distance Miles		Actual min sec		Speeds mph
0.0	Rugby	00	00	—
2.3	Hillmorton	5	11	46
7.3	Welton	10	19	68/80
12.9	Weedon	14	45	69
19.8	Blisworth	20	29	76
22.7	Roade	22	54	70
27.8	Castlethorpe	26	43	87
30.2	Wolverton	28	30	78
		pws		
35.9	Bletchley	33	50	20
42.4	Leighton	40	42	74/76
46.5	Cheddington	43	58	74
50.9	Tring	47	37	69
54.6	Berkhamsted	50	45	75
58.1	Hemel Hempstead	53	20	82/84
		sigs		
61.7	Kings Langley	57	09	—
65.2	Watford	60	45	
69.3	Hatch End	64	13	74
71.2	Harrow	65	42	79/82
74.5	Wembley	68	15	74
77.2	Willesden	70	35	—
		sigs		
82.6	Euston	79	42	

Net time: 73min

The outstanding incident of this run was the acceleration from the 20mph pw slack near Bletchley. The engine had done well enough in reaching even time near Roade in less than 23 miles from the Rugby start, but on being given the road again after the Bletchley slowing, the most exciting running was recorded. Mr Coster writes that in years of working on the LMR and many hundreds of miles behind Pacifics 'I have only heard the "Big Lizzies" opened out on six occasions. Five of these were on the northern banks. The noise from the chimney of

143

46228 was tremendous when pulling away from the pws at Bletchley station to Stoke Hammond. I could not believe my eyes when I was recording 75mph above Leighton Buzzard'. It is only fair to add that on many occasions when travelling on the main line in the 1950s Mr Coster made no attempt to time running which was either cut to pieces by checks or which required no effort worthy of the engine. His best runs were, however, some real compensation.

The 'Royal Scot' and the 'Mid-day Scot' were given XL bookings of 80min for the 82.6 miles to Rugby followed by 77min for the 75.5 miles Rugby to Crewe. More is known of the running of the 'Mid-day Scot', which attracted more train timers especially between Euston and Rugby. It was possible to travel down by the 'Mid-day Scot' and return on the 14.30 from Birmingham, which had a 79min booking. The 'Mid-day Scot' was usually the heavier train and was more interesting for that reason. It was, however, a ragged timekeeper and on a number of visits we made to the LNWR main line for lineside photography, this train was rarely observed on time between Rugby and Nuneaton. When it was on schedule the engine was almost invariably a 'Duchess'. Much of the lost time was not the fault of the engine, but there was little margin in hand against delays when the load approached the permitted 510 tons tare. The 77min to Crewe gave no trouble and a slightly late arrival at Rugby could be corrected by Crewe.

We are indebted to K. R. Phillips for a summary of his timing experiences and those of his friends on this booking. For comparative purposes a number of passing times by 'Jubilee' class engines on the Birmingham two-hour expresses have been corrected to the equivalent stopping time.

Type of Engine	No of runs	Average gross load	Average net time
'Duchess'	18	457 tons	79.8min
'Princess'	9	439 tons	81.5min
BR Class 8 No 71000	7	488 tons	83.2min
'Jubilee' (corrected times)	56	351 tons	81.6min

This is a far from satisfactory record in view of the fact that these are net times. Actual times would be longer. It shows the ascendency of the 'Duchess' class, but as some runs had net times well within schedule, on others time was lost to restore the average to something barely superior to the booked time. A collection of the best runs is, however, a convincing record of locomotive competence (see opposite).

While eight of the ten runs show a net gain on schedule only two actually arrived at Rugby in 80min. Several runs were approaching Rugby in time for a punctual arrival, only to get checked before

Above: No 46202 the Turbomotive, with post-war modifications, climbing
Camden Bank with the 8.30am Liverpool express from Euston./*F. R. Hebron*

Below: No 46202 rebuilt with 'Duchess'-type cylinders and named *Princess Anne*
at Edge Hill Shed./*Eric Treacy*

Above: No 46207 *Princess Arthur of Connaught* accelerates from a signal check near Bulkington with the up 'Manxman' in August 1952./*J. F. Clay*

Below: LMR Pacific No 46225 *Duchess of Gloucester* on test train passing Skipton old station on 23 March 1956./*W. Hubert Foster*

Above: No 46237 *City of Bristol* on test on the WR, heading the down 'Cornish Riviera' past Reading West./*M. W. Earley*

Below: No 46235 *City of Birmingham* passing Hay Fell on a Plymouth and Crewe to Glasgow express on 12 July 1963./*Derek Cross*

Above: No 46254 *City of Stoke on Trent* at Shap Wells on a Birmingham to Glasgow express./*Eric Treacy*

Below: No 46235 *City of Birmingham* leaving Beattock station with a Birmingham-Glasgow train./*T. G. Hepburn*

Left: No 46223 *Princess Alice* at Greskine Box with a Euston-Glasgow Sleeper with banking engine in the rear./*Eric Treacy*

Above: No 46256 *Sir William Stanier FRS* leaving Carlisle on the up 'Royal Scot'./*Eric Treacy*

Below: No 46257 *City of Salford* leaving Euston on the down 'Caledonian'./*Eric Treacy*

Above: No 46242 *City of Glasgow* climbs towards Shap with the up 'Caledonian'./*T. G. Hepburn*

Below: No 46251 *City of Nottingham* and WR 4-6-0 No 7022 *Hereford Castle* at Swindon shed on 9 May 1964./*J. F. Clay*

Above: No 46251 *City of Nottingham* on an SLS Special on Dillecar Troughs on 12 July 1964./*W. J. V. Anderson*

Below: No 46245 *City of London* approaching Stoke Summit on a return Home Counties Railway Society special from Doncaster to Kings Cross on 9 June 1962./*M. Mason*

Above: No 70049 *Solway Firth* south of Tring with the 11.25 Euston-Llandudno on 5 September 1964./*Brian Stephenson*

Below: No 70003 *John Bunyan* at Beattock station with a Glasgow-Carlisle slow./*T. G. Hepburn*

Above: No 72005 *Clan Macgregor* at Carlisle./*T. G. Hepburn*

Below: No 72008 *Clan Macleod* approaches Gleneagles with the 1.30pm Carlisle-Perth in May 1963./*W. J. V. Anderson*

Above: The morning Glasgow-Birmingham train passing Thrimby Grange hauled by No 71000 *Duke of Gloucester* on 2 August 1960./*Derek Cross*

Below: No 71000 *Duke of Gloucester* leaving Shrewsbury for Crewe on 17 July 1954./*H. A. Chelkley*

Above: Class A1 Pacific No 60152 *Holyrood* at Crewe on Birmingham-Glasgow express in May 1953./*J. F. Clay*

Below: Class A1 Pacific No 60161 *North British* climbing Shap with the Birmingham-Glasgow express on 9 April 1953./*Eric Treacy*

Above: SR Pacific No 35012 *United States Lines* climbing Shap at 60mph before the check at Scouts Green on the RCTS "Solway Ranger" rail-tour of 13 June 1964./*M. York*

Below: Class A4 Pacific No 4498 *Sir Nigel Gresley* climbing towards Shap Summit at 50mph with the RCTS "Border Limited" rail-tour of 28 October 1967./*T. G. Hepburn*

Above: Some outstanding European Pacifics:—Chapelon Class 231E compound Pacific No 231E41 at La Chapelle Shed./*J. Cliffe*

Below: Alsace-Lorraine Railway Class S16 2cyl Pacific No 1401 fitted with Caprotti valve gear./*Ian Allan Library*

Bottom: DB Class 10 4-6-2 No 10,002 leaving Wabern with the 12.30 Hamburg to Frankfurt express on 9 July 1966./*W. G. Sumner*

Above: The preserved No 6201 *Princess Elizabeth* at a Tyseley Open Day on 28 September 1969. Normally preserved at Ashchurch./*J. B. Mounsey*

Below: No 6203 *Princess Margaret Rose* at Butlin's Holiday Camp, Pwllheli. It is intended to display this engine at the Midland Railway Centre Derby./*Ian Allan Library*

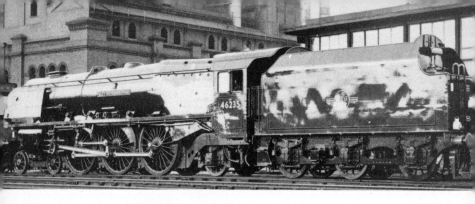

Above: No 46235 *City of Birmingham*, preserved in BR green, photographed at Birmingham on 22 May 1966./*J. W. Ellson*

Below: No 6229 *Duchess of Hamilton* preserved in LMS red at Butlin's Holiday Camp, Minehead. This engine is intended for exhibition at York Railway Museum./*Ian Allan Library*

Bottom: No 6233 *Duchess of Sutherland* steamed for the first time in public at Bressingham Steam Museum on 30 May 1974. *G. D. King*

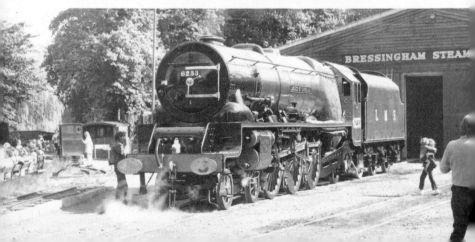

Euston-Rugby (82.6 miles)

Engine	Load tons	Actual min sec		Net time min
No 46249 *City of Sheffield*	493/530	85	03	79 ½
No 46240 *City of Coventry*	471/495	80	30	75
No 46244 *Princess Alexandra*	525/560	79	38	76 ½
No 46231 *Duchess of Atholl*	474/510	82	35	77 ½
No 46235 *City of Birmingham*	428/460	82	00	75 ½
No 46248 *City of Leeds*	473/510	78	53	77 ½
No 46212 *Duchess of Kent*	363/390	81	03	74 ½
No 46203 *Princess Margaret Rose*	423/455	82	25	79 ½
No 46201 *Princess Elizabeth*	455/490	87	35	81
No 46211 *Queen Maud*	459/490	86	36	83

entering the station. The second run in the table by No 46240 and 495 tons was exceptionally fast to Tring with a sustained 68mph up the 1 in 335 past Harrow, 73½mph at Watford and a minimum of 65mph at Tring. This run was timed by the Rev. R. S. Haines and has been published by Cecil J. Allen. The worst run with the slowest net time of 83min, by a 'Princess' with 490 tons, would have been considered to be excellent when the engine was new. The best net time with a 'Princess' and a heavy train was 81min with 490 tons, which does not quite equal Earl's run in 79½min net with 510 tons in 1937. The runs chosen for tabulation show the heaviest load with a Duchess and the shortest net time with a Princess.

The journey by No 46224 was perhaps the best ever recorded on this train. Two very similar logs from different correspondents were published by Cecil J. Allen and the resemblence is so strong that it is a justifiable assumption that the same run was timed independently by two recorders unknown to each other. The main difference between the logs was the allowance made for the weight of the passengers and their luggage and we have averaged the two figures. Where exceptional maximum speeds are different we have taken the lower figure. We would not presume to adjudicate between two experienced recorders, but two independent logs add proof to a most exceptional run.

The driver was H. Nicklin of Crewe North with Fireman Roberts. Driver Nicklin had a very high reputation in those days and some stop-watch enthusiasts, travelling mainly for train timing, used to seek out the trains he was booked to drive. The good work continued after Rugby with an actual time of 74min 57sec and a net time of 72½min for the 75.5 miles to Crewe. The run by the 'Princess' No 46212 was with a relatively light load, but the net time of 74½min was good. This run was timed by K. R. Phillips. Although we have evidence that a 'Duchess' could gain 2min on Earl's pre-war best time with 50 tons more, it must be concluded that the 80min booking was too tight for reliable time-keeping under the prevailing operating conditions.

Distance miles		Sched min	No 46224 Princess Alexandra 16, 523/560 tons Actual min sec	Speed mph	No 46212 Duchess of Kent 11, 363/390 tons Actual min sec	Speed mph
00.0	Euston	0	00 00	—	00 0C	—
1.1	Camden No 1		5 03	—	3 18	—
5.4	Willesden	9	10 58	57	9 13	57
8.1	Wembley		13 46	56	11 49	63
11.4	Harrow		17 12	59½	14 56	64
13.3	Hatch End		19 08	60	16 43	63½
					sigs	38
17.4	Watford Junct	21	23 06	68	21 23	54
20.9	Kings Langley		26 12	67	24 52	63
24.5	Hemel Hempstead		29 24	67	28 04	67
28.0	Berkhamsted		32 34	65½	31 09	66/67
31.7	Tring	35	35 56	65	34 30	70/80
					pws	30
36.1	Cheddington		39 08	84	38 32	—
40.2	Leighton Buzzard		42 28	75	42 55	69
			pws	32		
46.7	Bletchley	47	49 23	47	48 08	74
52.4	Wolverton		55 06	75	52 38	78
54.8	Castlethorpe		57 01	74½	54 31	75
59.9	Roade	58	61 16	71½	58 48	68
					pws	37
62.8	Blisworth	61	63 36	80½	61 18	—
69.7	Weedon	67	68 36	84	68 59	72
75.3	Welton		72 44	75	73 39	70/68
80.3	Hillmorton		76 38	81	77 47	77
82.6	Rugby	80	79 38	—	81 03	—

Net time:76½min   Net time: 74½ min

In June 1957 a new express was put into service between Euston and Glasgow. The up train left Glasgow at 8.30 and reached Euston in 6hr 40min, or at an average speed of 60.2mph, and the return journey began at 16.40. The time to Carlisle was 291min for the 299.7 miles against the 283min of the pre-war 'Coronation Scot'. The 1957 train was named the 'Caledonian' and was limited to eight bogies, seating 84 first-class and 120 second-class passengers, it weighing 265 tons tare or 275 tons gross. It proved to be a much more exciting train than the pre-war 6½hr service to Glasgow.

If the road was clear and there was no need for time recovery the 'Caledonian' was easy enough for a 'Duchess'. There have already been runs described in this chapter where the 'Caledonian' schedule was equalled or surpassed with over 500 tons over quite long sections of the road. There were other occasions when exceptional running was made by 'Duchesses' with their eight-coach loads. There appears to have been more occasions recorded when fast running for time recovery took place than ever was the case with the pre-war 'Coronation Scot'. In ordinary service there were such feats as topping Grayrigg Bank at 66½mph with 275 tons, Shap Summit at 60mph with 295 tons and Beattock Bank in the northbound direction at 54mph, which was all the more creditable in that the approach was balked and speed was only 63mph at Beattock station as compared with 80mph with which No 6201 approached the bank in November 1937. The 'Duchess' needed more hp than the 'Princess' on test in pre-war days and in the southbound direction Beattock Summit was passed on one run at 75mph compared with 67 by the 'Princess'. These were all excellent performances even for large locomotives with light loads and in some cases short bursts of up to 3000ihp were needed.

The most exciting occasion of all was on 5 September 1957, when the up 'Caledonian' reached Euston 37min early. The tragedy is that no experienced recorder had been invited to take detailed timings, but a sound reconstruction of the events of the day was made by D. H. Landau after extensive enquiries. Mr Landau's findings were published in the *1971 Trains Annual* (Ian Allan Ltd) and repeated in the June 1974 *SLS Journal*. We are grateful for permission to quote from this and a skeleton log is possible.

The greatest interest centres on the Crewe-Euston time of 118min pass to stop for the 158.1 miles. This compares with the start-to-stop time of 119min by No 6220 *Coronation* in 1937. As far as Rugby there seems little difference, with perhaps a slight advantage to the 1937 run, but after Bletchley the 1957 engine was given a real run up to Tring. It had long been an LMR legend that the late Laurie Earl once ran from passing Bletchley to Tring Summit in 9½min; the more gullible even claimed 8min, which is probably beyond the latest electrics and will have to await the Advanced Passenger Train! Driver Starvis had never run this stretch in under 10min and the fastest run actually recorded was 10min 13sec by No 6220 *Coronation* in 1937. The actual time by No 46244 in 1957 was 9min 40sec. This gives an average speed of 93.3mph for the 15 miles Bletchley to Tring. In Driver Starvis's own words: "After 80 through the Wolverton slack we were up to about 88 through Bletchley and over 90 by Leighton, then we opened her out a bit and went over the top without falling below 90". The time of 9min 40seconds accords with a speed of 91 or 92 at the summit. This suggests an ihp of around 2750, which is within the sustained steaming capacity of a 'Duchess'. Just what uphill or downhill possibilities there would have been with a short burst of over 3000ihp with a 275ton load remains a matter for conjecture.

The run from Carlisle to Euston, 299.1 miles in an actual 253min, represented an average of 70.8mph, the net time of 242min a start-to-stop average of 74mph. The passing times from Roade to Willesden, 54.5 miles, meant an average of 92mph compared with No 6220 in

The 'Caledonian,' 5 September, 1957

Engine: No 46244 *King George VI.*
Driver: W. Starvis, *Fireman:* J. Tumilty, Camden Shed.
Load: 8 cars, 265/275 tons.

Distance Miles		Schedule min	Actual min sec	
0.0	Carlisle	0	00	00
12.80	Plumpton	18	13	00
	sig stand 3min			
17.90	Penrith	21	21	00
31.40	Shap Summit	39	35	00
	Sigs Scout Green			
37.00	Tebay	45	40	00
50.00	Carnforth	57	51	30
62.80	Carnforth	68	60	00
	pws			
69.10	Lancaster	73	68	00
80.70	Garstang	83	77	00
90.10	Preston	93	84	30
105.20	Wigan	114	101	30
117.00	Warrington	126	112	00
	Sigs Norton Crossing			
124.80	Weaver Junction	133	121	00
141.00	Crewe	148	135	00
151.40	Whitmore	160	145	00
160.10	Norton Bridge	167	151	00
165.40	Stafford	172	155	00
174.70	Rugeley	181	163	00
189.00	Tamworth	193	172	30
201.90	Nuneaton	205	181	30
216.40	Rugby	219	193	00
239.10	Roade	238	210	15
252.30	Bletchley	249	219	00
267.30	Tring	262	228	40
281.50	Watford	273	238	00
293.60	Willesden	283	245	45
299.10	Euston	291	253	00

Net time: 242 min

1937 averaging 89.3mph. Driver Starvis said that No 46244 was the pick of a good bunch of 'Duchesses'; the weather was favourable and the coal good but not the best. It is doubtful if the coal was of the same superlative quality as the Grimethorpe coal used by No 6220 in 1937, but the steaming of No 46244 was assisted by the double chimney. Any engine working through from Glasgow had to be handled with care. The driver thought that on a shorter run the Crewe-Euston time could have been cut to 115min and with the improved signalling that accompanied electrification to slightly less. While such times are a tribute to the prowess of a well-handled 'Duchess' with a light load, it must be remembered that times of this

148

nature are now the daily schedule with heavier loads. Even this excellent high speed run did not satisfy everyone, as before the 'Caledonian' drew up in Euston station, 37min ahead of time, one passenger opened his door, jumped out and sprinted towards the Underground with a withering sideways look at the offending engine crew as he passed the footplate. His reactions to a late arrival defy imagination!

The 'Duchess' class did some good running on occasion on lines other than the actual West Coast Route. Some sleeping car trains were routed via the Glasgow and South Western "Long Road" between Carlisle and Glasgow. Although this did not involve a bank as long as Beattock, the southbound trains had to climb through the Barrhead Gap with Neilston Bank, 3½ miles of 1 in 67-70, while northbound trains had to surmount 1½ miles of 1 in 87 then, after a brief intermission of easier grading, 1¾ miles of 1 in 75. Between Dumfries and Kilmarnock there are gradients of 1 in 200 and 1 in 150, and northbound trains have to climb a continuous 6 miles of 1 in 150; those going south have to face 4½ miles at 1 in 100 or thereabouts soon after starting from Kilmarnock. Such a road is no place for weak engines when loads reach 500 tons or over. On the evidence of logs recorded by D. S. M. Barrie and those published by Cecil J. Allen the 'Duchesses' could work loads of from 500 to 550 tons over the 58 miles between Dumfries and Kilmarnock in 60-62min start to stop in either direction and climb through the Barrhead Gap at minimum speeds of around 30mph. One of the best runs was by No 46249 *City of Sheffield*, which followed a net time of 61½min from Dumfries to Kilmarnock with 555 tons with a minimum speed of 36mph on the climb to mp 17 and a net time of 33min for the 24.15 miles from Kilmarnock to Glasgow.

It should not be assumed that all 'Duchess' running was at the same high level. Cecil J. Allen had the sad task of giving details in *Trains Illustrated* of a number of occasions when deplorable running over a clear road made late running trains later still. Of course all engines were not always in good condition, but on some of these runs the gradients were descended more slowly than gravity alone would have moved the train. On the other hand Norman Harvey has published a run by No 46252 *City of Leicester* in bad condition and shy for steam in 1950 when schedules had not regained their pre-war standards. Some crews would have lost time heavily, but Frank Brooker, who drove the 'Royal Scot' class engines in the 1948 Exchanges, made a 525ton load seem like light work by gaining 11min on an easy booking of 181min to Crewe. There was no hard running, but an even pace was maintained over the gentle ups and downs.

The rate of failure on the road by the 'Duchesses' was very low and loads on the former LNWR were probably the heaviest in Britain in the 1950s. The 19.20 down in 1953, for example, frequently had vehicles added at Bletchley, bringing the load at times up to 21 vehicles or 650 tons tare, yet no time was booked against the engine on a relatively easy booking. Despite the excellent work performed on individual runs we cannot help wondering how the 'Duchesses' would have performed had they been owned by the SNCF and been run with regular crews and the incentive of timekeeping bonuses.

In the 1960s 'Duchess' class engines were used on a number of occasions on enthusiasts' rail tours over a variety of routes. On one of these, "The Borders Rail Tour" organised by the RCTS in July 1961, No 46247 *City of Liverpool* was provided to work a load of 365 gross tons over the Midland Leeds-Carlisle route over Ais Gill. This line had seen many epic performances by a variety of locomotives, but No 46247 proved to be the most potent of them all and set up the record time for steam. The comparable position is shown as follows:

Settle Junction to Blea Moor (13.9 miles, average grade 1 in 111)						
Class	No	Time min	Av speed mph	edbhp	ihp	ihp/ engine wt
MR 990 4-4-0	998	22.0	37.9	860	1010	17.3
LNWR 'Prince' 4-6-0	388	21.9	38.0	900	1070	16.1
Compound 4-4-0	1008	20.75	40.2	975	1155	18.75
'Jubilee' 4-6-0	5660	16.33	51.0	1155	1675	21.1
ER A4 4-6-2	60019	14.4	57.9	1850	2320	22.3
'Duchess' 4-6-2	46247	14.12	59.0	1970	2435	23.2

Those of us who rode on this train find that the memory of the crisp clear beat of *City of Liverpool* echoing back from the fells helps us to relive the great days of steam.

'Duchesses' found their way on to the Great Central main line and the East Coast line from Kings Cross to Doncaster and one made a fast run, though with a light load, over the GWR Birmingham to Paddington route. Time was, however, running out for steam as the 1960s ran their course, though there were a number of occasions when diesels failed and had to be replaced by 'Duchesses' at short notice, especially over the Crewe-Carlisle section. On some of these occasions notable runs took place, but much of the everyday work of the remaining Pacifics was on secondary services such as parcels trains. A suggestion was made that a number of 'Duchesses' should be transferred to the Southern Region to reinforce their Pacifics, but restricted clearances in the Southampton area prevented this.

It was, however, with something of a shock that it was learnt that the remaining 'Duchesses' were all to be withdrawn in September 1964 and that the RCTS Special "The Scottish Lowlander", run on 26 September, was to be the last run of a Stanier Pacific. Appropriately No 46256 *Sir William A Stanier F.R.S.* was chosen to work the

12-coach train of 416 tons tare, 450 tons gross from Crewe to Carlisle and back. The engine ran smartly on the short runs from Crewe to Warrington and Preston, which was a good omen for the sterner tasks that lay ahead. From Preston the start was brisk and 74mph was reached at Brock, but thoughts were centred on the road beyond Lancaster and as the hills loomed ahead excitement grew in the train. Would the last run of a Stanier Pacific be worthy of the epics of the past — by *Hardwicke, Ralph Brocklebank,* and *Duchess of Abercorn?*

A signal stop before Carnforth was not encouraging but speed was quickly regained and Grayrigg Bank was climbed at a sound but not exceptional 42mph. Then just as speed was picking up for a run at Shap the sickening feel of brakes caused dismay. Were we stopping for a banker from Tebay? The cause turned out to be a pw slack near mp 29. It only served to inspire Driver Johnson and Fireman White of Preston to an exceptional performance. The engine was immediately put hard at it and the effort was continued to the summit. Tebay was passed at 60mph and this increased on the 1 in 146 to Tebay North IBS to 61mph, which involved an estimated edbhp of 2400 and an ihp of 2800-2900 for a short time. The summit was passed in 6¾min from Tebay at a minimum speed of 38mph. Such a climb was worthy of a 'Duchess' at its best. The descent to Carlisle was delayed and restrained, but the net time of 90½min for the 90.1 miles over Shap from Preston to Carlisle with 450 tons was excellent. Many of us logged the train

---

Preston-Carlisle, 26 September 1964
Engine: No 46256 *Sir William A. Stanier, FRS.*
Load: 416/450 tons.
Driver: Johnson. *Fireman:* White (Preston Shed).

Distance miles		Sched min	Actual min sec	Speeds mph
00.00	Preston	0	00 00	—
9.5	Garstang	13	11 47	74/70
			sigs	
21.0	Lancaster	23	23 05	20
24.9			sig stop	
27.3	Carnforth	28	32 04	55/62
34.5	Milnthorpe		39 04	72
40.1	Oxenholme	43	44 36	52/54
47.1	Grayrigg		53 29	42min
50.5	MP 29 ½		pws	25
53.1	Tebay	59	61 27	60
54.5	Tebay North IBS		62 49	61
56.1	Scout Green Crossing		64 38	48
58.7	Shap Summit	69	68 14	38min
			sig stops	
90.1	Carlisle	104	108 56	

Net time: 90 ¼ min

that day, but the log overleaf is a condensed extract of the timings of H. G. Ellison, a most experienced recorder with a long association with this route.

"The Scottish Lowlander" continued its journey behind the Gresley A4 No 60007 *Sir Nigel Gresley*, but this lies outside the West Coast story. Some hours later the train arrived back in Carlisle behind A4 No 60009 *Union of South Africa* to find No 46256 *Sir William A. Stanier F.R.S.* waiting to make its last run over Shap. Finally, 12min late, we set off into the dark rainy night. The initial start was slow, but as the engine warmed up resolute hill climbing followed and a net time of 38¾min to Shap Summit with 450 tons was of comparable quality to the best efforts of the 'Duchesses' a few years earlier. Five of the lost minutes had been recovered and with falling grades ahead a punctual arrival at Preston and Crewe seemed probable. Alas this did not happen and the West Coast route presented the picture which was so familiar in the post-war world. A series of operating mishaps, culminating in a defective tail lamp at Wigan, put the special 40min late into Crewe. Perhaps this was symbolic, for now that the story can be written in historical perspective it has to be recorded that rarely indeed had operating efficiency matched the proven capacity of these great engines.

There was evidence enough that the maximum power of the engine was still there and the final run was a notable effort. No 46256 ran into Crewe, its fire was dropped and it never moved again until it went for scrap with, so it is rumoured, the rail tour reporting number still in place. So these great Stanier engines passed from the scene.

CHAPTER THIRTEEN

Other Pacifics on the
West Coast Route

After nationalisation locomotives from other Regions appeared more frequently on the West Coast route and the former LMS engines were reinforced by the standard locomotives built by the new owners. These were not West Coast Pacifics in the true meaning of the word, but three classes of Pacific were used over the former LNWR and Caledonian main lines and there is little doubt that the demands of the northern banks were in the minds of the designers when these engines were built. The 1948 Exchanges had shown that claims that only the engines actually designed for a certain route had any hope of performing well on their own metals were exaggerated, and that there would be occasions when the former boundaries could well be ignored. In 1950 there was a certain amount of experimental running of former LNER Pacifics over the Caledonian route from Glasgow to Carlisle. These engines were of the A4 and Peppercorn A1 classes and they were used on heavy sleeping car trains. Little has emerged as to how the A4 performed, but the A1 No 60161, as yet un-named, was recorded on one occasion. A contemporary proposal to use 'Duchesses' between Edinburgh and Newcastle was not put into practice.

The Gresley Pacifics had been designed for high-class performance in pre-war conditions, while the Thompson and Peppercorn Pacifics had not been intended to push the A4 standards of speed and power any higher, but rather to make these standards available under conditions of fuel and maintenance which were more exacting. The A1s proved to be the best of the post-Gresley Pacifics. They gave excellent mileage figures with low maintenance costs, but they were unpopular for their rough riding.

No 60161 had to take over a 14-coach sleeping car train weighing 500 tons tare and 525 tons full. The engine change was made outside Kingmoor shed and on gradients similar to those over the GNR main line the A1 passed Beattock, 37.7, miles in a very good time of 42min 5sec. This was much like the time which would have been expected of a good-steaming 'Duchess'. Beattock was passed at full speed and the bank was taken unassisted. The climb took 24min 10sec for the 10 miles with speeds of from 18 to 24mph. This latter time was not equal to a 'Duchess' at anywhere near its best, but many climbs by unassisted 'Duchesses' were no faster. We do not know if the A1 had been threatened by slipping, but the atmospheric conditions on Beattock Bank in the small hours were rarely favourable. One distinct advantage in favour of the A1 design was its 5000gall tender, which reduced anxiety that water would last out compared with the 4000gall tender of a 'Duchess'.

During the years 1951-53 A1s Nos 60152/60/1 had spells on loan to Polmadie Shed and they worked on the West Coast Main line as far as Carlisle on the 21.25 up sleeping car train, returning on the 3.34 down. Another was used on the lodging turn which involved taking the Up Postal to Crewe and returning on the Birmingham-Glasgow. A run on this train was published by Cecil J. Allen in 1952. No 60161, by then named *North British*, was at the head of a 12-coach load of 387 tons tare, 420 tons gross. The running was well up to average 'Duchess' standards and Beattock was passed in an actual time of 40min 50 sec or in 39½min net for the 39.7 miles, but the train in front, which had already caused some delay before Beattock, was not stowed away until Greskine by which time the A1 had been brought to a dead stand on the bank. When finally given the road *North British* started away up 1 in 79/74 with speed rising to 23mph at Greskine, 28 at Harthope and finally to 30mph at the summit. This very good effort was timed by W. Robertson, a very experienced recorder over this section.

The year 1951 also saw the first appearance of a standard BR Pacific on the West Coast Route, when No 70000 *Britannia* ran its initial test run from Crewe to Carlisle. The BR standard designs were intended to incorporate the best, fully-proven features of the Regional types, with emphasis on reliability and ease of maintenance rather than the ultimate in thermodynamic refinement. This was a movement towards American practice and away from the French compounds with their complication, superlative performance and economy but moderate mileage. The BR engines were to have two cylinders only, except in the case of the Class 8 Pacific, which was in any case deferred until some undefined date in the future. This conception was also broadly in line with the German pre-war standard range and certain German features were undoubtedly followed.

Emphasis was placed on a robust frame design. At first bar frames were considered for the larger engines, but although certain advantages were undoubtedly obtainable by their use, the difficulties likely to be caused by having to adapt the railway workshops to so revolutionary a change caused this idea to be abandoned. The best type of plate frames were adopted with the aim of obtaining freedom from cracking and fatigue, and to this end frames 1¼in thick with substantial cross-bracing were used. The use of two cylinders allowed space for the cross-bracing.

Like Bulleid's 'Merchant Navy' class Pacifics, the BR Pacifics had frames placed on the centre line of the axleboxes. This reduced offset

154

forces and the axleboxes had all-welded hornguides. Despite this there was a certain amount of trouble with the hornstays and spring attachments. This was probably made worse by the rather stiff springing adopted and the engines turned out to be rather hard riders. Compensated springing with equalizing bars which might have reduced the tendency of the Pacifics to slip was not used.

Roller-bearing axleboxes were fitted to the first batch of Class 7 Pacifics, but later, for comparative purposes, five were built with plain bearings for the leading and trailing coupled axleboxes, with roller bearings only on the drivers; later a further ten had plain bearings for all coupled axles. No significant difference in bearing performance was discernable. The axles were hollow-bored to compensate for the extra weight of the cannon boxes and this at first caused trouble with wheels moving on the axles due to insufficient interference fit. This aroused quite a stir in engineering circles causing elastic theory to be reconsidered; however, it was subsequently shown that the original fits were correct, but that manufacturing errors had occured. Nevertheless, it was deemed prudent to plug the ends of the hollow axles. The saving in weight was in any event marginal.

The first standard Pacific was the Class 7 type designed to undertake the duties given on the LMR to the 'Royal Scot' class 4-6-0, on the E and NE Regions to the V2 class 2-6-2s, on the WR to the 'Castle' class 4-6-0s and on the SR to the 'West Country' class Pacifics. The first was No 70000, which was named *Britannia*, giving its name to the class. The new Pacific had an amply-sized boiler with a grate area of 42sq ft and a free area almost as great as a 'Duchess' at 6.79 sq ft. For the first time on a Crewe-built Pacific there were adequately-sized superheater flues of 5½in diameter, which gave good A/S ratios in accordance with Wagner's rules, although Schmidt elements were used. On test adequate steam temperatures were attained. The ashpan was similar to that of Bulleid's 'Merchant Navy' with overhanging side hoppers, but with dampers at the front only. It was subsequently felt that provision for a rear air entry would have been an advantage at the highest steaming rates.

The cylinder design gave good clean valve events with 11in piston valves and 20in by 28in cylinders. The clearance volume was 10.3% and no exhaust clearance was necessary. A single blastpipe and chimney was fitted with a plain 5⅜in diameter blastpipe cap. The engine was thus deliberately restricted in its front-end limit with the aim of fitting it to the range of economic working. It was also fully in accordance with the general policy of the post-war period in that the ultimate in thermodynamic performance was not being sought.

The reciprocating balance was fixed first at 40% later at 50%, this being considered to be a good compromise between hammer blow and horizontal forces for a 94ton engine. There was, however, early trouble with drawbar hunting, which was subsequently cured with modified drawbar springs. Another early trouble was water carry-over from the dome, which was very low, making it difficult to provide a high steam collecting space. The regulator was of the multi-valve type positioned in the superheater header. A modified steam separator was fitted later.

In service the 'Britannia' class Pacifics had a mixed reception. The engine crews of the former GER section took to them most readily and the best work recorded by the class was on the GER and the Midland. The Midland men never thought them better than the 'Royal Scots'. They had the worst reception on the WR, whose men always had great pride in the products of Swindon. On the West Coast Route they had to face the standards established by the Stanier Pacifics and it was unreasonable to expect a Class 7 Pacific to rival a Class 8 'Duchess'. However, a number of good performances were recorded over LNWR and Caledonian lines.

On 12 January 1951, only ten days after completion, painted in temporary black while awaiting a final decision as to livery, No 70000 set off from Crewe with a train of empty stock with the dynamometer car weighing 442 tons tare. The booking was an easy 174min for the 141.5 miles, but it was intended to run hard up to Shap. The time of 35min 5sec from passing Carnforth to topping Shap Summit was comparable with the uphill running expected of the 'Princess' class engines in 1936, when the 'Mid-Day Scot' had such a hard schedule. The 'Princesses' usually took a load similar to the 442 tons tare of the 'Britannia', but at times they equalled this time with over 500 tons. No 70000 was, however, opened up rather more on the Tebay to Shap Summit section, where its time of 7min 5sec was almost exactly the same as that of No 6200 *The Princess Royal* on test in June 1935 with 460 tons. The 'Britannia', however, needed to be opened out more on the upper part of the bank as its speed at the foot was lower than that of the 'Princess'. The 'Britannia', with its smaller cylinder volume, had to be given longer cut-offs than the 'Princess' to achieve much the same hp and before the summit No 70000 was working at 50% with full regulator. The highest equivalent dbhp was 1870, corresponding at this relatively moderate speed to 2100ihp.

Some allowance had to be made for the fact that the 1935 test train of No 6200 consisted of 20 vehicles, including some light stock. This

Tebay-Shap Summit (5.5 miles)

Date	Locomotive	Load tons	Time	Speed at Tebay mph	Speed at Summit mph
6/35	No 6200	461/465	7min	69	35
1/51	No 70000	442/445	7min 5sec	64	36

would give a higher running resistance for the same weight than the train hauled by No 70000. On the climb, however, most of the hp would be used to overcome gravity and running resistance would only form a small percentage of the total power output. Although *Britannia* had been worked on long cut-offs at times on this run, such working was only of short duration and 38lb/mile and 3.26lb/dbhp/hr were very good figures over such a road; they were comparable with what might have been expected of any first-class British express engine tested in the same way at that time. It was a promising start for the new design.

South of Crewe the 'Britannias' took over some of the Class 7 duties, sharing the work with the 'Royal Scot' class 4-6-0s with roughly equal competence. These included the Manchester expresses routed via Stoke, such as the down 'Comet', which had an XL timing. The time to Stoke-on-Trent, 145.9 miles from Euston, was 146min and the intermediate bookings from Easton to the point where the Stoke line branched off at Colwich were similar to those of the down 'Lancastrian', 'Royal Scot' and 'Mid-day Scot', on which the 'Duchesses' were allowed 510tons tare. The Class 7 engines of the 'Britannia', the 'Royal Scot' or the rebuilt 'Patriot' classes were allowed 405 tons.

A journey on the down 'Comet' was timed by W. O. Knight and was published by Cecil J. Allen in his book *British Pacific Locomotives* (Ian Allan 1962). The Longsight engine No 70031 *Bryon* had a 12-coach load weighing 379 tons tare, 400 tons gross, and with it gained easily on schedule. The running was very similar to that of a 'Duchess' at its best on the down 'Lancastrian', although with 100 tons less. Tring summit was passed at 63½mph and a maximum of 84mph was reached near Cheddington, while Roade was topped at 67½mph. At Polesworth speed rose to 82mph and the minimum above Lichfield was 66mph. The main line was left at Colwich with the train 5min before time after a 25mph pws near Rugby. Had the train had a clear run in, Stoke would have been reached in 139½min, or in 138min allowing for the slack pw work near Rugby. Smart work continued on the short runs to Macclesfield, Stockport and Manchester. The 'Britannia' had shown its ability to reach Manchester by this route in three hours from Euston had the run been non-stop.

When the 'Duchesses' were all withdrawn in September 1964 — some thought inadvisedly — the 'Britannias' had often to deputise for failed diesels over the northern banks. Some times they were not able to manage and this added point to the arguments of those critics who though the withdrawal of the 'Duchesses' was premature. There were, on the other hand, a number of occasions when the loads were light when the Class 7 Pacifics showed their ability to gain on the 'Caledonian' schedule with 275ton loads. It is perhaps fair to say that, although the 'Britannias' ran very well on the West Coast route, they

157

showed no clear advantage in times and speeds over the 'Royal Scots' and the rebuilt 'Patriots', which were exceptionally efficient 4-6-0s. The Pacifics probably had an advantage in maintenance costs.

The Class 6 Pacifics were less successful. They were virtually identical with the 'Britannias' except for having a smaller boiler with a grate area of 36sq ft and a lower working pressure of 225lb against 250lb. A 35-element superheater was fitted instead of 40 elements, again with the same 5½in flues and barrel length. The result of this smaller boiler was a reduction in adhesion weight, which, was not an asset for a Pacific. The cylinders were reduced to 19½in in diameter and this, combined with the lower pressure, reduced the tractive effort from 32150lb for the 'Britannias' to 27520lb. The clearance volume was somewhat greater than that of the Class 7 Pacifics with the same valve settings and sizes and the optimum speed range was 45-90mph, making them perhaps more suited to fast express work with moderate loads than to hard mixed traffic duties. This was a quality shared by the Bulleid 'West Country' class Pacifics, which had perhaps been the inspiration of this design. The excellent performance of the Bulleid 'West Country' Pacific over the Highland main line in the 1948 Exchanges had suggested a Pacific for heavily-graded routes with restricted axle loadings. The fact that the Class 6 Pacifics were named after Scottish Clans suggests an original hope that they might be used on the Highland.

In actual fact they were never in regular service over the Perth-Inverness road and were allocated to Kingmoor and Polmadie, except for short periods on loan to other sheds, such as for experimental running on the Liverpool Street-Clacton-on-Sea services. They never seemed to have the strength of an effective mixed traffic engine and never surpassed the best efforts of the Stanier 'Black Five' 4-6-0-s, let alone the 'Jubilee' Class 6 engines. It would be hard to imagine a 'Clan' climbing Ais Gill in the manner of the 'Jubilee' class engine No 5660 *Rooke* on test in 1937, when ihps in the region of 1800 were attained. The turn for a 'Clan' to visit the Rugby test plant never came, but doubtless had one done so there would have been much scope for improved performance. No re-draughting at the Plant would, however, have altered the basic disadvantage of a Pacific as compared with a 4-6-0 for secondary duties. The adhesion weight of a 'Clan' was no better than that of a 'Black Five' and less than that of a 'Jubilee', while added to this 4-6-0s usually kept their feet better than Pacifics. It is the considered opinion of the writers of this book that, as claimed in our earlier books about 4-6-0 locomotives, the 4-6-0 had much to commend it for mixed traffic work.

In the original plan a design for a Class 5 Pacific was seriously considered, but this was later abandoned in favour of the 73000 class 4-6-0 based on the Stanier 'Black Five'. The success of the Bulleid 'West Country' class Pacific in high-speed running on moderate grades is well-known and a matter of historical record, but it is also true that their everyday running over the very steep banks of the S&DJR was a disappointment. When the weather was favourable and the engine in good form, then a 'West Country' could outclass a 'Black Five', but their record of slipping in bad weather was such that official load limits had to be fixed at the same figure for both types. Similar difficulties faced the 'Clans', which were used on secondary trains over the Stranraer line and on parcels and fish trains south from Perth. They came south over Shap on trains to Manchester and Liverpool and at times visited Leeds. One was once sent from Leeds up to St Pancras, but they never took on regular duties over the Midland main line. Despite their mediocre performance they were popular with engine crews. Many of the Kingmoor men preferred them to the 'Britannias', considering them lighter on coal and water and more comfortable to ride. Their more languid movements doubtless set up fewer stresses.

The most interesting engine in the standard range was very nearly never built. This was the Class 8 heavy Pacific to reinforce the 'Duchesses'. In the original plan this engine would have been based on a 'Duchess', but would have had bar frames, a larger ashpan and tender and a number of standard fittings. Possibly it would have had the larger 5½in superheater flues, which might have raised the steam temperature that was something of a disappointment with the Duchesses. The eight-wheeled tender, with its 5000gall of water, would have given this modified 'Duchess' a distinct advantage, especially if the standard Class 8 Pacifics had been used on other railways with water troughs further apart than those of the former LNWR. At the time the standard range of locomotives was being prepared the Class 8 was the design for which there was the least immediate need. There is little doubt that the modified 'Duchess' would have been a success and many will regret its failure to appear.

There were however other forces at work and other ideas as to the form of the ideal Class 8 Pacific. The ruling spirit behind one alternative design was J. F. Harrison, who had been one of the more promising young men trained by the late Sir Nigel Gresley. This Pacific was an alternative to the modified 'Duchess' and would have been an amalgam of many of the best features of Doncaster and Eastleigh practice under Bulleid. Instead of four cylinders and divided drive, as in the 'Duchess', the proposed Pacific would have had three cylinders all driving the middle coupled axle. The boiler was to be based on that of the Bulleid Pacifics, which had proven itself to be a prolific steam-raiser. The Bulleid motion enclosed in its oil bath would have been replaced by a more simple three-cylinder arrangement which anticipated the rebuilt Bulleid Pacifics that were to appear four years later. This engine, like the modified 'Duchess', might well have been an excellent performer on the road.

It was the result of a sad accident that a Class 8 Pacific was built at all. In October 1952 the terrible Harrow disaster destroyed the LMR Pacific No 46202 *Princess Anne* rebuilt from the Turbomotive. It was possible to build another Pacific as a replacement. So it was that, instead of a modified 'Duchess', or a three-cylinder Pacific of Gresley ancestry, the last Class 8 Pacific was developed as an enlarged 'Britannia'. The 'Britannia' boiler was enlarged by fitting a 48sq ft grate, but was otherwise unaltered, and the ashpan was given a rear damper in the centre section as a concession to the larger grate.

Three cylinders were accepted of necessity as two cylinders large enough could not be accommodated within our restricted loading gauge. The problem of the inside valve gear was neatly solved by using British Caprotti valve gear which was, at that time, giving some promising results on BR Class 5 4-6-0s of the 73000 class. A very robust inside big end was provided and this was intended to put an end once and for all to the trouble which had beset earlier three-cylinders locomotives. The same 6ft 2in driving wheel diameter as on the Class 6 and 7 Pacifics was accepted and with the free running characteristics of Caprotti gear and the results in service of 6ft 2in Pacifics on the Eastern and Southern regions, could be expected to allow of the highest speeds that the track would permit.

The aim of the design was not primarily to increase the power and speed capacity of the 'Duchess' class. Practical professional locomotive engineers realised that, with 66 tons of adhesion weight, the same basic limit would affect the new BR Class 8 as affected the best of the Regional Pacifics. The aim was rather the attainment of the best 'Duchess' standards with more consistency and with slightly lower fuel and maintenance costs. These aims, it is sad to say, were never realised, though there was some evidence that history should record a near miss rather than a failure.

The one and only BR Class 8 Pacific No 71000 was named *Duke of Gloucester* to commemorate the Duke's Honorary Presidency of the Sixteenth Railway Congress in May 1954. Whether this fashion of naming would have continued is not known as no more were ever built. The new engine was allocated to Crewe North Shed and it was understood that in course of time it would be transferred to Camden to replace the ill-fated *Princess Anne*. Had this been so we might have seen how it would have performed on the exacting booking of the down 'Lancastrian', but in actual fact it stayed at Crewe. We do have evidence of its behaviour on XL bookings from a number of recordings on the down 'Mid-day Scot', which was always worked by a Crewe engine.

It is well known now that the results in service were disappointing. The recorder in the train, with his stop-watch, noted no improvement on 'Duchess' standards of running and equality was rare. The fireman, with his shovel, felt no easing of his burden and if a special effort was made to extend No 71000 he was aware of an increase in coal consumption. The net result of this was that the new Pacific became a very unpopular member of the Crewe North stud. It was considered to be more comparable with the aging 'Princesses' than with the top-link 'Duchesses'. At first No 71000 worked over Shap and Beattock on the through working to Perth, but latterly it was restricted to the easier section south of Crewe. During the earlier period a few recordings were made over the northern banks, but nothing comparable with the best 'Duchess' standards emerged.

South of Crewe the engine was rather better, but the average of a random selection of runs timed by K. R. Phillips and his friends on the down 'Mid-day Scot' was a less than satisfactory record. The best run by No 71000 on this booking was published by Cecil J. Allen in 1956, when Rugby was reached in an actual time of 81min 42sec for the 82.6 miles or in a net time of 78½min. The load was 510 tons and the net time is close to the best average 'Duchess' time, though somewhat inferior to the best individual run. On another occasion when the recorder, R. I. Nelson, rode on the footplate of No 71000 hauling 485 tons gross, the cut-off positions were very low — down to 7-8% on the easier grades.

When the test results were published the story was made clear. The cylinder performance of No 71000 was excellent and much superior to that of the 'Duchess', but the boiler performance was poor and the superior steaming of the 'Duchess' more than redressed the balance. If it had been pointed out to a fireman, toiling hard with the shovel with little result, that the engine was showing a good steam per ihp/hr rate, then a cynical reply would follow with ample justification. The exact reason for the poor boiler performance of No 71000 has been the subject of much discussion but no final verdict has been reached. It was given extended consideration in an able article by D. H. Landau in the November 1974 issue of *Railway World*. This article was entitled 'The Fiery Duke' and the title was significant.

It appears that the trouble was associated with the problems inherent in the use of poppet valves on simple engines. High peak exhaust pressures were thought to cause high boiler combustion losses. Certainly the gun-shot blast of No 71000 was apparent to lineside photographers who sought out the engine and this inspired Mr Landau's title for his article of "The Fiery Duke". The test report showed that when the engine was working hard, 36% of the available energy was ejected up the chimney in the form of unburnt fuel. Similar trouble seems to have been experienced everywhere when poppet-valve gears were used at high steaming rates with simple engines; the table of test results in *World Steam in the 20th Century* by E. S. Cox (Ian Allan 1969) shows that exhaust pressure was a fantastic 25.9lb sq in at maximum output on the Pennsylvannia RR Class T1 4-4-4-4 type when tested on the Altoona Plant in 1942.

Earlier theories of rear-end vibration causing disintegration on the grate of No 71000 were discounted by tests at Swindon when the back end was tied down on the Plant. Despite the exceptional steam per indicated hp hr of 12.2lb, which was a British record, the figure at lower speeds within the normal operating range was no better nor worse than that of a piston-valve engine, such as a 'Britannia'.

One of the aims of the standard range of locomotives was lower repair costs. This seems to have been achieved in the case of the 'Britannia' and the 'Clan', but the Class 8 engine cost more than the 'Duchess', though as it was a single prototype rather than an established class the comparison may be unfair. No 71000 was built in 1954 and early in 1955 the Modernisation Plan was published forecasting the end of steam locomotive construction. While No 71000 was being designed there must have been stirrings of an anti-steam lobby. In 1956 the question of building more Class 8 Pacifics for the more important main-line services while diesel prototypes were being tested more fully was discussed, but the decision was made to press on with dieselisation and *Duke of Gloucester* remained a solitary engine. The wisdom of this policy has since been doubted and it is an interesting speculation as to whether further Class 8 Pacifics would have had Caprotti gear or whether the policy of Gresley, with his 2-8-2s of the *Cock o' the North* class, would have been followed, with the remainder of the class reverting to piston valves. Had this been done performance on the road by the BR Class 8s could have been expected to be very similar to that of the rebuilt Bulleid 'Merchant Navy' class Pacifics.

During the final few years of steam some interesting runs were made over the West Coast Route by Pacific locomotives from the other Regions on enthusiasts' specials. Many of these were organised by The Railway Correspondence & Travel Society, which is to be congratulated on the way it has left many of us with glorious memories of the prowess of steam. Several of these tours were ingeniously contrived so as to allow for the negotiation of Ais Gill and Shap Summits in the same trip.

On 30 June 1963 "The Three Summits Tour" included Beattock Summit as well, but behind one of the native 'Duchess' class engines, whereas the climb to Ais Gill and the return trip up to Shap were behind A4 class engine No 60023 *Golden Eagle*. The greatest interest was centred on the climb from Carlisle up to Shap Summit. The load was 10 bogies weighing 329 tons, tare, 360 tons full. Speed rose to 45mph on the initial 1 in 131 to Wreay and on the varied gradients to mp 53, which were between 1 in 228 and 1 in 114, the speed remained in the narrow limits of 57 to 58mph. Then, just as speed was rising to 68mph ready for a rush at the final climb, there was a dead stop before Penrith. Recovering from this speed rose to 54mph and then was held at an absolute minimum of 53mph on the 1 in 125 to the summit. This was not equal to some of the hps attained by 'Duchess' class Pacifics, but it was an exceptionally good effort for a visiting engine on a strange road.

On 13 June 1964 the RCTS ran "The Solway Ranger", which was hauled northwards over Shap and south over Ais Gill by the SR rebuilt Bulleid Pacific No 35012 *United States Lines*. The Bulleid Pacifics had an excellent boiler capable of much the same evaporation rate as a 'Duchess', but they were equally tricky as regards slipping. No 35012, however, showed that there were no terrors in the northern banks. The load was a comparatively light one of nine bogies — 303 tons tare, 325 tons gross — and from a dead stop at Carnforth speed rose to 65mph at Hincaster Junction before falling to 54½mph at Grayrigg Summit. The driver obviously had every intention of making a record time from Tebay to Shap Summit. Speed rose to 82mph before starting the climb and it was still as high as 60mph at Scout Green Box when the train was stopped for 3¼min. Had this not happened the summit would certainly have been topped at 50mph or over and one of the fastest ascents on record with steam would have resulted. The driver was Bert Hooker, who in the 1948 Exchanges had fired the SR 'West Country' class Pacific. His efforts with the shovel are still spoken of with respect by retired GCR and Highland locomotive men. He did very well on a strange road with "The Solway Ranger".

On 1 April 1967 the Gresley A4 class Pacific No 4498 *Sir Nigel Gresley* restored to blue livery was at the head of a 12-coach train weighing 424tons tare, 450 tons gross. It was not long before the traditional A4 capacity for fast running manifested itself as No 4498 reached 92 mph in 16 miles from a cold start. This was on a very slight down grade of 1 in 419 and there are no accurate records of such a speed ever having been attained at this spot by a 'Duchess' equally loaded, though of course this was largely a matter of opportunity. The last 'Duchess' had been withdrawn in 1964 and in 1967 the track had been improved for the electrics. Later in the journey No 4498 made a most competent climb to Shap with exactly the same minimum speed on Grayrigg Bank as the LMR Pacific *Sir William A. Stanier FRS* on its last run over Shap in 1964. Then followed almost exactly equal times from passing Tebay to the summit, but the A4 had passed Tebay at a higher speed than the 'Duchess', which had been delayed. The Stanier engine had reached the higher hp, but the A4 had made a notable run for a visitor. This trip had been organised by the A4 Preservation Society.

On 28 October 1967 No 4498 *Sir Nigel Gresley* ran once more from Crewe to Carlisle, this time on the RCTS special "The Border Limited". The start from Crewe was certainly a record for steam as a maximum of 96mph was recorded at the same spot as 92mph on the earlier occasion. The load, however, was less — 351 tons tare, 385 tons gross — as against 450 tons, so the merit was comparable. A real effort was made up to Shap with a time of 29min 58sec for the 31.4 miles and a rise of 887ft. Grayrigg Bank was topped at 52mph, but the real effort came between Tebay and the summit. This might have been even faster had there not been a speed restriction to 58mph near Low Gill, which meant that Tebay was passed at 73mph instead of over 80mph as was the case with the 'Merchant Navy' in 1964. The driver opened No 4498 out to — in his own words — "give the lads a good run" and the time of 5min 53sec was a record for such a load as 385 tons. The minimum speed at the summit was 47mph and the edbhp was 2090 for the final 4 miles. This would, of course, include a momentarary maximum rather higher, but the record hp of the Stanier Pacific No 6234 *Duchess of Abercorn* was not quite equalled. It was nonetheless an excellent effort for the smaller A4 and the crew, Driver B. Cadman and Fireman N. Stuart, deserve every credit. It is strange to reflect that one of the finest hill-climbing feats to the credit of the former LNER Pacific was performed by men from Crewe North Shed. The A4, after the manner of its breed, had proved to be very fast on the level.

There was a good deal of inter-Regional running in Scotland and there are photographs of A3 class Pacifics on the Caledonian main line between Glasgow and Carlisle. On 26 September 1964 the A4 No 60009 *Union of South Africa* had run in excellent fashion over the former G&SW route from Glasgow to Carlisle before handing its train over to No 46256 *Sir William A. Stanier FRS* for its final run over Shap. On 7 October 1966 a BR-sponsored excursion from Edinburgh to Carlisle and back was headed by the Peppercorn A2 class Pacific No 60532 *Blue Peter*. This train ran over the Waverley Route on the outer journey and returned over Beattock, where *Blue Peter*, with its eight-coach load of 280 gross tons, was pressing hard on the tail of a heavier diesel-hauled express and many signal checks followed. Up the 1 in 200 approaching Beattock *Blue Peter* was accelerating into the 70s when signals brought speed down to 52mph at the foot of the bank. Four miles further, when speed was sustained at a steady 46mph, another adverse signal brought it down to 38mph, when the road cleared and the A2 fought back to 45mph before the summit. The pass-to-pass time of 13min 37sec was very good in face of these difficulties. The Peppercorn A2s were similar to the A1s apart from their 6ft 2in driving wheels. The smaller wheels should in theory have made the A2s more effective on the banks than the A1s, with their 6ft 8in wheels, but in practice there was little difference as the limit was imposed by slipping before the engines were at their absolute maximum power outputs. The A2s have been timed at over 100mph despite their smaller wheels.

If the description "West Coast Route" is limited to London to Glasgow or Edinburgh, then there is little further to report of visiting Pacifics except to mention the RCTS "Moorland Tour" of 26 October

1968, which brought the preserved A3 Class Pacific No 4472 *Flying Scotsman* to the road over Shap. It is unfortunate that various delays balked the ascent, as there were indications that *Flying Scotsman* would otherwise have done very well. If, however, the route of the 1895 Race train right through to Aberdeen is considered as the West Coast Route, then some mention has to be made of the excellent running by A4 class engines on Glasgow-Aberdeen services during their final years.

The former Caledonian section men took very well to these Gresley engines and with light loads there was some very fast running, which included a start-to-stop time of 27min 28sec for the 32.5 miles Perth to Forfar with speeds rising to 89mph by No 60026 *Miles Beevor*, on 7 bogies weighing 265 tons gross. While no visiting Pacific beat a 'Duchess' on its own road, some did very well and a comparison of Pacifics is suggested.

CHAPTER FOURTEEN

Pacifics Compared

It has been said that comparisons are odious, but in the case of the steam locomotive it is difficult to see any better basis for assessment of merit than a comparison with other locomotives of about the same size. In absolute terms any steam locomotive was a wasteful user of fuel, but a designer who managed to build an engine of comparable efficiency to the best of his contemporaries achieved success. Comparisons must, however, be made on very qualified terms because our designers had to fit their engines to one of the more restricted loading gauges. A British Pacific can easily be compared with another engine in this country, but a comparison with a Continental Pacific has to be qualified by consideration of the restricted space into which it had to be fitted.

The Stanier Pacific, as first built, did not compare very favourably with the GWR 'King' or the LNER A3 class. It should have been better as it was slightly bigger, but in its original form it was a rather unreliable steamer. At its best it was perhaps roughly comparable with a GWR 'King', which had, to some extent, been the inspiration of the design; but the 'King' had a better and more consistent record in 1933/4. The 'King' was never intended to make a continuous run of 400 miles, such as was expected of the two original 'Princesses', but the latter were not performing this run with really conspicuous success in 1933/4. LNER A3 class Pacifics could have made the 400mile run easily enough, for they ran the 393 miles between Kings Cross and Edinburgh each summer with the non-stop 'Flying Scotsman'. The slightly larger LMS Pacific might have been expected to have been somewhat stronger on the banks had there been plenty of steam.

In terms of everyday running none of the British express engines of 1933 was equal to the continuous power outputs required of the French compound 'Super-Pacifics' of the Reseau du Nord, which were daily handling 550-650 ton trains on the Calais-Paris route. Even they were less potent in comparison with the rebuilt Paris-Orleans Pacifics, which were gaining daily in reputation with performances that made the name of Andre Chapelon famous in railroad circles all over the world. Even greater success attended the test-running of those PO Pacifics which had been rebuilt by Chapelon as 4-8-0s.

The improved boiler fitted to No 6200 in 1935 raised the Stanier

Pacific to new standards of running and in this form it was more than comparable with anything else in Britain. The average speed of 70.7mph with a 475ton train from Crewe to Euston and the climbs over the northern banks, achieved on test in June 1935, would not easily have been equalled either by a GWR 'King' or by an LNER A3 and this hard work was performed on a coal consumption, related to the work done, comparable with the best ever recorded up till then by any British express locomotive. In the summer of 1935, No 6200, with its improved boiler, was, with little doubt the best express locomotive in Britain, but in the autumn it was challenged in formidable fashion by the new Gresley A4 class Pacific, which promised to be its equal in power and efficiency and its superior in sustained and maximum speeds.

In its new form, capable of ihps of up to 2400-2500, the Stanier Pacific was approaching the standards of the Breville "Super-Pacifics" of the French Nord, but the later Collin Pacifics still had a distinct edge and the French compounds approached the standards of their best test running more frequently in everyday service. On test in 1933 the Collin Pacific No 3.1289 achieved short bursts of 1750-1800dbhp, which were roughly comparable with the edbhps achieved on test by No 6200 in 1935. It has been suggested that this particular Nord engine was rather less effective during the 1933 trials than other engines of the same class tested on other occasions, and it is certainly true that higher hps were recorded later when the Lemaitre multiple-jet exhaust was fitted.

The Chapelon Class 3722 4-6-2 of the Paris-Orleans Railway quite outclassed any British Pacific with its sustained edbhps of 2500. The British Pacifics regularly ran much higher annual mileages, with the 'Princesses' averaging 70,000 miles per annum before the war as against 46,500 miles for the Nord Pacifics. The French engines were, however, worked much harder for their size in everyday running than any British express engines of the 1930s.

When the new, larger Stanier Pacifics of the 'Duchess' class replaced the 'Princesses', higher standards were reached. After the double chimney had been fitted to No 6234 in 1939, it was possible, under test conditions, to reach edbhps of up to a maximum of 2800-2900 with ihps of over 3000 for 5-10min. This was approaching the best attained by the Chapelon Pacifics of Class 231E, which had been built for the Nord after the 1933 trials. It was, however, well below the sustained hps attained on test by the slightly larger compound Pacifics of P-O Class 231.722, which proved to be the most powerful Pacifics in Europe. One of these engines on the Vitry Test Plant ran for two solid hours with a rim hp of 3000 corresponding to an ihp of 3400. The best of British Pacifics only crossed the 3000ihp mark very briefly and very infrequently. The maximum sustained ihp for a 'Duchess' was 2900 and that was not kept up for two hours. But one aspect of

'Duchess' performance was a rather better ratio of drawbar to indicated hp, due partly to a lower specific running resistance and partly to a smaller and lighter tender.

There is no doubt at all that the French Chapelon compounds were more powerful and more thermally efficient than the 'Duchess' or any other British express locomotives, but that does not support a facile assumption that French design was inspired and British design was decadent. The designers had to face entirely different economic conditions and different climates of labour relations. The French compounds gave of their best when operated on the *Machine titulaire* system, with regular crews for each engine. The regular drivers were workshop-trained men of considerable knowledge, such as the famous *Mecanicien* Maillebuau, who took his annual holiday when his Pacific was away in Tours workshops so that he could follow it through and ensure by his presence an impeccable standard of repair. Added to this there was a system of timekeeping and economy bonuses which gave further encouragement to the skilled handling of complicated machines and achieving maximum efficiency. The French compounds were built to a more generous loading gauge and a few more inches of permitted width over the cylinders was a great help to the designer.

It is perhaps fair to consider France as one extreme and America as the other, with the British economic problems somewhere in between. In the United States mileage and availability were all-important, as the costs of labour were high and the distances were great. Wonderful power/weight ratios and wonderful fuel/dbhp/hr figures on test were of secondary importance to a rugged simplicity and a capacity to stand continuous hard work. In France labour costs, during the heyday of steam, were relatively low and the repair and maintenance costs of a complicated French compound, although higher than the corresponding costs for a British simple engine, were only about 60% of the fuel costs. It was essential for the French to seek the lowest possible fuel consumption. In the post-war world these conditions were changing and the proposed range of three cylinder compounds, which Chapelon would have built had there been no electrification, aimed at giving improved availability with little loss of thermal efficiency.

In some quarters there has been unfair criticism of British designers for their reluctance to build compounds on the Chapelon pattern, when a little thought should have convinced the critics that the solution to the British locomotive problem was to be found elsewhere. The restricted loading gauge made the building of British compounds on the Chapelon system difficult and the accompanying revolution in operating and maintenance methods would have been unacceptable. The French compounds should be honoured for their performance, but they did not point the way to the ideal British express locomotive. The simple engine was better for this country and a fairer comparison is that between a 'Duchess' and other simple express locomotives of the highest class. The most powerful simple 4-6-2 locomotive in Europe would appear to have been the two experimental S16 Class 4-6-2s of the Alsace-Lorraine Railway. These were slightly heavier than a 'Duchess' at 107 tons and they had a boiler pressure of 290lb/sq in and two cylinders with Caprotti valve gear. Had there been room within our loading gauge the BR engineers would doubtless have liked to build No 71000 with a similar two-cylinder layout. The S16 had a slight advantage over the 'Duchess' in power output, but this was obtained at a high cost in fuel and just like BR No 71000, the rate of coal consumption increased disproportionately as the engine was extended. The comparative figures for the Chapelon 231.722 Class compound, the S16 and the 'Duchess' are best tabulated:

	PO 231.722	AL S16	LMS 'Duchess'
Dbhp at 62mph	Welsh Coal lb/dbhp/hr	Sarre Coal lb/dbhp/hr	S. Kirkby Coal lb/dbhp/hr
1630	2.09	2.31	2.30
2400	2.24	2.90	2.80
2630	2.53	3.42	—

Uncorrected for calorific value of coal.

From the above figures it will be seen that the 'Duchess' compared reasonably well with the French simple locomotive, which had the advantage of a Kylchap exhaust and an ACFI feed water heater. The S16 showed the same characteristics as BR No 71000, with a falling-off in efficiency at the higher rates of working. The ascendency of the 231.722 is underlined, but neither of the French Pacifics would have fitted our loading gauge. Although the 231.722 was better at the drawbar than either of the simple engines, the specific locomotive running resistance was lower with the simples. In the case of the S16 the rigid bar frames may have helped by eliminating frame flexing. The proposed BR Class 8 based on a 'Duchess' would have had bar frames.

The German railway problems were similar to the British, but they normally worked their Pacifics for greater mileages than the British and for much greater annual mileages than the French. For many years it had not been their practice to run as hard, size for size, as was the custom in France, but for a few years leading up to the Second World War there was a period of high-speed running with diesel traction and with a few highly specialised steam locomotives, such as the 05 class streamlined 4-6-4s. The three-cylinder 01 class Pacifics, later fitted for oil firing and re-classified 012, were tested up to

350001b/hr and dbhps of just over 2000, which put them in a position better than a 'Princess' but slightly lower than a 'Duchess' at its best. Steam temperatures were, however, higher than those of the 'Duchess' and this was to be expected in view of the research carried out on superheating by German engineers from Schmidt to Wagner. The German contribution to locomotive science should not be underestimated.

The two experimental Pacifics turned out by Krupps in 1957 were the last high-speed steam locomotives built anywhere. Had steam continued they might well have been outstanding performers. They reached sustained evaporation rates of 39700lb/hr, which compares with 42000 for the 'Duchess', but the cylinder efficiency of the German Pacifics was greater and their sustained ihp of 3000 was slightly higher. The design of the steam passages had been submitted to Chapelon and some of his suggestions had been adopted while, uniquely for Germany, a double exhaust was fitted. The steam temperature was superior to that of the 'Duchess'. On test steam rates of 12.07lb/ihp/hr were attained by this piston-valve engine, which was very slightly better than the 12.2lb of the poppet-valve BR No 71000. The German Pacific was, however, very heavy with an engine weight of 113½ tons and a tender weighing 84½ tons. The superiority in cylinder performance, as compared with a 'Duchess', was to some extent used up before the horsepower reached the drawbar. The solid construction of the German Pacific almost certainly gave it an advantage in maintenance costs, though definitive figures are lacking. The Type 10s exceeded the 100000 miles-a-year target that LMR Nos 46256/7 failed to reach.

If the German Pacific seemed massive by comparison with the British and French engines it was delicate compared with its American equivalent. The classic 4-6-2 design in the US was the Pennsylvania Class K4S, which was first built as a hand-fired Pacific in 1914. In its original form the K4S reached ihps of up to 3200 on the Altoona Plant, which was less than that of the much lighter Chapelon 231.722 and was not all that much more than the figure for a 'Duchess'. But by the time these European Pacifics were running the K4S had been fitted with mechanical stoker and the Kiesel star-shaped blastpipe, and the ihp had climbed to 3530. In the 1940s experiments were made on No 5399 fitted with the Franklin poppet valves, and with this machine, ihps of over 4200, probably a world record for the Pacific type, were reached. These high hps were reached with steam/ihp/hr rates of around 17, while the piston-valve engines needed about 20lb/ihp/hr at maximum output. There were further experiments with steam-operated poppet valves on No 5436, but there was no move to convert the whole class. The Franklin poppet valves were used on the T1 class 4-4-4-4 Duplex locomotives, which gave impressive results on test, but which were something of a disappointment in everyday service. The K4S Pacific weighed 138 tons without its tender, but following American tradition it far surpassed the French and British Pacifics in availability and mileage.

The comparative position of the 'Duchess' and various foreign Pacifics is best shown in a table.

Locomotive	ihp	Engine weight
Pennsylvania K4S 2cyl simple FPV	4267 sustained	140.1 tons
Paris Orleans 231.722 4cyl comp. OCPV	3550 sustained	102.5 tons
Pennsylvania K4S 2cyl simple piston valves	3530 sustained	138 tons
Alsace Lorraine S16 2cyl simple CPV	3300 sustained	107.4 tons
German DB Type 10 3cyl simple piston valves	3000 sustained	113.5 tons
LMS 'Duchess' 4cyl simple piston valves	2910 sustained	105.3 tons

FPV: Franklin poppet valves. OCPV: Dabeg oscillating cam poppet valves. CPV: Caprotti poppet valves.

A comparison based on drawbar hps would have been more significant, but such a comparison would have been meaningless unless made at the same speed and the relevant dbhps for the above sustained ihps are not available in every case. The 'Duchess', thanks to a relatively light tender and to a low running resistance, had a ratio of dbhp to ihp which compared favourably with most Pacifics.

The true comparison by which the 'Duchesses' should be judged is not, however, with Pacifics built in other lands to different loading gauges and to face different economic conditions. The more valid comparison is with other British Pacifics of much the same size. There is no intention to boost the reputation of the West Coast Pacifics by denigrating others and it must be said at once that there were also excellent Pacifics on other British lines. No British express locomotive has a higher reputation, especially in the higher speed ranges, than the Gresley A4 class first introduced in 1935 and subsequently improved by the addition of the Kylchap double exhaust system. No A4 was given a full test on the Rugby or the Swindon Plants so a comparison has to be based on the more limited evidence of the 1948 Exchanges, the record of the A4 in ordinary service and some deductions made from the test report on the V2 2-6-2 tested at Swindon. The V2 had similar cylinders and valves.

If discussion is limited to established fact, the A4 was Britain's fastest steam locomotive. The maximum speed recorded behind an A4 was over 10mph more than Britain's next fastest. The next fastest was No 6220 *Coronation*, but its attempt was made on a stretch of line which had very limited space for a safe deceleration. There is little doubt that No 6220 could have travelled faster than its 113 or 114mph had it been tested where there was more space. It is unquestionable that *Mallard* was driven harder than *Coronation* with the confidence given by an excellent piece of road with ample space for slowing down. The trend of *Coronation's* acceleration curve, as far as it goes, supports the conclusion that a 'Coronation' class Pacific, especially one fitted with a double chimney, would have attained a speed very similar to that of *Mallard* had it been tested under similar conditions down Stoke Bank. Conjecture as to the exact figure knows no limit, but *Mallard's* record remains one of the established facts of British railway history.

A similar conclusion can be gained from a consideration of the more significant question of sustained high speeds. The average speed of 89mph for the 72 miles from Welton to Kilburn by *Coronation* in June 1937 called for an average ihp slightly less than that of A4 No 2509 averaging 91.8mph from Finsbury Park to Fletton in September 1935, but the average of 92mph for the 52 miles from passing Roade to Willesden by No 46244 in 1957 was marginally higher. Again, a fair comparison returns a verdict of near equality of merit and we are still unable to improve on the "honours easy" verdict of the late Cecil J. Allen. There is, however, little doubt that in everyday service the A4 class had the more distinguished record of high-speed running. This may partly be due to opportunity, partly the result of running traditions and partly the inevitable result of the contours of the line. It would, nevertheless, have been impossible for the A4 to have returned such a record in the absence of ability. There is no reason to doubt the ability of a double-chimney 'Coronation' to have proved at least equal had the same opportunity been given.

A consideration of the dimensions supports the theory of near equality. The valve cylinder ratios of the 'Duchess' suggest a capacity for high speed and were, on paper at least, better than those of the A4s. Against this they had a higher clearance volume tending to increase steam consumption. The full Kylchap exhaust of the A4 was probably superior to the simple double chimney of the 'Duchess', but the LMS arrangement made for easier tube cleaning. The 'Duchess' was bigger than the A4 and so, other things being equal, might have been expected to reach higher sustained and maximum hps. This seems to have been fulfilled in practice, but the A4 came very close to the 'Duchess' maximum on at least two occasions. One was during the high-speed flight of *Mallard* in 1938, when the ihp curve must have crossed the 3000 mark, and the other occasion was over a quarter of a century later when the same engine was driven very hard from Werrington to Stoke Box with a 415ton train and a speed of 80mph was sustained on the 1 in 200 above Little Bytham. This would most likely have required 3000-3100ihp. It is perhaps significant that all the highest ihps attained by the A4s were in the higher ranges of speed. The A4 was the racehorse among British Pacifics, but in a trial of strength the 'Duchess' would have proved the more powerful.

The slight edge of the A4 in terms of coal/dbhp/hr during the 1948

Exchanges is perhaps hardly significant, as such a narrow margin may lie within the limits of testing error. One 'Duchess' went through the entire testing period on every Region, but the A4s were troubled by failures of the fallible inside big end. In later years, under the influence of K. J. Cook from the GWR, a modified big end, incorporating some features of the De Glehn/Swindon pattern, brought about some improvement. Both the A4 and the 'Duchess' were built for high speed and proved to be faster than their immediate predecessors, but in terms of coal/dbhp/hr figures attained on variable speed pre-war dynamometer car tests neither was better than the 'Princess' or the A3. The A4 and the 'Duchess' were, however well ahead of the other Class 8 engines tested in 1948.

The A4 and the 'Duchess' may be regarded as the last express locomotives built in Britain, with performance on the road the main aim of the design. Later Pacifics had to be designed to meet deteriorating operating conditions. They may be regarded as adaptations for the survival of steam power, which was being threatened as these later Pacifics went on to the drawing boards. The most interesting of these was perhaps the Bulleid design for the Southern, which first appeared during the war. Had the hopes of the designer been fulfilled these engines would have outclassed all other Pacifics on the road and would have been easier to maintain. They combined an excellent boiler with a patent chain-driven valve gear enclosed in an oil bath and the whole engine was under an air-smoothed casing. The boiler was at least the equal of that of the 'Duchess' in steaming capacity, but the steam was not used to advantage, as over 16lb of steam were needed for each ihp against 14.5lb for a 'Duchess'. Slipping was, if anything, an even worse problem and the fear of twisted rods prevented a full extension of the engine on the Rugby Test Plant or in controlled road tests between Skipton and Carlisle.

In 1956 the first example was rebuilt on more conventional lines and the steam rate was improved to a figure comparable with that of a 'Duchess'. The result was an engine roughly equal to a 'Duchess' in potential power output, which in service came near to but never actually excelled the Stanier engines in maximum or sustained power output. In high-speed running they enjoyed a number of eleventh-hour romps during the 1960s and they finished with more 100mph maximum speeds to their credit than the 'Duchesses', though the A4 total, which was swollen by a period of pre-war fast running denied to later engines, still remained unchallenged. There is little doubt that an original or a rebuilt 'Merchant Navy' class Pacific, given the opportunity, would have travelled very fast down Stoke Bank, but just how near it would have got to an A4 or a Duchess is something which we shall never know. The 6ft 2in driving wheels of the Bulleid Pacific did not seem to have any adverse effect up to 105mph, but what would have happened at 115-120mph is something which only a special trial would have answered. There is an example of a rebuilt 'Merchant Navy' reaching 3000ihp near Roundwood Box, calculated by the same formula that credits the A4 with a similar figure.

Another British Pacific which just touched the 3000ihp mark on one test occasion was the Peppercorn A1 class. This design was an attempt by Doncaster to obtain similar performance to that of an A4 but with less trouble in maintenance, with higher mileages and with lower repair costs. There are no definitive figures to say how far this aim came to fulfilment, but we do know that the A1s, especially those with roller bearings, ran some very high mileages. According to figures published by E. S. Cox in *British Railways Standard Steam Locomotives* (Ian Allan 1966), the A1s had lower repair costs than the 'Duchesses' or the Bulleid Pacifics and they were only marginally higher than those for the two-cylinder 'Britannia' class BR Pacifics. The corresponding figures for the A4s are not available. An A1, No 60128 *Bongrace*, was selected to run test trains examining the new AWS equipment and one test demanded a start from Grantham with a 465ton train and a maximum speed of 90mph at Corby. During the course of this acceleration the dynamometer car recorded an average edbhp of 2295 between mps 99 and 100 and the engine continued downhill at a long cut-off to reach the required 90mph, at which point the ihp is calculated to have reached the 3000 mark. The A1s have, with some justice, been described as "Britain's most under-rated Pacifics." They had a reputation for rough riding, but attained a number of 100mph maxima.

Britain's largest 4-6-0, the GWR 'King', was categorised as Power Class 8 along with the largest Pacifics. The 'Kings' did not match the very high dbhps attained at high speeds by the best of the 4-6-2s, but at the lower end of the scale they were the best starters in Britain, starting heavy trains with a crisp beat and little or no slipping. They were also very strong at low speeds up short, very steep banks. This pattern of performance was the result of being a 4-6-0 rather than a Pacific, of a high adhesion weight and a sensitive regulator. The 'Kings' were admirably suited to GWR duties, but their smaller boilers would hardly have been suitable for the 400mile continuous Euston-Glasgow workings. A number of 100mph maxima have been recorded by the 'Kings' on the easier roads.

It is possible to summarise 'Duchess' performance. According to the established facts they were Britain's most powerful express loco-motives and they were among the fastest and most economical. The evidence supporting the "most powerful" claim is tabulated opposite.

The 'Duchesses' had their faults as did all engines. The worst of these was the tendency to slip, which might have been lessened by using equalising bars as was seriously proposed for one of the original 'Princesses'. The steam temperature was disappointing, but this could have been rectified if more modern ideas of the correct A/S ratios in

IHP outputs of British Pacific locomotives

'Duchess'	Maximum	3300	Calculated from recorded dbhps
'Duchess'	Sustained	2910	Recorded on Test Plant
A4 Kylchap	Maximum	3100	Calculated by resistance formulae
A1 Peppercorn	Maximum	3000	Calculated from recorded dbhps
'M Navy' (orig.)	Sustained	2480	Recorded on Test Plant
'M Navy' (reblt.)	Sustained	*2215	Calculated from steam flow and heat drop
'M Navy' (reblt.)	Maximum	3000	Calculated by resistance formulae
BR Class 8	Sustained	2650	Recorded on Test Plant
BR Class 7	Sustained	2220	Recorded on Test Plant

*The sustained figure of 2215ihp for the M Navy was calculated from steam flow and heat drop on a controlled road test when the evaporation rate was 32000lb/hr. This was not the limit of the boiler and it is in close agreement with 2250ihp for a Duchess on 32000lb/hr.

superheater flues as used in the BR standard range had been introduced. The Peppercorn A1s and the Bulleid Pacifics were also unsatisfactory in this respect, but the Gresley A4s and the BR standard types were satisfactory. The 'Duchesses' were very large engines for hand firing and this limited maximum efforts on ordinary service to relatively short bursts. To some extent this same criticism applied to other Class 8 engines, while even some medium-sized 4-6-0s needed two firemen when extended on test runs. The mechanical design of the 'Duchess' was good and they ran high mileages by British criteria, maintaining a high standard of reliability with few failures on the road.

The question has often been asked as to whether the life of steam in this country should have been prolonged. It would be completely unrealistic to imagine that steam trains could ever top Shap at over 90mph — the requisite power/weight ratios are unobtainable: but a much stronger case could be made for the suggestion that the phasing out of steam power in this country was unduly precipitate. Something more akin to the German policy, with perhaps some use of oil firing or mechanical stokers on the largest engines, would have allowed a longer period for the testing of diesel prototypes. Fewer but better diesel classes would have been an advantage in the earlier stages of modernisation. Extravagant claims for the hand-fired Pacific should not be made. In the 1939 tests No 6234, for short periods, gave dbhps which compared favourably with those of the 'Deltic' diesels at the same speeds, but these efforts could never have been sustained with hand firing.

Had the 'Chapelonised Duchess' proposed in 1939 been built it may well have been that the disappointing steam temperatures would have been cured by the Houlet-type superheater. This superheater had been used with success on the PO 231.722 class Pacifics, but there had been some trouble with burnt elements which had been countered with a better grade of chrome alloy steel. The first batch of Chapelon

Pacifics for the Nord had Houlet elements, but the 5P4 type of superheater was substituted in the later series. Expert drivers of the Nord were adamant that the older rebuilds with the Houlet superheater were slightly stronger. The whole question of the value of boiler pressures as high as 300lb and very high steam temperatures has been the subject of some debate. The Kylchap double-exhaust system might have proved better than the simple LMS-type double blastpipe, but the experiment on No 6245 was short-lived. The Kylchap made access to the tubes for cleaning more difficult, but it gave excellent results if properly proportioned. Although it has not actually been stated there is little doubt that, had the BR Standard Class 8 4-6-2 based on a 'Duchess' ever been built, modified elements reflecting the experience gained on the 'Britannia' would have been used with beneficial results. The 5000gal tender proposed for this engine would have been an operational advantage, especially when heading north over Beattock Summit on the former Caledonian main line, where the troughs were more widely spaced.

When thoughts turn to possible modifications which might have

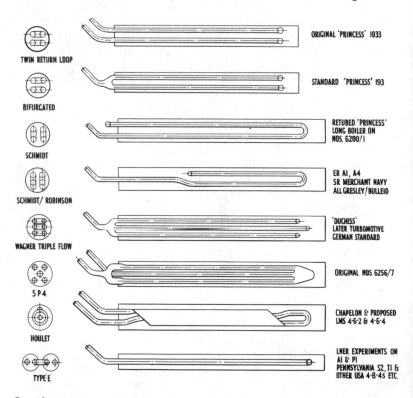

Superheater arrangements.

prolonged the life of steam the turbine engine No 6202 must not be overlooked. The simple non-condensing turbine locomotive did not end its history with No 6202, for others were built in France, Germany and the US. The SNCF built a 4-6-4 turbine locomotive designated Class 2-3-2 Q1. This was constructed by Schneider and was completed in 1941. The driving wheels were 4ft 11½in diameter and each axle was driven by a 1000hp turbine with a reversing stage on its own shaft, without disengaging gear in the manner of a marine reversing stage. The boiler pressure was 355lb/sq in, one of the highest ever used on a conventional boiler. It developed 2600hp at the wheel rims on test at Vitry in 1941. In service windmill and back pressure losses from the reversing stages impaired the running. There was some overheating and the economy was disappointing. In service it used 7% more fuel than a four-cylinder compound Pacific. It was taken out of service in 1944 following damage to one of the turbines.

In Germany Krupps were building two streamlined 2-8-4 turbine locomotives in 1941. These were designated Class 09 and had coupled wheels driven by a jackshaft from a single 3160hp turbine working on a boiler pressure of 310lb. Both locomotives were destroyed during an RAF air raid on Essen in 1943.

The Pennsylvania RR engine was built by Baldwins in 1944 with the 6-8-6 wheel arrangement. A single Westinghouse turbine with six stages drove the eight coupled wheels. The boiler pressure was 310lb and the grate area 120sq ft. This enormous locomotive was tested on the Altoona Plant and attained a maximum hp of 7245 at 66mph. The corresponding steam rate was 14.86lb steam per ihp/hr, which compared with 14.51lb for the 'Duchess'. Despite the very high exhaust back pressure of 19.51lb/sq in the steam consumption rate was more satisfactory than that of the T1 class 4-4-4-4 piston engines at the same speed. In ordinary service speeds of over 100mph were reached despite the 5ft 8in coupled wheels and on one run 50 miles were covered at 100mph with a load of 1000 US tons. The main trouble was staybolt breakage due to the high pressure and high evaporation rates. It was put on less arduous duties in 1949, following damage to the turbine, and was finally scrapped in 1957 after a period out of service. The T1s were out of service by 1949 and they had all been scrapped by 1953.

The simple non-condensing turbine locomotive had achieved more success than the more complicated condensing engine, especially those with electric drive. The original Swedish non-condensing turbine-driven freight locomotives of 1932 were still in service in 1954 when the line was electrified and they were put into reserve. As far as is known they were still in existence in store in 1971. Had the turbine principle been carried further on the LMS, advantage might have been taken of the fact that smaller driving wheels could have permitted the highest speeds. A 4-8-2 turbine locomotive with 5ft driving wheels and a 'Duchess' boiler might have been a logical development of No 6202 and the greater adhesion weight would have permitted heavier loads over the banks without slipping, while equally high speeds on the favourable grades would have been possible. The possibilities of turbine drive remain one of the unresolved issues of steam locomotive history.

Conjecture, however, knows no limits. The engines which were actually built had an interesting history and they leave varied and happy memories. Thoughts go back to the first sighting of No 6200 on the up 'Royal Scot' in its early days before the line had lost its LNWR atmosphere; and to an occasion a few years later when No 6204 was observed passing Rugby on the same job at a holiday weekend, but this time with an 18-coach load of over 600 tons though only a mere three minutes late. Memories recall an easy mastery over the job as the blue and silver 'Coronation Scot' flitted smoothly and silently along at 80mph, while the red-and-gold 'Coronations' looked even better. Great was the joy when first we read of over 3000ihp from a British locomotive as the results of the test running of No 6234 in 1939 were first published, but shortly after this come sombre memories of black and unkempt Pacifics doing their best in the national interest. After the war trips behind blue or green 'Duchesses' in the 1950s left a picture of easy competence on 17-coach loads if only the road were clear. Finally, the crisp, clean beat of red Pacifics climbing the northern banks on Society railtours comes echoing back through the years.

In 1928 a well-written book entitled *Engines* by Professor E. N. da C. Andrade was published by Bell. In it the Professor foretold a time in the future when the steam locomotive would hold an affection in the minds of men similar to that held by the memory of the sailing ship in 1928. Today, almost half a century later, this forecast has sadly come to pass. The analogy was an excellent one, for the great days of the clipper ships were not quite the end of the large sailing vessel. It became necessary before the end to build ships where speed alone had to take second place to ease of operating if sail was to hold any place on the oceans of the world. In just the same way steam locomotives designed for mileage and availability followed those designed for high-quality performance alone, just as sailing vessels more easy to man followed the fully-rigged clippers. In 1928 steam power in Britain had not reached its zenith and the first West Coast Pacific was still almost five years away. The zenith of high-speed steam was reached when the A4s and the 'Duchesses' attained the peaks of recorded performance during the years 1937-39, with the 'Duchess' being a splendid *Thermopylae* to the A4's *Cutty Sark*.

Test Results, Comparison with Foreign Pacifics

Country	Railway	Class of engine	Evaporation lb/hr	Duration	IHP	Speed mph	Steam rate lb/ihp/hr	Remarks
USA	Pennsylvania	K4S Franklin poppet valves 2cyl simple	70000 47770	Sustained Sustained	4267 3190	75 85	16.4 15.0	(A) 1939 Test Plant (B) 1939 Test Plant
USA	Pennsylvania	K4S 15in piston valves	70000	Sustained	3530	65	19.8	(A) 1937 Test Plant
		K4S 12in piston valves	67000	Sustained	3250	47	20.5	(A) 1915 Test Plant
		K4S 12in piston valves 2cyl simple	28000	Sustained	1750	66	16.1	(B) 1915 Test Plant
France	Paris-Orleans	231.722 class 4cyl compound Dabeg poppet valves	— 54000 49000 31750	Maximum Sustained 1hr Sustained 2hr Sustained 1hr	3800 3550 3300 2650	75 75 62 69	— 15.2 14.85 11.9	(A) Vitry Test Plant (A) Brake Loco Test (A) Vitry Test Plant (B) Brake Loco Test
France	Alsace-Lorraine	S16 2cyl simple Caprotti valves	48000	Sustained	3200	62	15.0	(A) Brake Loco Test
Germany	Bundesbahn	DB Type 10 3cyl simple	39700	Sustained	3000	–	13.2	(A)
Great Britain	LMS	'Duchess' 4cyl simple	— 42000 36000	Maximum Sustained Sustained	3300 2910 2550	63 80 90	— 14.5 14.2	1939 Road Test (A) Rugby Test Plant (B) Rugby Test Plant
Great Britain	SR	'M. Navy' (original)	42000	Sustained	2480	60	16.9	(A) Rugby Test Plant
		'M. Navy' (original)	28000	Sustained	1770	60	15.8	(B) Rugby Test Plant
		'M. Navy' (rebuilt) 3cyl simple	32000	Sustained	2215	80	14.4	(L) Controlled Road Test

(A) At maximum evaporation (B) At minimum steam consumption (L) Limit of test (not maximum possible)

Appendices

Leading Dimensions

While every endeavour has been made to present tables of dimensions as accurate as possible these figures are subject to the normal hazards affecting all statistical information about locomotives. Published dimensions are notoriously unreliable and often bear no relation to the actual dimensions of an individual engine. Cylinders are bored out or lined up, frames are strengthened, wheel tyres are turned down and boiler heating surfaces vary between different batches of boilers.

Boiler heating surfaces are not always in themselves significant. Superheating surface area does not always give a true indication of steam temperature. The Stanier Pacifics in their final form had very large nominal superheating surfaces but their actual steam temperatures were disappointing. Dimensions which are rarely quoted such as boiler free gas areas, tube A/S ratios and the percentage of air space through the grate are often of much greater significance. A brief indication of the meaning of some of these may be of interest.

Nominal Tractive Effort

This frequently used figure is perhaps the most misleading of all locomotive dimensions. It is the mean pull that a locomotive could exert during one revolution of the driving wheels in full gear with full boiler pressure, assuming that there is sufficient adhesion weight to allow the engine to start without slipping. It gives no indication at all of the drawbar pull which the engine could sustain at speed.

T = tractive effort.
d = diameter of cylinders.
S = stroke of cylinders.
p = boiler pressure.
n = number of cylinders.
D = diameter of driving wheels.

$$T = \frac{d \times S \times 85\% \ p}{D} \times \frac{n}{2}$$

The above formula is for a simple locomotive, a more complicated calculation is needed for a compound.

A consideration of the performance records of a number of British

180

and foreign locomotives underlines the limited value of tractive effort as a qualification of power.

A/S Ratio

This is the area to surface ratio of tubes and flues, defined as the free cross-sectional area open to gas divided by the internal swept surface, including any due to the external gas surface of superheater tubes. It is the measure of the resistance to gas flow of a tube and for plain smoke tubes can be restated as the length to diameter, ratio L/D. In this case $A/S = 4 + L/D$. The value stated to be good practice by Dr Wagner of the German State Railways in 1930 for engines with single blastpipes was A/S 1/400. More recent practice suggests that double blastpipes permitted a slightly higher ratio.

Free Gas Area

This is the total area available for gas flow through a boiler and is obtainable from the sum of the individual tube cross-sectional areas open to gas flow. It is a measure of the steaming capacity of a boiler and is sometimes stated as a percentage of the grate area. Some authorities consider that a minimum percentage is necessary for good steaming.

Clearance Volume

Clearance volume is the space left at the end of the piston stroke between the piston and the cylinder cover to allow for mechanical clearance and also for compression space for cushioning. It includes the steam space in cylinder ports and valve chests after the point of cylinder cut off and is increased by large piston valves and steam passages. For a given amount of work done, a higher clearance volume enables a shorter cut-off to be used but there is a marginal increase in steam consumption.

A consideration of the tables shows that it is unwise to define rigid limits of what constitutes good practice, because these tables describe locomotives with very different A/S ratios, free gas areas and clearance volumes all showing good steaming and free running qualities. It is most probably true to say that in a complete locomotive what might have been a design defect in one feature was compensated by a good feature elsewhere.

Table 1 Pacific Dimensions Compared

Class	Driving Wheel Dia	No and Size of Cylinders	Boiler Pressure lb/sq in	Nominal Tractive Effort lb	WEIGHTS (tons) Adhesion	Engine	Tender	Total	VALVE DIMENSIONS DIA	LAP	LEAD	Exh Clear	Clearance Volume %	Water Gall	Coal Tons
'Princess Royal'	6ft-6in	4-16¼in x 28in	250	40,300	67.5	104.5	54.7	159.2	8in	1¾in	¼in	Nil		4000	9
'Coronation' 'Duchess'	6ft-9in 6ft-9in	4-16½in x 28in 4-16½in x 28in	250 250	40,000	67 67	108 105	56.5 56.5	164.5 161.5	9in	1¾in	¼in	.062in	12.5	4000	10
BR7	6ft-2in	2-20in x 28in	250	32,150	60.75	94	52.5	146.5	11in	1.69in	¼in	Nil	10.3	4250	7
BR 6	6ft-2in	2-19½in x 28in	225	27,520	56.8	88.5	49.1	137.6	11in	1.69in	¼in	Nil	10.8	4250	7
BR 8	6ft-2in	3-18in x 28in	250	39,100	66	101.2	56.5	157.7	7in	Poppet valves Rotary cam Caprotti			13.0	4725	7
ER A1	6ft-8in	3-19in x 26in	250	37,940	66.9	105	60.5	165.5	10in	1⅝in	⅛in	Nil	8.5	5000	9
ER A4	6ft-8in	3-18½in x 26in	250	35,455	66	102.9	64.9	167.8	9in	1⅝in	⅛in	Nil	7.9	5000	9
SR 'Merchant Navy'	6ft-2in	3-18in x 24in	280‡	37,500	63	94.75	49.7	144	11in	1⅝in	⅛in	Nil	9.8	6000	5
LMS Proposed 4-6-4	6ft-6in	4-17½in x 28in	300	56,000	72	119	68	187						5000	12

‡ Later reduced to 250lb/sq in.
Tractive effort 33495lb.

182

Table 1 Pacific Dimensions Compared — continued

Class	Driving Wheel Dia	No and Size of Cylinders	Boiler Pressure lb/sq in	Nominal Tractive Effort lb	WEIGHTS (tons) Adhesion	Engine	Tender	Total	VALVE DIMENSIONS DIA	LAP	LEAD	Exh Clear		Clearance Volume %	Water Gall	Coal Tons
Chapelon 231.722	6ft-4¾in	2 (HP) 16½in x 25.6in 2(LP) 25.5in x 27.2in	242	47,500	56.5	101		51.5† 152.2	9.5in HP Poppet valves 10.4in LP oscillating cam Dabeg					25% HP 16% LP	7500	10.5 *

† Test weight half full, 77tons fully loaded.
* Including 1 ton for briquettes.

Table 2 'Princess Royal' Class Boilers

Boiler Nos	Locos First Fitted	Tubes + Flues No	Dia	Superheater Tubes Dia	Type	Free Areas Ft² Tubes	Flues	Total	Total % Grate Area	A/S Ratios		Heating Surface Ft² Tubes	S/H	F'box
		Original long tube boilers with short firebox						Built 1933						
6048 6049	6200 6201	170 + 16	2¼in + 5⅜in	1⅛in	(1)	3.78	1.55	5.33	11.8	1:495	1:450	2523	370	190
Retubed		119 + 32	2⅜in + 5⅜in	1¼in	(2)	2.98	2.88	5.86	13.0	1:474	1:469	2429	594	190

Table 2 'Princess Royal' Class Boilers — continued

Boiler Nos	Locos First Fitted	Tubes + Flues No	Dia	Superheater Tubes Dia	Type	Free Areas Ft² Tubes	Flues	Total	Total % Grate Area	A/S Ratios Tubes	Flues	Heating Surface Ft² Tubes	S/H	F'box
Prototype enlarged superheater boiler retaining long tubes and short firebox														
6050	6200 (4/35)	110 + 32	2¼in + 5⅛in	1¼in	(2)	2.44	2.88	5.32	11.8	1:495	1:474	2240	594	190
Retubed		110 + 32	2⅜in + 5⅛in	1¼in	(3)	2.75	2.88	5.63	12.5	1:469	1:474	2310	623	190
Standard short tube boilers with long firebox Built 1935														
9100/5 9235	6202/7 6212	112 + 32	2¼in + 5⅛in	1¼in	(3)	2.49	2.88	5.37	11.9	1:458	1:448	2097	653	217
Retubed		112 + 32	2⅜in + 5⅛in	1¼in	(3)	2.80	2.88	5.68	12.6	1:435	1:448	2167	623	217
9101-4	6203-6	141 + 24	2¼in + 5⅛in	1¼in	(3)	3.13	2.16	5.29	11.7	1:458	1:448	2218	467	217
Retubed		123 + 32	2⅜in + 5⅛in	1¼in	(3)	3.08	2.88	5.96	13.2	1:435	1:448	2299	598	217
9106-9	6208-11	112 + 32	2¼in + 5⅛in	1¼in	(3)	2.49	2.88	5.37	11.9	1:458	1:448	2097	623	217
Retubed		123 + 32	2⅜in + 5⅛in	1¼in	(3)	3.08	2.88	5.96	13.2	1:435	1:448	2299	623	217

Superheater Element Types:
(1) Twin Single return loops 1⅛in. 11SWG.
(2) Schmidt double return bend 1¼in. 11SWG.
(3) Bifurcated 1¼in. 11SWG, 1¼in. 13SWG, (653sq ft),,11SWG altered loop (598sq ft).

Table 2 'Princess Royal' Class Boilers — continued

Boiler Nos	*Locos First Fitted*	*Tubes + Flues No*	*Tubes + Flues Dia*	*Superheater Tubes Dia*	*Superheater Tubes Type*	*Free Areas Ft²: Tubes*	*Free Areas Ft²: Flues*	*Free Areas Ft²: Total*	*Total % Grate Area*	*A/S Ratios: Tubes*	*A/S Ratios: Flues*	*Heating Surface Ft²: Tubes*	*Heating Surface Ft²: S/H*	*Heating Surface Ft²: F'box*
			Special turbomotive boiler			Built 1936								
9236	6202 (7/36)	81 + 40	2¼in + 5⅛in	1in	(3)	1.79	4.04	5.83	12.9	1:458	1:383	1951	577	217
Modified		81 + 40	2¼in + 5⅛in	1in	(4)	1.79	3.61	5.41	12.0	1:458	1:428	1951	832	217
Retubed		101 + 40	2⅜in + 5⅛in	1¼in	(3)	2.52	3.61	6.13	13.6	1:435	1:448	2232	720	217

(4) Triple flow 1in. 13SWG.

Some diagrams show engines with 1½in. 9SWG elements, probably wartime double return bend type giving A/S 1:540, free area 2.41, S/H 586sq ft.

Table 3 Pacific Boilers Compared

Class	*Grate Area Ft²*	*Flues + Tubes No*	*Flues + Tubes Dia*	*Superheater Tubes Dia*	*Superheater Tubes Type*	*Free Areas Ft²: Tubes*	*Free Areas Ft²: Flues*	*Free Areas Ft²: Total*	*Total % Grate Area*	*A/S ratios: Tubes*	*A/S ratios: Flues*	*Heating Surface Ft²: Tubes*	*Heating Surface Ft²: S/H*	*Heating Surface Ft²: Fi'box*
'Princess Royal'	45			See Table 2										
'Duchess'														
6220-55	50	40 + 129	5⅛in + 2⅜in	1in	(3)	3.23	3.66	6.89	13.8	1:436	1:553	2807	822	230
6256/7	50	40 + 129	5⅛in + 2⅜in	1in	(4)	3.23	3.32	6.55	13.1	1:436	1:664	2807	979	230

Table 3 Pacific Boilers Compared — continued

Class	Grate Area Ft²	Flues + Tubes No	Dia	Superheater Tubes Dia	Type	Free Areas Ft² Tubes	Flues	Total	Total % Grate Area	A/S ratios Tubes	Flues	Heating Surface Ft² Tubes	S/H	Fi'box
BR 7	42	40 + 136	5½in + 2⅛in	1⅜in	(1)	2.66	4.13	6.79	16.2	1:436	1:423	2264	718	210
BR 6	36	35 + 108	5½in + 2⅛in	1⅜in	(1)	2.11	3.61	5.72	15.9	1:436	1:423	1878	622	195
BR 8	48.6	40 + 136	5½in + 2⅛in	1⅜in	(1)	2.66	4.13	6.79	13.9	1:436	1:423	2280	718	226
ER A1	50	43 + 121	5¼in + 2¼in	1½in	(2)	2.62	3.59	6.21	12.4	1:414	1:443	2216	680	245
ER A4	41.25	43 + 121	5¼in + 2¼in	1½in	(2)	2.62	3.59	6.21	15.1	1:437	1:464	2344	749	231
SR 'Merchant Navy'	48.5	40 + 124	5¼in + 2¼in	1½in	(2)	2.76	3.33	6.09	12.5	1:404	1:492	2176	662	275
Chapelon 231.722	46.6	28 + 125	5¼in + 2⅛in	1.57 3.90	(5)	2.62	2.40	5.02	10.8	1:482	1:670	1904	877	201
LMS Proposed 4-6-4	70							9.8	14					

Superheater element types:
(1) Schmidt double return bend 1⅜in x 10SWG.
(2) Schmidt/Robinson short return bend 1½in x 9SWG.
(3) Wagner triple flow 1in x 11SWG (856sq ft) 1in x 10SWG (822sq ft).
(4) 5P4 finned return tubes. (4) 1in x 11SWG + (1) 1½in x 9SWG.
(5) Houlet concentric tube.

Table 4 Designs proposed but never built

Year	Class	Driving Wheel Diameter	Number and Size of Cylinders	Boiler Pressure	Nominal Tractive Effort lb	Weight Tons Adhn.	Engine	Tender	Total	Grate Area SQ Ft²	Surface SQ Ft² Tubes	S/Heater	Firebox
1913	McIntosh 4-6-2	6ft 6in	4-16in x 26in	180	24576	55	90	56	146	36	2440	516	158
1924	Hughes 4-6-2	6ft 9in	4-18½in x 26in	180	33600	60	95	54	149	42	2715	600	230
1926	Fowler Compound 4-6-2	6ft 9in	2HP-16¾in x 26in 2LP-23⅝in x 26in	240	34600	63	101	42½	143½	43.5	2357	631	221
1932	Stanier 3cyl 4-6-2	6ft 9in	3-19in x 28in	250	39700	67½	104½	52½	157	45	-	-	-
1939	Stanier "Chapelonised" 4-6-2	6ft 9in	4 - -	300	-	-	-	-	-	50	-	-	-
1939	Stanier 4-6-4	6ft 6in	4-17½in x 28in	300	*56000	72	119	68	187	70	-	-	-

*Based on normal TE formula. It was intended to limit this to 42800lb by fixing cut-off at 65%

Stanier Pacifics Building and Withdrawal Dates

'Princess' class

Number	Name	To Traffic	Withdrawn
6200	The Princess Royal	6/33	11/62
6201	Princess Elizabeth	11/33	10/62†
6202	*Princess Anne	6/35	10/52
6203	Princess Margaret Rose	7/35	10/62†
6204	Princess Louise	7/35	10/61
6205	Princess Victoria	7/35	11/61
6206	Princess Marie Louise	8/35	11/62
6207	Princess Arthur of Connaught	8/35	11/61
6208	Princess Helena Victoria	8/35	10/62
6209	Princess Beatrice	8/35	9/62
6210	Lady Patricia	9/35	10/61
6211	Queen Maud	9/35	10/61
6212	Duchess of Kent	10/35	10/61

*Ran without a name until rebuilt from turbine propulsion to conventional engine in 8/52. Damaged in Harrow accident 8/10/52; remains held awaiting decision until 5/54, when it was scrapped as replacement locomotive BR Class 8 No 71000 entered service.
Preserved.

'Coronation and Duchess' class

Number	Name	To Traffic	Withdrawn
6220	*Coronation	6/37	4/63
6221	Queen Elizabeth	6/37	5/63
6222	Queen Mary	6/37	10/63
6223	Princess Alice	7/37	10/63
6224	Princess Alexandra	7/37	10/63
6225	Duchess of Gloucester	5/38	9/64
6226	Duchess of Norfolk	5/38	9/64
6227	Duchess of Devonshire	6/38	12/62
6228	Duchess of Rutland	6/38	9/64
6229	*Duchess of Hamilton	9/38	2/64†
6230	Duchess of Buccleuch	6/38	11/63
6231	Duchess of Athol	6/38	12/62
6232	Duchess of Montrose	7/38	12/62
6233	Duchess of Sunderland	7/38	2/64†
6234	Duchess of Abercorn	8/38	1/63
6235	City of Birmingham	7/39	9/64†
6236	City of Bradford	7/39	3/64
6237	City of Bristol	8/39	9/64
6238	City of Carlisle	9/39	9/64
6239	City of Chester	9/39	9/64
6240	City of Coventry	3/40	9/64
6241	City of Edinburgh	4/40	9/64
6242	City of Glasgow	5/40	10/63
6243	City of Lancaster	6/40	9/64
6244	City of Leeds/King George VI 4/41	7.40	9/64
6245	City of London	6/43	9/64
6246	City of Manchester	8/43	1/63
6247	City of Liverpool	9/43	5/63
6248	City of Leeds	10/43	9/64

Number	Name	To Traffic	Withdrawn
6249	City of Sheffield	4/44	11/63
6250	City of Lichfield	5/44	9/64
6251	City of Nottingham	6/44	9/64
6252	City of Leicester	6/44	5/63
6253	City of St Albans	9/46	1/63
6254	City of Stoke on Trent	9/46	9/64
6255	City of Hereford	10/46	9/64
6256	Sir William A. Stanier FRS	12/47	10/64
6257	City of Salford	5/48	9/64

*No 6220 was renumbered 6229 1939 to 1942 while the real No 6229 renumbered 6220 was on tour in USA. The original numbers were restored when the engine returned.
†Preserved.
Nos 6220-6229, 6235-6248 were streamlined. The streamlining was removed from all the engines between 4/46 and 5/49. After removal of streamlining the altered engines had a sloping top to the smokebox. These were replaced by normal cylindrical smokeboxes as these needed replacement between 7/52 and 5/60.

In the early days of nationalisation the prefix M was added to numbers. Between 4/48 and 9/49 40000 was added to all former LMS engines.

There are slight differences in official figures for the building dates of engines, usually occurring when a locomotive was finished at the end of one month and first put into traffic early in the next.

The official description of the larger Pacifics was the 'Princess Coronation' class. This clumsy title was not popular and it has not been used in this book. The more logical class titles are 'Coronation' for the streamlined engines and 'Duchess' for the non-streamlined engines. Ultimately they all became 'Duchesses'. The names chosen were respectable but unimaginative. They lacked the popular appeal of some of the LNER names, which had a more sporting flavour. The names could be misleading to the uninitiated as some 'Princesses' were 'Duchesses' and some 'Duchesses' were 'Princesses'. The 'Princesses' were nicknamed the 'Lizzies' and the 'Duchesses' were the 'Big Lizzies.'

Tenders

The first LMS Pacifics appeared with a new enlarged type of tender carrying 9tons of coal and 4000gal of water. This was similar in appearance to the standard Derby tender but was larger, although it was dwarfed by the length of Nos 6200/1. Three of these tenders were built, two of them with roller bearings. One of the three went with the 'Royal Scot' exhibition train on its American tour of 1933. The coal did not trim forward by gravity as had been hoped and the closing stages of a continuous run with a heavy train in unfavourable weather could be exhausting.

A new design of tender was introduced in 1935 when No 6202, the

189

Turbomotive, and the 6203-6212 batch were built and the tenders of 6200/1 were replaced. These tenders had the Stanier type of high sides with curved coping and carried 9tons of coal and 4000gal of water. The original tenders of Nos 6200/1 were fitted with curved coping and were mated with various 'Jubilee' class 4-6-0s.

In course of time it was found that 9 tons of coal was little enough for a continuous run between Euston and Glasgow with a heavy load in bad weather. A new version with higher sides carrying 10 tons of coal was built in 1936. One of these tenders, normally attached to No 6206, was fitted with a steam coal pusher.

The streamlined 'Coronation' class Pacifics had tenders basically similar to the 10ton type used on the 'Princesses' from 1936, but they were very different in external appearance in that the side sheets were raised to full height and extended to the rear so as to bridge the gap between tender rear and the front coach of the train. This gave the illusion of a longer tender. All the 'Coronations' had steam-driven coal pushers. There was a 10½in cylinder connected to wedge-shaped rams which pushed the coal forward. The exhaust escaped, with explosive sound, through a pair of pipes on the bunker backplate. The unstreamlined 'Duchess' class engines had the standard 10ton type of tender as used on the 'Princesses', but with the coal pusher on every engine. Nos 6249-52 were originally intended to be streamlined but were built without the casing mated with tenders which had been completed earlier. These were modified to the standard design in due course.

The water capacity of the LMS Pacific tenders was limited to 4000gal, which was considered to be adequate on the former LNWR, where the water troughs were close together. It was less satisfactory on the former Caledonian main line, where there was a gap of nearly 66 miles between Floriston troughs and the next set near Strawfrank Junction. This could be managed as it was on the trial run of 6234 with 610 tons in 1939, but a poor pick-up at Floriston could make a stop for water and the banker at Beattock station inevitable. The low water capacity could restrict the power output of a 'Duchess' on other Regions. The BR standard Class 8 designs either projected or built had greater tender water capacity.

Liveries
The original livery of the 'Princesses' as built in 1933-5 was the LMS crimson lake lined out in yellow with a black edging. This was derived from the Midland livery and officially was the same shade of red, but Midland purists always claimed an extra lustre for the original livery. Actually there was probably more variation between individual Midland or individual LMS engines over the years than there was between a Midland and an LMS engine as first turned out. The letters were in gold, shaded with black and were 14in high, while the numbers were

12in. As originally built the numbers and letters were in the same straight line. This was easily done as the letters appeared in the centre of the lower panel on the lined tender. When the larger tenders with higher sides were introduced the letters were raised so that they were again on the centre line of the tender side, but the numbers were left in the original position in the centre of the cabside panel. This spoilt the sideways viewpoint as compared with the original pair.

In 1936 there was a change of typeface for letters and numerals, as some 'Princesses' were turned out after shopping with the numerals reduced in size and given a sans-serif style in gold with red shading. Before all the class had been altered there was a return to the scroll/serif style and the larger size but with red shading. So the 'Princess' class entered the war. The whole class officially retained the pre-war red livery until painted in post-war livery.

The fact that these 'Princesses' were officially still in LMS red was of academic interest only. All engines were covered in a mixture of grime and rust by the end of the war. Occasionally a patch where constant rubbing had worn away the grime revealed a hint of the old livery. In 1946 the LMS chose their post-war livery. This was a brave attempt to face reality and to use a livery which was practical under the adverse conditions which seemed likely to last for several more years. The express engines were painted black with maroon and straw-coloured lining. The numerals and the tender letters were now in the same straight line. This livery was badly received by enthusiasts, who contrasted it with the declared intention of the LNER to restore all locomotives to apple green and the A4s to their pre-war garter blue. Soon, however, it was realised that nothing more than a few token paintings in the pre-war colours could be expected for some time and that the LNER locomotives soon got as dirty as those of the LMS. Although the new LMS livery had only a vestigial hint of the pre-war red, now called maroon, a really clean locomotive could look attractive and the LMS representative in the 1948 Exchanges, *City of Bradford*, was admired wherever it went.

After nationalisation a few 'Princesses' were painted black with the LNWR-style lining. There were strong representations in the councils of BR that the locomotives should all be painted black, but the public reaction was most unfavourable and various experimental liveries were tried, resulting in a decision to paint the larger express engines blue, which was said to be based on that of the old Caledonian railway. This was short-lived from 1949 to 1951, when it was decided to paint the larger express engines in the Brunswick green used for the medium-sized engines. This had proved to be more durable than the blue. It is uncertain if all the 'Princesses' had been painted blue before the decision to standardise the green was made; some photographs taken by the writers certainly look as if the engines were black, but whether this impression was the result of dirt or intention is uncertain.

All the 'Princesses' were green by 1957/8, when it was decided to paint 20 LMR Pacifics red. Among these were four Princesses, Nos 6200/4/7/8. The two preserved 'Princesses' are red, but LMS purists claim that only No 6201 is really in the authentic LMS style. However, where there are slight differences they are usually rather better and the over-ruling thought must be that all preservation is good preservation.

The 'Coronation' class started with the five blue streamliners. The blue was a medium shade, different from the garter blue of the LNER A4s. The silver lines started from a point in the front of the engine and ran in parallel, thick at top and bottom with two thin lines in between, right along the sides of engine, tender and the 'Coronation Scot' coaches. Officially the lines were in aluminium paint, but some observers claimed that close inspection revealed that they were really white. The explanation lies in the probabilities that different people, though not colour blind by normal standards, have slightly different colour vision and by the possibility that the 'silver' weathered to something closer to white after a time in service. The numbers and the letters were in the same straight line between the upper and lower broad stripes.

When the 1938 batch was introduced a change was made to red with gold lines. The gold stripes were edged by a black line almost ½in wide, which picked out the gold stripes more clearly. The 1938 batch of non-streamlined engines, the true 'Duchesses', were finished in red but with small differences in lining detail as compared with the 'Princesses'. The out-of-line letters and numerals formed a point of possible criticism on these otherwise impressive locomotives. The 1939 batch reverted to streamlined form and the intention was to re-paint the blue engines and to provide new red stock for the 'Coronation Scot' early in 1940 had peace continued. These engines were turned out at a slower rate during the early part of the war and they were completed by mid-1940. The 1943 batch of 'Coronations', beginning with No 6245, were turned out in wartime unlined black with insignia in yellow with red shading, and engines formerly blue or red were repainted in this colour. This batch of four engines built in 1943 completed the streamlined 'Coronation' class. The new engines built in 1944 reverted to the non-streamlined 'Duchess' class, though in some cases with streamlined tenders already completed. By the end of the war and for some years after the normal state of a locomotive was a dirty grey, so there is a certain amount of doubt as to whether or not individual engines did or did not receive the wartime black.

The first post-war 'Duchesses' were Nos 6253/4/5, built in 1946, and these were given the LMS post-war black with the maroon and straw lining. The majority of the 'Coronations' and 'Duchesses' received this livery. In 1946 No 6234 was given an experimental slate blue livery and it has been debated as to whether this was a serious attempt to investigate a new colour or whether it was merely a case of leaving an engine in shop grey while a decision was being made. In early BR days a number of 'Duchesses' were painted in black with LNWR-style lining, which livery was later standardised for mixed traffic locomotives. Others were given an experimental dark blue with LNWR style lining. It has been suggested that this blue was nearly the same as the former GER Royal Blue. The actual number of engines given these experimental liveries is not quite clear, but it would seem that seven or eight were given LNWR black and six were painted in experimental dark blue.

In 1949 a lighter shade of blue was adopted for Class 8 engines and it was claimed that this was close to the Caledonian shade. The BR lion-and-wheel emblem replaced the words British Railways on the tender. In mid-1951 it was decided to use the GWR-style Brunswick green of the Class 6 and 7 engines on the Class 8 locomotives and the blue was abandoned, being considered less durable in service. All the 'Duchesses' ultimately received the green livery and many kept it until withdrawal. They looked very well in it. The lion-and-wheel was replaced by a more heraldic device.

In 1958 it was decided to paint a number of 'Duchesses' in red and 16 of the larger Pacifics received this livery. Some red 'Duchesses' had the BR style of lining, but others were lined out in a style very close to that of the former LMS Pacifics, Nos 6230-4. The numerals were, however, at a higher position on the cabsides, at the same height as the emblem on the tender. In this respect they were an improvement on the LMS engines.

Two 'Princesses' and three 'Duchesses' have been preserved and four out of the five have been restored to LMS red, although only 6201 is quite in the authentic pre-war livery. The remaining engine, No 46235 *City of Birmingham*, has been preserved in BR green and this has been criticised, but is seems fitting that one engine survives in the livery carried when much of the best work by the class was performed. Where the red survivors differ from the original LMS livery the change has been an improvement, for the wrong position historically for the cabside numerals is the right position aesthetically.

Preservation
The following Stanier Pacifics have been preserved:

Number	Name	Livery	Location as at 1/76
6201	Princess Elizabeth	LMS red	Ashchurch
6203	Princess Margaret Rose	LMS red	Midland Rly Centre, Derbys.
6229	Duchess of Hamilton	LMS red	York Railway Museum
6233	Duchess of Sutherland	LMS red	Bressingham Steam Museum
46235	City of Birmingham	BR green	Birmingham Transport Museum

While it is good that as many as five Stanier Pacifics are preserved it is to be regretted that at the moment only No 6201 is able to haul rail-tours on main lines.

Accidents

The Stanier Pacifics were involved in a number of accidents, but there was no question of faulty design of the locomotive being responsible. On 10 September 1940, No 6224 was, owing to the exigencies of war, put in charge of a passed fireman and a passed cleaner and these inexperienced men allowed the firebox crown to become uncovered, resulting in a boiler explosion between Cleghorn and Carstairs. The fireman was killed, but there was little damage to the train. By a strange coincidence the same engine suffered almost exactly the same mishap at much the same spot on 5 March 1948 when in charge of an experienced crew. The driver was killed, but defective water gauges were blamed for the accident.

On 15 May 1944 No 6225 was derailed on poor track near Mossband Box south of Gretna and three passengers were killed. When working the 13.00 from Glasgow to Euston, No 6231 over-ran signals and ran into a freight train which was being shunted. Both enginemen were killed but there was no loss of life among passengers although the train was badly damaged. In 1947 No 6235 was in collision with a light engine near Lambrigg Box on Grayrigg Bank, but although the collision was on a high viaduct no coaches went over the side. Also in 1947, No 6244 was derailed between Atherstone and Polesworth on track that had deteriorated during the heavy snows earlier in the year. Five passengers were killed. On 16 April 1948, No 6251, on the southbound 'West Coast Postal', ran into the rear of the 17.50 from Glasgow to Euston which had stopped after the communication cord had been illicitly pulled. The crash was due to signalman's error in admitting the 'Postal' into a section already occupied.

The worst disaster of all involving Pacifics was the terrible multiple collision at Harrow and Wealdstone on 5 October 1952, when No 46242, hauling a southbound sleeping-car train, ran into a local train and the northbound 8.30 Liverpool, with the former turbine engine No 46202 *Princess Anne* piloted by a 'Jubilee', ran into the wreckage with results that were only excelled in death roll and horror by the Quintinshill accident of 1915. No 6202 was scrapped and replaced by the poppet-valve No 71000, but No 46242 was repaired. The 'Princess' class Pacific No 46207 was derailed at Weedon when hauling the 8.20 Liverpool-Euston in the same year.

Although this may seem to be a gloomy list of casualties it must be remembered that the Pacifics ran 71million miles and that on two occasions the excellent design of the larger Stanier Pacifics as vehicles prevented what might have been disasters. The first was the fast approach to Crewe by No 6220 on its famous press trip of 29 June

194

1937 and the other was when No 46236 *City of Bradford* during the 1948 Exchanges approached Peterborough unduly fast owing to lack to communication between the ER pilotman and the LMR driver. Had not the chassis design of the Stanier Pacific been excellent derailments would have happened on both these occasions. The Stanier Pacifics had the reputation for excellent riding at high speeds.

Allocations

The first 'Princesses' were first allocated to Camden and Polmadie and were joined by Nos 6203-12. When the larger Pacifics were built in 1937-8 most of the Princesses were transferred to Crewe North and Edge Hill. In 1939 three were allocated to Longsight for the Manchester-Euston services, but the war cut this plan short. During the war some were sent to Holyhead for a short time, but in post-war days Crewe and Edge Hill were their principal depots. Towards the end of their lives a few were stationed at Rugby, Carnforth, and Carlisle (Kingmoor).

The larger Pacifics were at first divided between Camden, Polmadie and Crewe North Sheds, but later Edge Hill and Carlisle (Upperby) had small allocations. In October 1939 a few were sent to Holyhead for the 'Irish Mails', but this was short-lived. Towards the end some were sent to Kingmoor and when Camden Shed was closed the remaining Pacifics were sent to Willesden.

Four LMR Pacifics, Nos 46207/10 and Nos 6254/57, were loaned to Old Oak Common Shed (London) while a number of 'Kings' were in Swindon Works for bogie modifications and in 1955 No 46237 was sent to the WR for comparative tests with the redraughted 'Kings'. The plan to use LMR Pacifics over the Edinburgh-Newcastle section of the NER while A1 Pacifics were used by Polmadie was not carried out nor was the suggestion over ten years later to transfer some LMR Pacifics to the Southern Region.

Detailed Modifications

Apart from No 6202 the turbine engine there were few major variations from the two basic designs. Known variations were:

Nos 6200/1	Long-tube boilers as detailed in Table 2.
No 6201	Experimental double chimney for a short time in 1934.
No 6205	Fitted with two sets of valve gear for four cylinders in 1938.
No 6206	Fitted with coal pusher in tender in 1938.
No 6212	Built in 1935 with smokebox door secured by 11 lugs.
No 6245	Built in 1943 with Kylchap double exhaust. This was removed later.
Nos 6253/4/5	Rocking grates.

Nos 6256/7	Built in 1947/8 with modifications intended to assist availability. These were redesigned Delta-type trailing truck, modified boiler proportions, reversing gear and cab side sheets of reduced depth.
No 6220-57	Smoke deflector plates fitted from 1946 onwards.

Mileage and Availability

Some of the Princesses ran over 80000miles a year before the war. Had peace continued some outstanding mileage figures might have been attained by the larger Pacifics, but the original five, running mainly on the 'Coronation Scot', ran relatively low annual mileages. Better figures would have followed the more general use of the red streamliners. The average annual mileage of the Princesses in 1937 was 74992, which was almost equalled by the 'Duchesses' during 1956, when they ran 74597 miles per annum. The 'Princesses' had fallen to between 50000 and 58000 miles in the post-war years, while the 'Duchesses' averaged between 67000 and 74000. Throughout their lives of 18-26 years the 'Duchesses' in the LM Region averaged 60000 miles per year, but those in the Scottish Region ran rather lower mileages. It had been hoped to reach a yearly mileage of 100000 with Nos 6256/7, but this was never attained. Had it been possible to have given these engines the same favourable treatment as was given to the 'Princesses' before the war the aim would almost certainly have been fulfilled. The 'Duchess' class, however, ran mileages which compared favourably with other British Class 8 express locomotives, with the roller-bearing A1s of the E and NE Regions being the only possible rivals.

Load Limits (Tons)

Euston-Carnforth	Full Load	Limited Load	Special Limit	XL Limit
Class 6	495	430	390	350
Class 7	550	495	475	405
Class 8	–	655	600	510
Carnforth-Carlisle				
Class 6	415	380	345	–
Class 7	465	420	285	–
Class 8	570	500	450	–

The 'Caledonian' had a special 280ton limit for Class 8 engines.

The pre-war 'Coronation Scot' was limited to nine coaches weighing 297 tons tare. The test running of November 1937 with the dynamometer car added to the nine bogies showed that 330 tons tare could easily be handled and had peace continued formations of 10 or 11 bogies of articulated stock would have been introduced in 1940. The XL limit for the pre-war 7hr 'Royal Scot' of 1938 was 420 tons for a

Pacific. This train had the same 80min to Rugby as the post-war 'Royal Scot' and 'Mid-day Scot', which were allowed 510 tons, but the 1938 train had its load trimmed to suit a 300min schedule to Carlisle in summer, while in the winter it was allowed 151min Crewe to Carlisle and 79min Carlisle to Symington.

The post-war limits applied to schedules between Euston and Crewe of:

Full load	187 min	158.1 miles
Limited load	176 min	158.1 miles
Special Limit	165 min	158.1 miles
XL Limit	155 min	158.1 miles
'Caledonian'	145 min (passing time)	158.1 miles

In LMS days the Pacifics were all Class 7P. In the early days of nationalisation it was decided to uprate the Classes 5XP, 6P and 7P to Classes 6, 7 and 8P so as to eliminate Class 5XP. There was no official differentiation between the 'Princesses' and the 'Coronations' or 'Duchesses', but it was recognised that the larger Pacifics were more powerful and it was usually arranged that they had the harder duties. Exceptions were the occasional use of 'Princesses' on the down 'Lancastrian' or the down 'Mid-day Scot'.

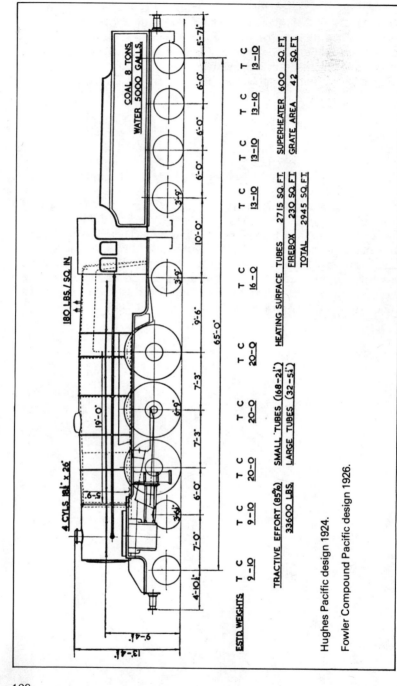

Hughes Pacific design 1924.

Fowler Compound Pacific design 1926.

198

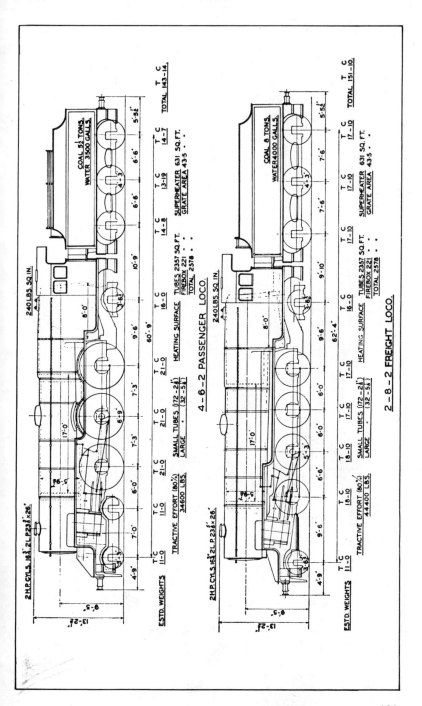

199

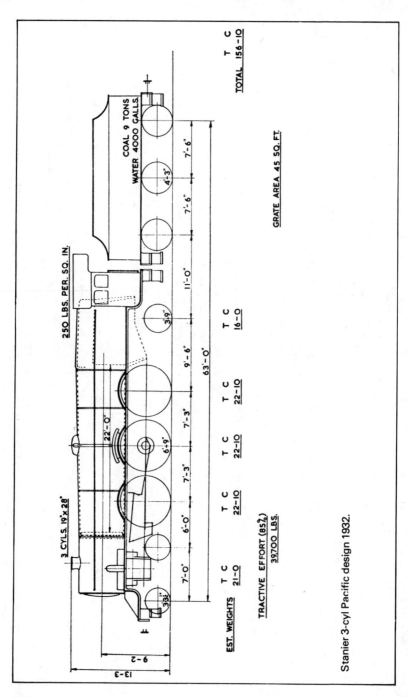

3 CYLS. 19" x 28"

250 LBS. PER. SQ. IN.

COAL 9 TONS
WATER 4000 GALLS.

GRATE AREA 45 SQ. FT.

EST. WEIGHTS						
T C	T C	T C	T C	T C	T C	
21-0	22-10	22-10	22-10	16-0		TOTAL 156-10

TRACTIVE EFFORT (85%)
39700 LBS.

Stanier 3-cyl Pacific design 1932.

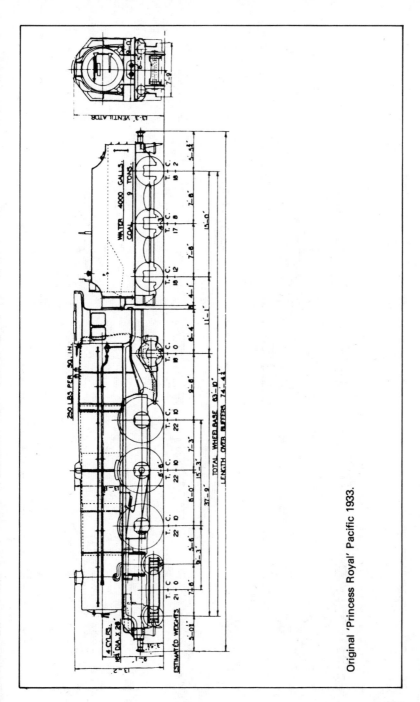

Original 'Princess Royal' Pacific 1933.

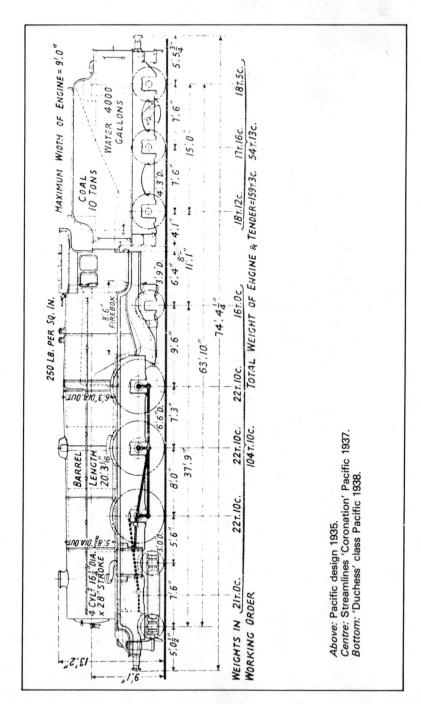

MAXIMUM WIDTH OF ENGINE = 9'0"

250 LB. PER SQ. IN.

WATER 4000 GALLONS

COAL 10 TONS

3'6" FIREBOX

BARREL LENGTH 20'.3¹⁄₁₆"

6'.3" DIA. OUT.

5'.8" DIA. OUT.

4 CYL.S 16¹⁄₂" DIA. × 28" STROKE

3'.0 0.

5'.6"

8'.0"

6'.6 D.

7'.3"

9'.6"

3'.9 D.

6'.4" 4'.1"

8'.7"

11'.1"

15'.0"

7'.6"

7'.6"

5'.5³⁄₄"

4'.3 D.

37'.9"

63'.10"

74'.4¹⁄₄"

5'.0¹⁄₄"

7'.6"

13'.2"

9'.1"

WEIGHTS IN WORKING ORDER

21T.0c.   22T.10c.   22T.10c.   22T.10c.   22T.10c.   16T.0c.   18T.12c.   18T.0c.   17T.16c.   18T.5c.

104T.10c.   547.13c.

TOTAL WEIGHT OF ENGINE & TENDER = 159T.3c.

Above: Pacific design 1935.
Centre: Streamlines 'Coronation' Pacific 1937.
Bottom: 'Duchess' class Pacific 1938.

202

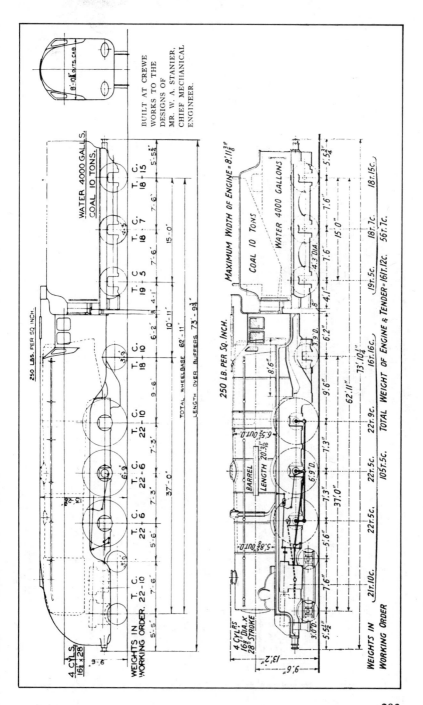

BUILT AT CREWE WORKS TO THE DESIGNS OF MR. W. A. STANIER, CHIEF MECHANICAL ENGINEER.

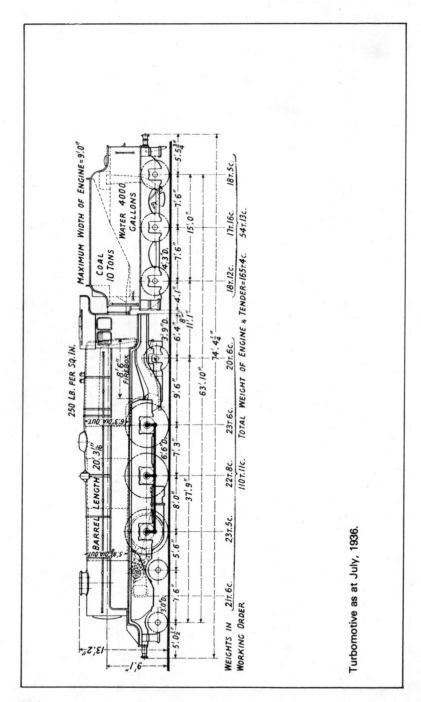

Turbomotive as at July, 1936.

204

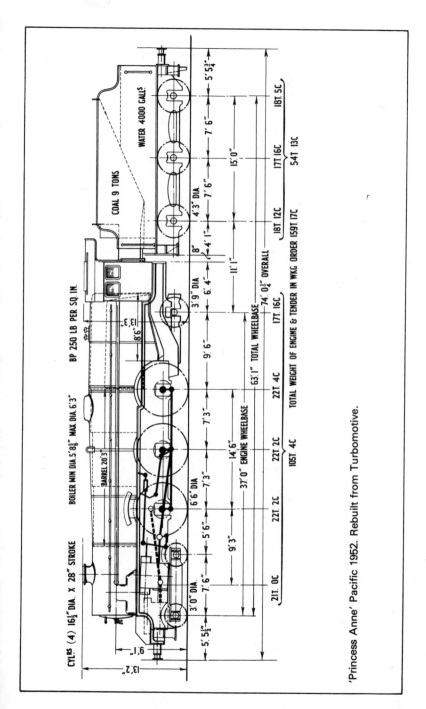

'Princess Anne' Pacific 1952. Rebuilt from Turbomotive.

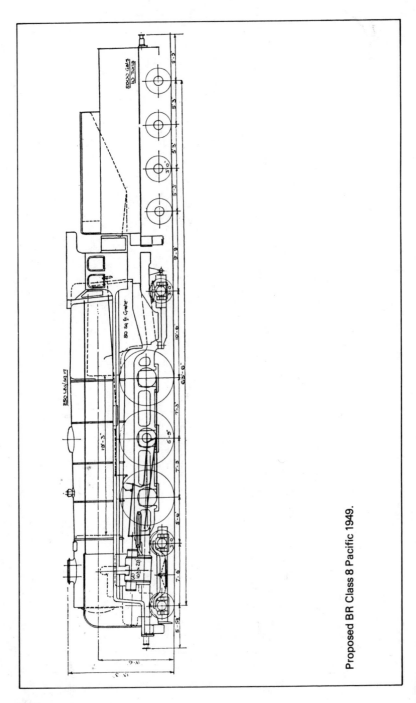

Proposed BR Class 8 Pacific 1949.

Bibliography

The Locomotive Performance and Efficiency Test Bulletins, B.T.C., 1953-1957.
A Modern Locomotive History, E. S. Cox Paper presented to the Institution of Locomotive Engineers Jan. 1946. Reprinted by the RCTS.
British Pacific Locomotives, Cecil J. Allen, Ian Allan 1962.
Locomotive Exhanges, Cecil J. Allen, Ian Allan 1949.
New Light on the Locomotive Exchanges, Cecil J. Allen, Ian Allan 1950.
William Stanier, O. S. Nock, Ian Allan 1964.
The British Steam Railway Locomotive Vol 2 1925-1965, O. S. Nock, Ian Allan 1966.
The Master Builders of Steam, H. A. V. Bulleid, Ian Allan 1963.
Locomotive Panorama Vol 1, E. S. Cox, Ian Allan 1965.
Locomotive Panorama Vol 2, E. S. Cox, Ian Allan 1966.
British Railways Standard Steam Locomotives, E. S. Cox, Ian Allan 1966.
Chronicles of Steam, E. S. Cox, Ian Allan 1967.
World Steam in the 20th Century, E. S. Cox, Ian Allan 1969.
British Steam Since 1900, W. A. Tuplin, David & Charles 1969.
The Last Locomotive Engineer, H. C. Rogers, Allen & Unwin 1970.
Essays in Steam, SLS Anthology, Ian Allan 1970.
Locomotive Liveries of the LMS, D. Jenkinson & R. J. Essery, Ian Allan 1967.
Stanier Locomotives, B. Haresnape, Ian Allan 1970.
The LMS Duchesses, Ed D. Doherty, Model & Allied Publications Ltd. 1973.
The LMS Pacifics, J. W. R. Rowledge, Profile Publications 1974.
Railway Reminiscenses, G. Vuillet, T. Nelson 1968.
Chapelon Genius of French Steam, H. C. Rogers, Ian Allan 1972.
The Steam Locomotive in America, W. J. Bruce, W. W. Norton 1952.
London Midland Fireman, M. F. Higson, Ian Allan 1972.
Die Dampflokomotiv, Meineke & Rohrs, Berlin 1949.
La Locomotive a Vapeur, A. Chapelon, Bailliere et Fils, Paris 1938. 2nd ed 1952.
La Machine Locomotive, E. Sauvage et A. Chapelon, Paris 1948.

Les Locomotives a Vapeur Francaises, L. M. Vilain, Paris 1959.
Dampfturbinen Locomotiven, R. Ostendorf, Frankfurt 1971.

Various issues of:
The Railway Magazine, The Locomotive, The Engineer, Railways, The Railway World Trains Illustrated, Modern Railways, The Railway Observer, The Journal of The Stephenson Locomotive Society, Proceedings of The Institution of Locomotive Engineers, The Institution of Mechanical Engineers, The Bulletins of the Locomotive Society of Scotland, The Meccano Magazine, The LMS Magazine.